International Perspectives on Voluntary Action

International Perspectives on Voluntary Action:
Reshaping the Third Sector

Edited by David Lewis

Earthscan Publications Ltd, London

First published in the UK in 1999 by
Earthscan Publications Limited

A catalogue record for this book is available from the British Library

ISBN: 1 85383 555 2 (paperback)
       1 85383 556 0 (hardback)

Typesetting and page design by PCS Mapping & DTP, Newcastle upon Tyne
Printed and bound by Biddles Ltd, Guildford and Kings Lynn
Cover design by John Burke
Cover photo © Panos Pictures/Neil Cooper

For a full list of publications please contact:

Earthscan Publications Limited
120 Pentonville Road
London N1 9JN
Tel: (0171) 278 0433
Fax: (0171) 278 1142
Email: earthinfo@earthscan.co.uk
http://www.earthscan.co.uk

Earthscan is an editorially independent subsidiary of Kogan Page Limited and
publishes in association with WWF-UK and the International Institute for
Environment and Development.

List of Contents

List of Figures, Tables and Boxes

FIGURES

TABLES

BOXES

List of Acronyms and Abbreviations

ADAB	Association of Development Agencies in Bangladesh
AKRSP	Aga Khan Rural Support Programme
AOSIS	Association of Small Island States
ARNOVA	Association for Research on Nonprofit Organizations and Voluntary Action (US)
BCSD	Business Council for Sustainable Development
BNP	Bangladeshi Nationalist Party
BRAC	Bangladeshi Rural Advancement Committee
CBO	community-based organization
CEO	chief executive officer
CIDE	Centro de Investigacion y Desarrollo de la Educacion
CITES	Convention on International Trade in Endangered Species
CSE	Center for Science and Environment (New Delhi)
CVO	Centre for Voluntary Organisation (London School of Economics and Political Science)
DAC	Development Assistance Committee of the OECD (qv)
DFID	Department for International Development (UK)
GNP	gross national product
GSS	Gono Shahajjo Sangstha (Bangladesh)
ICNPO	international classification of nonprofit organizations
IDA	International Development Association
IDR	Institute of Development Research (US)
IDS	Institute of Development Studies (UK)
IIED	International Institute for Environment and Development (London)
IISD	International Institute for Sustainable Development
IRN	International Rivers Network
ISTR	International Society for Third Sector Research
KENGO	Kenyan Energy and Environment Organization
LETS	local exchange trading system
LICROSS/ VOLAGS	League of Red Cross and Red Crescent Societies and Voluntary Agencies
MAN	Movimiento Ambientalista Nicaraguenese (Nicaragua)
MDB	multilateral development bank
NAFTA	North American Free Trade Agreement
NCS	national conservation strategy
NGDO	non-governmental development organization
NGO	non-governmental organization
NIC	newly industrializing country

NNGO	Northern NGO (qv)
NPI	New Partnership Initiative
ODI	Overseas Development Institute (UK)
OECD	Organisation for Economic Cooperation and Development
PCMA	Program in Conflict Management Alternatives (University of Michigan)
PIEDAR	Pakistan Institute of Environmental Development Action Research
PLA	participatory learning and action
PR	participatory research
PRA	participatory rural appraisal
PRIA	Society for Participatory Research in Asia
PRIP	Participatory Rural Initiatives Project (Bangladesh)
PSSRU	Personal Social Services Research Unit (London School of Economics and Political Science)
PVO	private voluntary organization
RMI	Rocky Mountain Institute (Colorado, US)
Sida	Swedish International Development Cooperation Agency
SNGO	Southern NGO (qv)
SO	support organization
TAA	total activities analysis
TEC	training and enterprise council
TIRN	Tennessee Industrial Renewal Network
TSO	third sector organization
UNEP	United Nations Environment Programme
UNCED	United Nations Conference on Environment and Development (Rio de Janeiro, 1992)
USAID	United States Agency for International Development
VO	voluntary organisation
WALHI	Indonesian Environmental Forum
WRI	World Resources Institute (Washington, DC)

Foreword

Most of the papers in this volume were first presented at the conference 'NGOs and Voluntary Organizations in North and South: Learning from Each Other?' organized by the Centre for Voluntary Organisation (CVO) and held at the London School of Economics on September 18–19 1997. The CVO was opened at the London School of Economics in October 1987 and is part of the School's Department of Social Policy and Administration. The focus of the Centre's work is the organization and management of non-governmental organisations (NGOs) and voluntary agencies and the implications for social policy. It attempts to develop usable theory by working with agencies in responding to current problems and issues.

Many people have worked hard to make both the conference and this book possible. The Centre is grateful to the Charities Aid Foundation for providing generous financial support for the conference. I would like to thank David Billis, Margaret Harris and Colin Rochester at the Centre for their constant support and encouragement, and Jane Schiemann and Sue Roebuck for their thorough and good-humoured administrative support. During the conference itself, the voluntary assistance of Sofia Frech, Zoe Marriage and Lucy Koechlin helped to make the event a success. A very great debt is also due to Lilly Nicholls, whose organizational and planning skills were invaluable and who worked well beyond the call of duty before and during the conference. Finally, I would like to thank Romayne Hutchison for preparing this material for publication in a very short space of time.

David Lewis
London School of Economics
April 1998

Contributors

Helmut K Anheier is Associate Director of the Johns Hopkins Comparative Nonprofit Sector Project, and Associate Professor of Sociology, Rutgers University, New Jersey, USA. He can be contacted at HAnheier@aol.com

Qadeer Baig is Programme Coordinator of the NGO Resource Centre, a project of the Aga Khan Foundation, in Pakistan. He can be contacted at info@ngorc.khi.sdnpk.undp.org

L David Brown is President of the Institute for Development Research (IDR) and Professor of Organisational Behaviour at the Boston University School of Management. He can be contacted at dave_brown@jsi.com

Michael Edwards is a freelance consultant and writer based in London and can be contacted at 106076.2125@compuserve.com

Alan Fowler is a freelance consultant and writer currently based in Addis Ababa, Ethiopia and can be contacted at alanfowler@compuserve.com

John Gaventa is a Fellow of the Institute of Development Studies (IDS), University of Sussex, UK and can be contacted at J.P.Gaventa@ids.ac.uk

Margaret Harris is Assistant Director of the Centre for Voluntary Organisation, London School of Economics (LSE) and may be contacted at M.Harris@lse.ac.uk

Syed M Hashemi is Director of the Grameen Trust's Programme for Research on Poverty Alleviation in Bangladesh and can be contacted at hashemi@citechco.net

Mirza Hassan is a Research Fellow at the Centre for Policy Dialogue in Dhaka, Bangladesh and is currently working on his PhD thesis at the Institute of Commonwealth Studies, University of London

Jeremy Kendall is Research Fellow in the Personal Social Services Research Unit (PSSRU) at LSE. His email address is J.Kendall@lse.ac.uk

Martin Knapp is Professor of the Economics of Social Care and Deputy Director of the Personal Social Services Research Unit (PSSRU) at LSE and can be contacted at M.Knapp@lse.ac.uk.

David Lewis is Lecturer in Non-Governmental Organisations at the Centre for Voluntary Organisation, LSE. His email address is D.J.Lewis@lse.ac.uk

Adil Najam is Assistant Professor of International Affairs and Environmental Policy at Boston University and Associate Director of the MIT-Harvard Programme on Public Disputes at the Harvard Law School, and can be contacted at anajam@mit.edu

Rob Paton is Senior Lecturer in Management at the Open University Business School, UK and can be contacted at R.C.Paton@open.ac.uk

Roger Riddell is Senior Research Fellow of the Overseas Development Institute (ODI) in London and can be contacted at r.riddell@odi.org.uk

Lester M Salamon is Director of the Johns Hopkins University Institute for Policy Studies and Director of the Johns Hopkins Comparative Nonprofit Sector Project. He can be contacted at lsalamon@ jhunix.hcf.jhu.edu

Marilyn Taylor is Senior Lecturer at the Department of Community Studies, University of Brighton, UK and can be contacted at mt49@brighton.ac.uk

I

Introduction: The Parallel Universes of Third Sector Research and the Changing Context of Voluntary Action

David Lewis

There has been a growth of interest during the past decade among researchers on what have been variously termed non-governmental organizations (NGOs), nonprofit organizations and voluntary organizations, in both the industrialized and the aid-recipient countries (Salamon, 1994; Smillie, 1995). This has reflected the heightened profiles of these types of organizations amongst policy makers and activists in both domestic and international contexts. In development studies, the new interest in NGOs has arisen partly in response to the perceived failure of state-led development approaches during the 1980s and the 'new policy agenda' which combines neo-liberal economic policy prescriptions with that of 'good governance' (Robinson, 1993). It has also reflected the post-Cold War policy context in which international NGOs have been brought centre stage in relief and emergency efforts (Fowler, 1995b). Within social policy research, interest in the third sector has been associated with the restructuring of welfare policies in the industrialized countries (eg Kramer et al, 1993; Smith and Lipsky, 1993). Renewed social science interest in the concept of 'civil society' in relation to the 'third world', the former socialist 'transitional' countries and Western industrialized contexts has also focused considerable research attention on the third sector in recent years (eg Brown and Tandon, 1994; Chambre, 1997).

The origin of this collection can be found in my own recent professional experience in moving from a background in developing country research to an academic centre which has its roots in the study of the British voluntary sector.[1] As a researcher from a development studies background working on NGOs and rural development in South Asia I have become intrigued by the existence of what might be loosely termed two 'parallel research universes' in the study of different types of non-governmental, voluntary and nonprofit organizations around the world.

Academic research into third sector organizations (ie those organizations which are neither part of the state nor part of the business sector) can be categorized broadly into two distinct groupings: work which focuses on these organizations and their activities in industrialized countries, and work which examines related types of organizations in developing or aid-recipient countries.[2] The NGO corpus of literature is a growing set of interdisciplinary writings within development studies which has concerned itself with the role of NGOs in development (eg Clark, 1991; Edwards and Hulme, 1995; Korten, 1990). Non-profit literature consists of research on what are variously termed 'voluntary', 'nonprofit' or 'third sector' organizations working in Western industrialized societies (eg Billis, 1993; Harris, 1998; Powell, 1987; Salamon, 1994).

These two research universes do not form entirely watertight categories and some points of overlap are briefly discussed below. While recognizing that there is some permeability in the boundaries of these two universes, it is suggested that this dichotomy is a useful way of representing and conceptualizing an important problem. A distinction is therefore maintained throughout this chapter between NGO literature on the one hand and nonprofit literature on the other.

THE CHARACTERISTICS OF THE TWO LITERATURES

There is considerable overlap in the subject matter of the two literatures. In a recent review article, Leat (1997: 47), herself a nonprofit researcher with a UK focus, reflects on this discovery. Acknowledging the odd sense of strangeness and familiarity, Leat describes her reactions while reviewing two collections of papers on NGOs by Edwards and Hulme (1992 and 1995) as 'akin to visiting New York from London':

> *The language, structures, culture, tensions and challenges are the same but different, more vivid, more urgent, both more complex and starker. The world in which NGOs operate is bigger, more culturally and politically diverse, the poor poorer and relatively more disadvantaged. The issues are familiar: what is the relationship between service provision and campaigning; how do you combine delivery of service with participation and democratization; how should/could effectiveness be assessed and when, why and how are voluntary organizations most effective; how do you combine multiple accountabilities upwards and downwards, and what is accountability anyway; by whom and how is the organization managed; how are associational roots and ideologies combined with bureaucratic structures; does he who pays the piper always call the tune, does sector matter, and so on.*

With so many research concerns in common, the existence of the two parallel research universes is perhaps surprising. In country contexts as different as, say, Britain and Bangladesh it is apparent that organizations may be struggling in different ways with essentially similar sets of issues (eg Kramer, 1994; Wood, 1997). Both literatures are interdisciplinary social science fields which seek to combine insights from economics, political science, sociology and anthropology and yet they remain different and largely separate from one another.

Difference

The NGO literature has been concerned with the growth and evolution of NGO roles in development and relief work, with policy issues of NGO relations with states and donors and with community-based action and social change (Clark, 1991; Drabek, 1987Farrington, 1993). In general, the NGO literature has focused on NGO roles within the aid industry (Clark, 1991; Fowler, 1997; Hulme and Edwards, 1997), and on development practice (eg Carroll, 1992; Korten, 1990; Smillie, 1995).[3] Its tone, while sometimes critical of the attention currently being given to NGOs, is usually one which documents and suggests the potential of NGOs to transform development processes in positive ways (eg Clark, 1991; Edwards and Hulme, 1992; Korten, 1990).[4]

By contrast, the nonprofit literature has ordered its priorities slightly differently. This has included considering theoretical questions such as the different explanations for the existence of the third sector (eg Anheier, 1995; Powell, 1987), and policy issues such as the growth of contracting (eg Kramer, 1994; Smith and Lipsky, 1993). It has concentrated on service delivery and welfare organizations more than advocacy and social change organizations (Billis, 1993; Salamon, 1994) and has given a higher priority than the NGO literature to organizational structure and management issues (eg Billis and Harris, 1996; Butler and Wilson, 1990; Young, 1992). It is perhaps surprising to note that organizational issues have hardly featured at all in the NGO literature.[5]

There are a number of other differences. The NGO literature has tended to see NGOs as one of a number of key actors in processes of development alongside the state, local government, foreign donors and private corporations (eg Farrington and Bebbington, 1993; Hulme and Edwards, 1997; Wuyts et al, 1992). In contrast to this relatively integrated approach, the nonprofit literature has to a greater extent focused on the organizations themselves and on the concept of the 'sector' as a distinctive subject for research (eg Billis, 1993; Salamon and Anheier, 1992 and 1997). This is also reflected in the appearance of specialized nonprofit journals such as *Nonprofit and Voluntary Sector Quarterly, Voluntas* and *Nonprofit Management and Leadership*. Research papers on NGOs, which in recent years have begun to appear in large quantity, are still published in general development journals such as *World Development* or the *Journal of International Development*.

Each literature also has its own distinctive sets of specialized terms. In the British nonprofit literature the term 'voluntary organization' is commonly used for domestic third sector organizations. The term 'NGO' is usually reserved for organizations of both North and South working in aid-recipient countries. In the US nonprofit literature, the term 'nonprofit organization' is widely understood in the domestic context, while the term 'private voluntary organization' (PVO) is sometimes used for US organizations working in the international context. By contrast within the NGO literature the umbrella term 'non-governmental organization' is generally used throughout, although the category 'NGO' may be broken down into specialized organizational sub-groups such as 'public service contractors', 'people's organizations', 'voluntary organizations' and even 'governmental NGOs' (Korten, 1990) or 'grassroots support organizations' and 'membership support organizations' (Carroll, 1992).

It is difficult to escape the conclusion that there is an arbitrariness to the different usages of these terms and categories both within and between the two literatures, and that these terms are culture bound. Sometimes the different labels reflect genuine organizational distinctiveness and difference while at other times the varied usages simply generate conceptual confusion. Why for example does the nonprofit literature tend to use different terms for essentially similar kinds of organizations working at home or internationally? Why does the NGO literature continue with a negative definition which expresses what these organizations are *not*? Najam (1996) has identified as many as 47 different and largely bewildering organizational terms in common use around the world which express the scale of the classificatory problem. Vakil (1997) has recently provided a useful taxonomy of NGOs, but does not address directly the question of different usages in the two literatures.[6] It is refreshing to find that some researchers do not make arbitrary cultural or geographical distinctions in the terms which they use. For example, a recent article by Kumar and Hudock (1996: 195) on accountability simply refers to 'NGOs ... [which] ... provide social services in Britain' and 'NGOs based in the "South", for example African NGOs' and does not reserve different terminologies for third sector organizations based on whether they are related to the so-called developed or the developing areas of the world.[7]

Separateness

The two literatures are not only different, but they are also largely separate and relatively little cross-referencing takes place between them. One reason given for this separation is that there are vast differences in the scale and order of problems in poor and rich countries which require very different research approaches and terms, and ultimately different kinds of organizational and policy solutions. For example, Billis (1984: 64) in his discussion of UK welfare agencies makes a point of distinguishing between two different sets of priorities in welfare provision. The relief of 'social discomfort' is contrasted with the more extreme need to address 'social breakdown'. Following from this idea a terminological distinction is later developed in his work in which the term 'non-governmental organization' is used in the developing country context and 'voluntary agency' is used in the UK context, reflecting in part the different levels of need in the different contexts (Billis and MacKeith, 1993: 3).

Another reason for the separation is the geographical disciplinary division of labour which has existed in many areas of the social sciences. A line has frequently divided domestic research from that with an international or third world focus.[8] A growing awareness of the importance of nonprofit and voluntary organizations in Europe and the US has gradually attracted attention from social policy and organization researchers, leading to the establishment of a distinct field of nonprofit studies. Development studies has concerned itself with understanding the lower income countries of Asia, Africa and Latin America, and the study of NGOs has gradually grown to form part of this research. Many academic departments in the UK still contain people working on similar research subjects – such as social exclusion – which *either* have a domestic *or* an international focus, but who only rarely or informally compare ideas across these boundaries. Each field has established its own professional associations, so that for example while the UK Development Studies Association has its own specialized NGO sub-group, nonprofit researchers have gone further and created an Association for Research on Nonprofit Organizations and Voluntary Action (ARNOVA) and the International Society for Third Sector Research (ISTR).

However, it would be wrong to suggest that the two literatures are *entirely* insulated from each other. Some researchers can be seen partly at least to straddle both camps (eg Fisher, 1994; Najam, 1996; Vakil, 1997). The nonprofit literature has begun to make efforts to internationalize its research perspectives (eg Anheier, 1990). This change is signified by the establishment of the ISTR and by the growth of comparative research projects such as that of Salamon and Anheier (1992 and 1997) and Kramer et al (1993).

However, one rarely finds researchers from the NGO literature writing in the internationalizing nonprofit literature and vice versa. Only a handful of researchers have begun the process of building links between the two literatures. For example Billis and MacKeith (1993) have used concepts drawn from research within the UK voluntary sector to explore organizational change among a sample of British development NGOs. Edwards and Hulme (1995) have drawn attention to connections between work on contracting in the South and its implications for development NGOs. Fisher (1994) has linked Western organizational theory with work on development NGOs and has suggested that Michels' iron law of oligarchy is challenged by the experience of some large Southern NGOs which have maintained more participatory management styles. Tandon (1995) has examined organizational issues around the accountability of NGO governing bodies, covering some similar ground to work in this area undertaken in the UK and US contexts. Fowler (1995b) has attempted to draw on the organizational work of Kanter and Drucker to assess NGO performance. However, this kind of cross-fertilization is comparatively unusual.

SOME IMPLICATIONS OF THE SEPARATION

If the two literatures are studied side by side it is difficult to escape the conviction that their separateness creates a set of problems which need to be addressed. These problems are essentially of two types, one related to *learning and exchange*, the other related to *relevance*.

Firstly, the separation of the two literatures may reduce opportunities for learning by researchers across different contexts. As third sector issues are increasingly prioritized by researchers and policy makers in different parts of the world there is a danger of re-inventing the wheel unless more comparative work is undertaken and more exchange of conclusions from existing work within the two literatures takes place. For example, while we might not expect the current growth of contracting arrangements between NGOs, governments and donors in developing country contexts to bring *exactly* the same sets of challenges faced within the British voluntary sector during the onset of welfare pluralist policies and enterprise culture in the 1980s, it might be extremely useful to compare aspects of the two experiences.

Despite the different order and scale of problems in rich and poor countries, there are many common approaches to poverty eradication and welfare provision (eg experiments with empowerment, credit provision and participation) and joint learning and exchange may therefore be possible. Ideas from the South are also reaching the North, creating new levels and layers of global exchange and learning:

> *As savings and credit schemes invented in Bangladesh catch on in the ghettos of Chicago, as African urban activists help community officials in the* banlieus *of Paris cope with social decay, and as local government officials from Europe make pilgrimages to Curitiba, Brazil to see how cities can be made more sustainable, fresh policy ideas will get transmitted at low cost, and know-how created in 'poor' countries will be revalued (Sogge, 1996: 169).*

Linking the two literatures more effectively may allow a more efficient use of what is known by filling gaps in knowledge through comparative research.

Secondly, the relevance of both of these literatures may be diminished unless their research agendas can react to the changing international contexts of voluntary action. Research structured by concepts of 'North' and 'South' (or the many other euphemisms for rich and poor countries) may be ill-suited to forces of globalization which may ultimately be dissolving such distinctions, or at least complicating them further. In addition, researchers need to engage with international third sector linkages which are already evolving between organizations in different parts of the world outside the lines of the conventional aid industry. It is this second set of issues which the remainder of this paper seeks to develop.

The chapters in this book represent a first systematic attempt to bridge the gap between the two parallel universes, and key writers from both research traditions contribute the chapters which follow. Closer links between the two literatures would bring potential complementarities of knowledge which would greatly enrich the research process. But more importantly, it would also allow research to link more closely with current policy and practice, which may be well ahead of research in terms of North–South third sector links. The separateness of the two literatures may inhibit understanding of examples of practical linkage, collaboration and learning which are already taking place among third sector organizations.

THE CHANGING CONTEXTS OF VOLUNTARY ACTION

The economic and political forces of globalization are creating new patterns of similarity and difference across a social, cultural, economic and political landscape which is undergoing massive change (Giddens, 1993). The usefulness of the concept of the 'third world' has been under attack for some time (Harris, 1986) with the economic growth of the newly industrializing countries (NICs) and the growing numbers of middle income countries in Asia and Latin America. As Escobar (1995) has argued, the construction of a discourse about the third world had as much to do with the assertion of Western economic and political power in the period after 1945 as it did with local realities in the countries of the South.

Given the fragility of many of these assumptions, there are certain pitfalls for third sector researchers. It is perhaps instructive to link Escobar's analysis of development discourse with our discussion of the parallel universe problem. Models and concepts of the nonprofit sector have so far tended to be developed in the North and then applied to the South (Salamon and Anheier, 1997). The problem of ethnocentricity or Eurocentricity is already well documented in the case of the application of Western models of development economics to the developing world (see Mehmet, 1995). Similar problems may be apparent in the efforts of Northern scholars to label, quantify and understand third sectors in other parts of the world. The power of development agencies to shape research on NGOs is visible in much of the published material on NGOs. Northern researchers are often funded in their research by official donors or write up work as a by-product of consultancy assignments.[9] This is a situation which has potentially dangerous implications for the objectivity of third sector research (Edwards and Hulme, 1995).

Sogge (1996: 146) has drawn attention to the fact that a central tenet of the aid paradigm has been the idea that

> ... the Problem is 'out there' on a poor periphery of the world, whose misfortunes have no connection with acts and omissions by the powerful in the wealthy core of the world.

As well as an emphasis on linking the causes and stressing the interconnectedness of poverty on a global level, we are also currently witnessing a convergence of research concepts across North and South.

Within British academia, research traditions such as development studies and social policy have for some time been widening well beyond their established North or South focus. Some social policy researchers are attempting to construct stronger links with development issues (eg Midgley, 1995), while in development studies there is a growing tendency to link concepts and research from both the developed and the developing world (eg Putzel, 1997). At a recent UK Development Studies Association seminar, for example, papers were presented on urban NGO work which mixed experiences from the South and from the UK. A recent collection of work on poverty and identity in urban areas by Beall (1997) combines writing on urban areas in both North and South, written by researchers from both contexts.

There are now debates taking place about whether or not concepts developed in the North may have relevance to the South. Relatively new social science concepts such as 'social exclusion' (Bhalla and Lapeyre, 1997; Gaventa, 1997) and 'social capital' (Harriss, 1997; Putzel, 1997) may be encouraging new insights and action around development and poverty issues, while much older ones such as 'civil society' both animate and complicate contemporary debates about democracy and voluntary action (Hann and Dunn, 1996; Harbeson et al, 1994). The research literature on social movements has an increasingly global focus and work within both the nonprofit (eg Hall and Hall, 1996) and the NGO literatures (Fox, 1996) has begun to make relevant links with work in this field.

A particularly striking example of the choices faced by third sector organizations within these changing landscapes is the case of the UK NGO Oxfam, which recently decided that it would establish projects to address poverty in the UK instead of working solely in the third world. Oxfam argued that its expertise which had been acquired through many years of working in developing countries might be transferable to the UK and that common problems of poverty and exclusion might exist in both North and South. The decision proved a controversial one. In the UK, the *Daily Mail*'s headline when Oxfam announced its new programme was 'Stick to the Third World!' (*NCVO News*, 1996). It was not clear whether this reflected a view on the political right that poverty is not a feature of British social life and only exists in the third world, or that if poverty did exist in the UK, it was not the place of an international development NGO to address the problem. The parallel universe problem can in a sense be seen as a microcosm of the research and policy challenges generated by trends towards globalization and the continuing dominance of Western discourses of knowledge and power about poverty and development (Gardner and Lewis, 1996).

Current research is again beginning to highlight the fact that poverty, along with resistance, is not confined to the third world but is found in the growing inequalities between social groups in the North. This is apparent if we consider the efforts of women to organize in response to the rise of neo-liberal policy change at the global level, in the face of the restructuring of welfare systems in the North and the structural adjustment process in the South. Within a global conceptual framework linking gender and organizational responses to poverty, comparisons and connections can be made between women organizing communal soup kitchens in Peru, influencing policy in Bolivia and fighting violence against women in New York (Lind, 1996).

Within the global third sector, conceptual and practical boundaries are therefore breaking down. Links between organizations in North and South are increasingly being constructed and assumptions about the separateness of the two parallel research universes can easily be challenged. For example, Local Agenda 21 efforts since the 1992 UN 'Earth Summit' conference in Rio to promote environmental action and sustainable development have released funds to community organizations in both North and South and within both contexts many common challenges have been observed (NGLS, 1997). Third sector organizations in the two parts of Ireland receive funds from the European Union intended to promote social and economic development. The relationships which result from these funding inflows create challenges, such as the management of relations with multilateral donors and the building of community participation, which are reminiscent of those involving NGOs in a developing country context (eg Williamson, 1996). Conversely, in some developing countries such as Ethiopia and India there are growing numbers of NGOs which raise money from private individual donors as well as corporate funds, in a manner usually associated only with rich European and North American countries (Norton, 1996).

Ideas are spreading from third sectors in the South to organizations in the North, as well as vice versa. For example, the Grameen Bank's approach to credit in Bangladesh has been replicated all over the world, including in the US (Holcombe, 1995). Participatory rural appraisal (PRA) has its roots in non-governmental and public sectors in the South (Biggs and Smith, 1998) and has been successfully used in the North (Cresswell, 1996). There is a history of community linking for solidarity between communities in North and South, such as the UK and the Gambia (Bond, 1996). There may be other less well documented examples of learning between North and South which would support the need for nonprofit and NGO researchers to pay closer attention to each other's work. For example in Brazil the efforts of the Catholic Church in developing local community base organizations have spread to other church communities in the US, initially among Latin Americans but increasingly now among other groups of people.[10]

If it continues to influence action and policy, other practical problems may follow from the parallel research universe problem. One is the question of resource allocation. What for example will be the impact on public giving if organizations such as Oxfam find that working with poverty at home is unpopular   with   their   supporters?   What   are   the implications for bilateral aid donors such as the Swedish International Development Cooperation Agency (Sida) if it follows trends in some of its own offices in its partner countries (such as Bangladesh and India) to fund Southern NGOs directly instead of working through the Swedish NGOs whose roots are in the church, trade unions and cooperatives within Swedish society (Lewis and Sobhan, 1999)? The roles of Northern NGOs working in development in particular are currently being rethought. For example, at a recent bilateral donor meeting reported to the author the issue was raised as to whether Northern development NGOs were the most appropriate intermediaries between donors and specialized Southern NGOs, or whether links should be promoted between UK voluntary sector organizations working on, say, child poverty in London with an Indian organization working with similar issues in New Delhi.[11] The resource implications of these questions may turn out to be significant for domestic voluntary organizations, NGOs and governments alike during the coming years.

LINKAGES AND LEARNING

The papers in this book bring together researchers from both literatures in order to explore common themes, different emphases and international linkages side by side. Part 1 explores global third sector themes and analyses connections which already exist between NGOs working in the North and those working in the South. The chapter by Lester Salamon and Helmut Anheier is based on ongoing research from the Johns Hopkins University Comparative Third Sector Research Project. It presents an international comparative perspective on third sector organizations which seeks to move beyond the two parallel universes of terminologies, assumptions and research foci. This approach calls into question the Western biases in the nonprofit literature and throws into sharp relief the diversity of third sector organizations beyond those generally reflected in the existing NGO literature, which have tended to be larger, bureaucratic development agencies linked to the provision of international development assistance. This is pioneering work because it forces us to look beyond NGOs (if these are defined as organizations linked to the development industry) towards more diverse and culturally specific types of non-state organizations. There is a serious gap in both the NGO and the nonprofit literatures when it comes to small scale, informal or associational organizations within the third sector.

John Gaventa, combining both activist and academic research perspectives, traces the exchanges between NGOs and community-based organizations in poor regions of the South of the US and Appalachia and counterpart organizations in Mexico and India. This chapter makes a convincing case for the need to understand the increasing level of parallel and convergence between poor communities in the North and the South and the resultant similarities of working methods displayed by NGOs and community-based organizations (CBOs) in both contexts. The research described by David Brown explores the growth of social learning as a means to facilitate response by organizations and networks to rapid levels of change in a world increasingly characterized by interdependence and diversity. Brown's case studies show the complexities and fragilities of learning processes which can easily generate misunderstanding and conflict. Yet difference, Brown suggests, can be put to good use in the formation of learning coalitions between organizations in North and South.

CONTRASTS AND COMPLEMENTARITIES

Part 2 brings together researchers from the two research universes in order to compare research findings on themes of potential common interest. This part contains overviews of current thinking on key third sector themes: governance, legitimacy and values, policy advocacy, and evaluation and effectiveness. Authors were asked to write on one of these themes and present current thinking from the perspective of their own research traditions. Each chapter offers a perspective from either the nonprofit literature or the NGO literature on a particular theme. It is clear that there are enormous differences of preoccupation and emphasis, but it is also evident that there is a surprising degree of common ground. This was apparent from the debates and informal discussions which followed each group of presentations at the conference.

Organizational issues are far more strongly represented within the nonprofit literature than they are in the NGO field. For example, Harris is able to outline a detailed set of research findings relating to governing bodies of voluntary organizations in the UK and the US which increasingly analyses the distinctive problems they face and the conceptual issues which underpin these problems. By contrast, as Baig shows, NGO researchers are by and large taking their first tentative steps in this direction having largely ignored organizational governance issues in favour of wider debates about NGO accountability. Baig shows that NGO researchers and practitioners could learn a great deal from this Northern research but he also draws attention to distinctive aspects of the governance problems faced by NGOs in Pakistan, the origins of which lie well beyond the boundaries of the organization in the unstable, risk-prone and resource-scarce environment in which NGOs in Pakistan operate.

These differences in emphasis are continued by Hashemi's work on NGO legitimacy in Bangladesh and Paton's chapter on legitimacy and values. Whereas Hashemi presents a historical perspective on Bangladeshi NGOs' changing legitimacy vis à vis the state and the poor, Paton's chapter examines values and legitimacy from a management perspective and raises important questions about value-based conflicts and tensions implicit in voluntary agencies, and in a sense shares Hashemi's emphasis on external resource dependence on social embeddedness. In his paper, Edwards shares Paton's discomfort with assuming that NGOs are able to operationalize the stated primacy of values in their mission statements and points to a crisis of values and legitimacy as NGOs drift away from their original commitment to social solidarity and become increasingly reluctant to face up honestly to problems and failures.

Looking outwards from the organizations themselves, Najam's chapter on NGOs as policy entrepreneurs outlines the importance of viewing NGOs as actors in the policy arena whether they are explicitly engaged in conscious attempts to influence policy or not. This view argues that NGOs have certain strengths in asserting themselves in areas of policy change, but exposes the tensions and contradictions implicit in the different policy perspectives of NGOs in the North and the South. Fowler presents a slightly more pessimistic picture in his chapter which attempts a composite view of advocacy efforts in both North and South in the face of economic globalization and the growth of communication technology. While there are new opportunities for advocacy work, the resource dependency of many NGOs draws them away from the necessary levels of civic rootedness required to maintain credibility. Taylor's overview of issues of policy influence in the UK voluntary sector shifts the focus to agency efforts to address problems of poverty and social exclusion in the North, but reminds us that despite their claims, voluntary agencies cannot necessarily be relied upon to maintain democratic norms and values.

Finally, it is interesting to compare Kendall and Knapp's review of evaluation issues in the UK voluntary sector and Riddell's analysis of evidence emerging from international aid donors' attempts to evaluate the impact of the NGOs which they support. While Kendall and Knapp demonstrate the firm theoretical basis on which the question of evaluation is considered by nonprofit researchers and the apparent methodological intractability of undertaking adequate evaluation efforts, Riddell shows how disappointing the accumulated findings of donor evaluations have been for those who may have assumed that NGOs are effective at what they do.

The papers collected in this volume form only a beginning in what it is hoped will eventually become a more established set of global third sector research agendas in which knowledge and experience are shared and relevance is emphasized. While maintaining a global approach, it will nevertheless be essential to retain an openness which will allow the richness and detail required to understand the contexts and particular types of organization which make up different third sectors. While the third sector is being reshaped, researchers and practitioners will more than ever need to share the commonalities and the diversity of their experience.

CONCLUSION

This chapter has argued that there are now two parallel universes of academic literature dealing with third sector organizations in North and South which are both different and separate such that they barely acknowledge each other. This is a problem because the two literatures actually cover many comparable issues and potential learning opportunities are therefore being missed. Secondly, this separateness runs counter to the phenomenon of globalization as well as the potential theoretical convergences apparent in North and South around such concepts as civil society, social exclusion and social capital. Thirdly, there is now a varied and dynamic spectrum of international third sector linkages already existing between North and South which the third sector research literature should perhaps reflect more fully.

Nevertheless, in sketching out potentially new third sector research agendas and a possible era of enhanced cooperation between nonprofit and NGO researchers, there are many potential hazards to be faced. On a practical level, there is evidence that learning across contexts and the replication of approaches can be a difficult process (Hulme, 1993). There is the risk of continuing domination of Southern policy agendas by the North as Northern nonprofit researchers move into wider transnational research work. We might lose sight of the scale of problems of poverty in the South as compared to the North. However, if the parallel research universes as presently constituted are allowed to solidify further, then opportunities for further learning may be missed and the relevancy of future third sector research may be diminished.

Future research on third sector roles and contexts in both North and South will need to take account of the changes and challenges outlined in this paper. Are NGOs to be seen merely as humanitarian relief organizations ('ladles for the global soup kitchen', as Fowler (1995a) has suggested) to mop up during complex political emergencies or are they catalysts contributing to the promotion of social and economic change? Are nonprofit organizations increasingly being asked to bear the brunt of state withdrawal from public services in industrialized countries or do they form part of a pluralistic civil society? Will international connections between third sector organizations contribute to the formation of 'global civil society' (Macdonald, 1994)? Such concerns are as central to the voluntary sectors of the UK or the US as they are to those in aid-recipient countries.

ENDNOTES

1 This introduction is a revised version of the overview paper presented at the conference 'NGOs and Voluntary Organizations in North and South: Learning From Each Other?' organized by the Centre for Voluntary Organisation and held at LSE on September 18–19 1997.

2 While recognizing the limitations of such a simple dualist terminology, the terms 'North' and 'South' are used for the purposes of argument in this paper to distinguish rich industrialized countries from low income, aid-recipient ones.

3 Brett (1996) is an important exception to the latter generalization.

4 Exceptions to the pro-NGO tone found in much of the literature can be found in Tendler (1982) and Sogge (1996). Much of the more 'critical' research literature focuses on the emergency relief work of 'Northern' NGOs in Africa, such as Abdel Ati (1993) and Hanlon (1991).

5 There are some notable exceptions, such as Tandon (1995), Fisher (1994) and Fowler (1997).

6 In order to make more constructive links between the two literatures we need to find a way through the terminological and conceptual confusion which exists around the international third sector. It is suggested here that many of the differences of terminology, emphasis and focus may derive as much from the histories of these different fields of study as from differences between third sector organization structures, activities or contexts. For example, organizational differences might be reflected more accurately if a conceptual distinction is made between 'grassroots membership associations' and 'formal bureaucratic organizations' or between 'welfare organizations' and 'social change organizations'. This might provide a sounder basis for comparative research than the current practice of drawing taxonomic distinctions on the basis of whether organizations are working in developing country or rich country contexts.

7 In recognition of this problem, no attempt has been made in this book to standardize terminology and it has been left up to each contributor to define their own terms.

8 A notable exception is the community development literature which has apparently avoided this problem (eg Craig and Mayo, 1995).

9 The present author is not blameless in this regard and has himself published material on NGOs by this route.

10 Personal communication, Peter Robinson, Humanitas Foundation, New York.

11 Personal communication, staff member of the British Department for International Development (DFID).

BIBLIOGRAPHY

Anheier, H K (1990) 'Themes in international research in the nonprofit sector', *Nonprofit and Voluntary Sector Quarterly*, Vol 19, No 4, pp371–391

Anheier, H K (1995) 'Theories of the nonprofit sector: three issues', *Nonprofit and Voluntary Sector Quarterly*, Vol 24, No 1, pp15–23

Abdel Ati, H R (1993) 'The development impact of NGO activities in the Red Sea province of Sudan: a critique', *Development and Change*, Vol 24, No 1, pp103–130

Beall, J (ed) (1997) *A City For All: Valuing Difference and Working With Diversity*, Zed Books, London

Bhalla, A and Lapeyre, F (1997) 'Social exclusion: towards an analytical and operational framework', *Development and Change*, Vol 28, No 3, pp413–434

Biggs, S and Smith, G (1998) 'Beyond methodologies: coalition-building for participatory technology development', *World Development*, Vol 26, No 2, pp239–248

Billis, D (1984) *Welfare Bureaucracies: Their Design and Change in Response to Social Problems*, Heinemann, London

Billis, D (1993) *Organising Public and Voluntary Agencies*, Routledge, London

Billis, D and MacKeith, J (1993) *Managing NGOs*, Centre for Voluntary Organisation, London School of Economics, London

Billis, D and Harris, M (1996) *Voluntary Agencies: Challenges of Organisation and Management*, Macmillan, London

Bond, B (1996) *North/South Linking: Who Benefits?* UK One World Linking Association, Chesterfield, UK

Brett, E A (1996) 'The participatory principle in development projects: the costs and benefits of co-operation', *Journal of Public Administration and Development*, Vol 16, No 1, pp5–21

Brown, L D and Tandon, R (1994) 'Institutional development for strengthening civil society', *Institutional Development*, Vol 1, No 1, pp3–17

Butler, R and Wilson, D (1990) *Managing Nonprofit and Voluntary Organizations*, Routledge, London

Carroll, T (1992) *Intermediary NGOs: The Supporting Link in Grassroots Development*, Kumarian, Connecticut

Chambre, S (1997) 'Civil society, differential resources, and organizational development: HIV/AIDS organizations in New York City', *Nonprofit and Voluntary Sector Quarterly*, Vol 26, No 4, pp466–488

Clark, J (1991) *Democratizing Development: The Role of Voluntary Organizations*, Earthscan, London

Craig, G and Mayo, M (eds) (1995) *Community Empowerment: A Reader in Participation and Development*, Zed Books, London

Cresswell, T (1996) 'Participatory appraisal in the UK urban health sector: keeping faith with perceived needs', *Development in Practice*, Vol 6, No 1, pp16–24

Drabek, A G (ed) (1987) *World Development* (Supplement), Vol 15, ppix–xv

Edwards, M and Hulme, D (1992) *Making A Difference: NGOs and Development in a Changing World*, Earthscan, London

Edwards, M and Hulme, D (1995) *NGO Performance and Accountability: Beyond the Magic Bullet*, Earthscan, London

Escobar, A (1995) *Encountering Development: The Making and Unmaking of the Third World*, Princeton University Press, Princeton

Farrington, J and Bebbington, A J with Wellard, K and Lewis, D (1993) *Reluctant Partners?: NGOs, The State and Sustainable Agricultural Development*, Routledge, London

Fisher, J (1994) 'Is the iron law of oligarchy rusting away in the Third World?', *World Development*, Vol 22, No 2, pp129–143

Fowler, A (1995a) 'Capacity building and NGOs: a case of strengthening ladles for the global soup kitchen?', *Institutional Development*, Vol 1, No 1, pp18–24

Fowler, A (1995b) 'Assessing NGO performance: difficulties, dilemmas and a way ahead', in Edwards, M and Hulme, D (eds) *NGO Performance and Accountability: Beyond the Magic Bullet*, Earthscan, London

Fowler, A (1997) *Striking A Balance: A Guide to Enhancing the Effectiveness of NGOs in International Development*, Earthscan, London

Fox, J (1996) 'How does civil society thicken? The political construction of social capital in rural Mexico', *World Development*, Vol 24, No 6, pp1089–1104

Gardner, K and Lewis, D (1996) *Anthropology, Development and the Post-Modern Challenge*, Pluto, London

Gaventa, J (1991) 'Building a worldwide NGO movement', speech to InterAction Forum, 1991, US

Gaventa, N (1997) 'Participation, poverty and social exclusion in the North and South', *Participation and Governance*, Vol 4, No 11, pp6–10

Giddens, A (1993) *The Consequences of Modernity*, Polity Press, Cambridge

Hall, L M and Hall, M F (1996) 'Big fights: competition between poor people', *Nonprofit and Voluntary Sector Quarterly*, Vol 25, No 1, pp53–72

Hanlon, J (1991) *Mozambique: Who Calls the Shots?* James Currey, London

Hann, C and Dunn, E (1996) *Civil Society: Challenging Western Models*, Routledge, London

Harbeson, J W, Rothchild, D and Chazan, N (1994) *Civil Society and The State in Africa*, Rienner, London

Harris, M (1998) *Organising God's Work: Challenges for Churches and Synagogues*, Macmillan, London

Harris, N (1986) *The End of the Third World*, Penguin Books, Harmondsworth

Harriss, J (1997) '"Missing link" or analytically missing? The concept of social capital', *Journal of International Development*, Vol 9, No 7, pp919–938

Holcombe, S (1995) *Managing to Empower: The Grameen Bank's Experience of Poverty Alleviation*, Zed Books, London

Hulme, D (1993) 'Replicating finance programmes in Malawi and Malaysia', *Small Enterprise Development*, Vol 4, No 4, pp4–15

Hulme, D and Edwards, M (1997) *Too Close For Comfort?: NGOs, States and Donors*, Macmillan, London

Korten, D C (1990) *Getting to the 21st Century: Voluntary Action and the Global Agenda*, Kumarian, Connecticut

Kramer, R (1994) 'Voluntary agencies and the contract culture: dream or nightmare?', *Social Service Review*, Vol 63, No 1, March, pp33–60

Kramer, R M; Lorentzen, H, Melief, W B and Pasquinelli, S (1993) *Privatisation in Four European Countries: Comparative Studies in Government–Third Sector Relationships*, M E Sharpe, New York

Kumar, S and Hudock, A (1996) 'Grants, contracts and NGO accountability in north and south', *Soundings: A Journal of Politics and Culture*, Issue 4, Autumn, pp195–202

Leat, D (1997) 'Review article: visiting the world of NGOs', *Nonprofit Studies*, Vol 1, No 2, pp47–51

Lewis, D and Sobhan, B (1999) 'Routes of funding, roots of trust? Northern NGOs, Southern NGOs, donors and the rise of direct funding', forthcoming in *Development In Practice*, Vol 9, No 1

Lind, A (1996) 'Gender, development and urban social change: women's community action in global cities', *World Development*, Vol 25, No 8, pp1205–1223

Macdonald, L (1994) 'Globalizing civil society: interpreting international NGOs in Central America', *Millennium: Journal of International Studies*, Vol 23, No 2, pp267–285

Mehmet, O (1995) *Westernizing The Third World: The Eurocentricity of Economic Development Theories*, Routledge, London

Midgley, J (1995) *Social Development: The Development Perspective in Social Welfare*, Sage, London

Najam, A (1996) 'Understanding the third sector: revisiting the prince, the merchant and the citizen', *Nonprofit Management and Leadership*, Vol 7, No 2, pp203–219

NCVO News (1996) *Tackling Injustice In Our Own Back Yard*, National Council for Voluntary Organisations, London

NGLS (1997) *Implementing Agenda 21: NGO Experiences From Around the World*, UN Non-Governmental Liaison Service, Geneva

Norton, M (1996) *The Worldwide Fundraiser's Handbook*, Directory of Social Change/International Fundraising Group, London

Powell, W W (1987) *The Non-Profit Sector: A Research Handbook*, Yale University Press, Yale

Putzel, J (1997) 'Accounting for the "dark side" of social capital: reading Robert Putnam on democracy', *Journal of International Development*, Vol 9, No 7, pp939–950

Robinson, M (1993) 'Governance, democracy and conditionality: NGOs and the new policy agenda', in Clayton, A (ed) *Governance, Democracy and Conditionality: What Role for NGOs?* INTRAC, Oxford

Salamon, L (1994) *Partners in Public Service: Government–Nonprofit Relations in the Modern Welfare State*, Johns Hopkins, Baltimore

Salamon, L and Anheier, H (1992) 'In search of the non-profit sector: in search of definitions', *Voluntas*, Vol 3, No 2, pp125–152

Salamon, L and Anheier, H (1997) *Defining the Nonprofit Sector: A Cross-National Analysis*, Manchester University Press, Manchester

Smillie, I (1995) *The Alms Bazaar: Nonprofit Organizations and International Development*, Intermediate Technology, London

Smith, S R and Lipsky, M (1993) *Non-profits for Hire: The Welfare State in the Age of Contracting*, Harvard University Press, Cambridge

Sogge, D (1996) 'Northern Lights', in *Compassion and Calculation: The Business of Foreign Aid*, Pluto, London

Tandon, R (1995) 'Board games: governance and accountability in NGOs', in Edwards, M and Hulme, D (eds) *NGO Performance And Accountability: Beyond the Magic Bullet*, Earthscan, London

Tendler, J (1982) 'Turning private voluntary organizations into development agencies: questions for evaluation', Program Evaluation Discussion Papers No 12, Washington, DC

Vakil, A C (1997) 'Confronting the classification problem: towards a taxonomy of NGOs', *World Development*, Vol 25, No 12, pp2057–2070

Williamson, A P (1996) 'Citizen participation, local social and economic development and the third sector: the influence of the European Union on policy innovation in the two parts of Ireland', paper to Second International Conference of the International Society for Third Sector Research, Mexico: July

Wood, G D (1997) 'States without citizens: the problem of the franchise state', in Hulme, D and Edwards, M (eds) (1997) *Too Close for Comfort? NGOs, States and Donors*, Macmillan, London

Wuyts, M, Macintosh, M and Hewitt, T (eds) (1992) *Development Policy and Public Action*, Oxford University Press, Oxford

Young, D (1992) 'Organising principles for international advocacy organizations', *Voluntas*, Vol 3, No 1, pp1–28

Part 1
Linkages and Learning

1

Crossing the Great Divide: Building Links and Learning Between NGOs and Community-Based Organizations in North and South

John Gaventa

INTRODUCTION

NGOs involved in development face a great geographical divide. On the one hand, we have those organizations which work on issues of poverty, community regeneration and the strengthening of civil society in the North. On the other hand, we find a vast range of NGOs, community-based organizations (CBOs) and others which focus on similar development issues in the South. Historically there is little sharing and learning between these groups across the hemispheres. While many larger NGOs working in the South are in fact based in the North, they have had little contact with issues in their own countries similar to those upon which they focus elsewhere.

Increasingly, especially in a context of globalization, this division must change. For NGOs, globalization offers a series of challenges for developing new models for linking and learning on strategies for approaching common problems in both North and South. Fortunately, we are beginning to see a number of attempts by NGOs in North and South to forge such new ways of working.

In this chapter, I will share some concrete examples of exchanges of experience between NGOs and CBOs in poor regions of the US with their Southern counterparts. These exchanges took place, on the whole, in conjunction with the work of the Highlander Research and Education Center, based in Tennessee. Highlander has worked as an NGO for over 60 years in the poor regions of the US, especially in the rural south and the Appalachian regions. Its work in education for community empowerment and community development has contributed significantly to the strengthening of popular participation in areas of labour rights, civil rights, poverty alleviation, community regeneration and the environment. From 1976–1993, I worked as a staff member, and later as Director, at Highlander.

I will first of all look further at the context in which we worked – what we came to know as the 'South within the North'. Secondly, I will examine the context of the voluntary sector in the US, suggesting that there are very differing understandings of its nature and character. Finally, I will turn to four examples of exchange of experience between NGOs and CBOs in the North and South, with some reflections on the lessons learned in the process.

THE 'SOUTH WITHIN THE NORTH'

While we often think of poverty in the South and wealth in the North, these distinctions are increasingly misleading. While the North clearly is a place of relative wealth, it also contains within it large-scale poverty, increasing inequality and highly uneven development. In the US, we find areas within inner cities and vast rural areas where levels of poverty, unemployment, relatively poor education, illiteracy, lack of access to health care and so on provide similarities to certain parts of the South. With growing inequality in industrialized countries, the movement of jobs and industry to newly industrialized regions of the South, increasing issues of access to basic services such as health care for the poor in many countries, and the globalization of goods, services and information, the traditional distinctions between North and South need to be re-examined. In our work in the US, we came to recognize that there are 'Souths within the North', just as there may be 'Norths within the South' (Gaventa, 1991).

In a recent seminar series at the Institute for Development Studies on Social Exclusion in North and South, Simon Maxwell (1997) suggested that we could examine the new relationships between North and South in terms of comparisons, convergences and connections. Each is helpful in understanding issues of poverty, participation and social exclusion.

Comparisons

While poverty may not be of the same scale, nor perhaps in many places as desperate in poor areas in the North as in other parts of the world, there are parallel issues, including those of illiteracy, access to health care, environmental degradation, distribution of land and natural resources and the like. While globally, for instance, the levels of inequality are known to be increasing in the South and North, it is not often realized that the level of income inequality in the US is higher than in many other countries, including those in the South. According to one study:

> *The share of income among the lowest 40% of American households,
> in 1985, places the United States behind every one of the 25 nations
> with high-income economies, except for Australia and Singapore,
> according to the World Bank. Of the 21 low-and moderate income
> nations reporting income distribution, the U.S. falls behind nine of
> them, including Bangladesh, Ghana, India and Pakistan. The
> United States' income distribution is more 'equitable' than only its
> client states of Central and Latin America: Guatemala, Peru,
> Colombia, Jamaica, Costa Rica, Venezuela, and Brazil (Couto, 1994:
> 22, quoting World Bank, 1991: Table 30).*

In addition to these comparisons of conditions, there have also been
comparative analyses and explanations for the underlying causes of these
conditions. It has not been uncommon in literature on community and
regional development in the US for rural areas such as Appalachia, the
Black Belt south or native reservations to be analysed using colonial or
third world analogies, or to be understood as peripheral regions in the
larger world economy.

Convergences

The growth of parts of the South and the decline of parts of the North argue
for a convergence of conditions in the 'low end' of the North and the 'high
end' of the South. For instance, industries which used to look to low-wage
rural areas for resources and labour, such as the Appalachian Region of the
US or the Welsh valleys in the UK, have now left for other parts of the
world, leaving behind large scale areas of de-industrialization. These
convergences have led in some instances to new reversals – for instance, a
South Korean plant recently came to South Wales, lured by the low-wage
labour and favourable business incentives.

Connections

Beyond parallels and convergences there are also increasingly connections
between poor regions of the North and South, as we are reminded by the
literature on globalization. While these connections are often articulated in
terms of economic connections brought on by multinationals or capital
mobility, or by cultural connections encouraged by global media and information technologies, there are also social and intellectual connections
involving shared development strategies and concepts – including in the
voluntary sector.

THE ROLE OF NGOS AND VOLUNTARY ASSOCIATIONS IN THE US – TWO VIEWS

Around the world, especially in the context of a development crisis, NGOs are increasingly being put forward as a vehicle for development, for social action and as a means of popular participation in social problem-solving. NGOs are becoming a measure of citizen's participation, and in turn, the civil society of which they are a part is seen as a critical part of democracy. As in other areas, there are important parallels between the roles that NGOs and CBOs are being called upon to play as civil society actors in the South, and the role which they have played in the North. The strength of these parallels depends, though, on what kind of voluntary organization we choose to examine.

In the US, for instance, there is a long history of voluntary associations and CBOs. Though the US has lagged behind many other Western democracies (and indeed democracies in other parts of the world) in terms of voter participation or worker participation, it has long been known for its 'civic culture'. In his book *Democracy in America*, written in 1835, the French scholar Alexander de Tocqueville wrote of this American art of forming associations:

> *Nothing, in my view, deserves more attention than the intellectual and moral associations in America ... In democratic countries knowledge of how to combine is the mother of all other forms of knowledge; on its progress depends that of all the others ... (de Tocqueville, 1966: 666).*

Following de Tocqueville's lead, many others have written of the importance of voluntary organizations as mediating organizations between large, bureaucratic institutions such as the state and the corporation, and the individual. Others acknowledge that voluntary organizations have been at the cutting edge of major social reforms and social movements, ranging from the temperance movement to the civil rights movement.

In modern times, the voluntary sector is composed of thousands of groups, many of which are organized and registered as nonprofit organizations – that is, as private groups which exist for a public or charitable purpose. In the last 20 years, these nonprofits have grown rapidly, joining the public and private sectors as key forces for social and economic action. As a generic group, these nonprofits are a vast category, including churches, schools, colleges and universities, research institutions, hospitals, foundations, social action movements, welfare agencies, arts and cultural organizations, community development groups, mutual benefit societies and others (see, for instance, work by Lester Salamon).

Drawing upon this rich but diverse tradition of civic association, there are those who have argued that such a model of civil society should be developed and promoted for strengthening democracy and development in other parts of the world. The number of associations or NGOs is seen as a proxy indicator for a pluralist and robust civil society. Yet perhaps we need to look more closely and critically at the nature of association in American society. While the contribution of voluntary, nonprofit organizations has been great, there is nothing inherent in the status of a voluntary nonprofit organization which leads it to work to remedy the inequalities or problems of society, or to strengthen the participation of the poor in dealing with development issues. In fact, within the literature on participation in the US itself, a number of critiques have been made of pluralist and open models of democracy and civil society which we often seek now to export to other parts of the world.

First, while many may participate in civic life and voluntary associations in the US, some are more able to participate than others. It is a well-known sociological fact that those who are the most privileged in socio-economic status are also the ones most likely to participate in such civic organizations. This produces a paradox of democracy: those that are most badly affected by the pressing problems of poverty, and may need to participate the most to change their conditions, are often the least able or likely to do so (see for example, Verba and Nie, 1972). The increasing inequality between the rich and poor in the US and other countries also has profound effects upon patterns of participation and organization.

Secondly, another body of literature has argued that the lack of participation in civil society is partly the result of barriers which have developed through power relationships that impede participation of certain actors and prevent certain issues from being raised. Rather than looking at who participates to understand civil and political life, we must examine who does not, and why (see, for instance, Bachrach and Baratz, 1970; Gaventa, 1980). From this point of view, American democracy is not necessarily as open to voluntary action as we often suggest, and the pluralism of American democracy is more a pluralism of elites than an indicator of democracy at the grassroots.

Thirdly, recent evidence suggests that civic engagement in the US may itself be on the decline. Robert Putnam (1995: 65), for instance, writes:

> To those concerned with the weakness of civil societies in the developing or postcommunist world, the advanced Western democracies and above all the United States have typically been taken as models to be emulated. There is striking evidence, however, that the vibrancy of American civil society has notably declined over the past several decades.

Despite the declines, we often continue to present to the rest of the world an image of a healthy civil society.

A View from the Grassroots

Within the US, partly in response to these arguments about shortcomings in civic participation, we have seen the growth of a new kind of organization: the grassroots community organization, or community-based group, as a vehicle for participation by the most disenfranchized. While this grassroots, community-based movement also has deep historical roots, its particular form grew out of the War on Poverty, and the civil rights and women's movements of the 1960s and 1970s. With the vacuum in social services and social policy left by the 1980s, this sector has continued to play more of a leadership role in social change. Boyte (1980; Boyte et al, 1986) and others have written about a new American populism, as communities organize to re-democratize the political system. In a recent report, Delgado (1993) argues that there are now over 6000 community organizations in operation in the US, mostly 'local, unaffiliated groups, initiated out of local residents' need to exert control over development in their communities' (10). Among the accomplishments of community organizations has been 'the redress of the balance of power – by holding public servants accountable, CO has managed in many localities to put the "dispossessed at the table" with bankers, planners and politicians' (10–11).

These grassroots organizations are as diverse as the rest of the nonprofit world. They may be organized around communities, neighbourhoods or issues. They are usually local, but increasingly are organizing into state, regional and national associations. They are supported by a vast array of intermediary organizations and NGOs which help to provide funding, training, technical assistance, research and education for their efforts. While diverse, this grassroots movement within the nonprofit sector is bound together by a common set of values and characteristics, as outlined below.

- They give organization and voice to the under-represented in society, and usually are controlled by them. Grassroots organizations have played important roles in the civil rights movements, the women's movement and poor people's movements.
- They raise key issues for the rest of society, serving as a conscience for the nation, advocates for change and sources of innovation and action.
- They often work to deliver needed services – such as housing, education or child care – to groups not reached by, or failed by, the government programmes. In doing so, they seek not just to provide charity to the poor and powerless, but to organize them and to deal with the causes of the problems rather than the symptoms.
- They serve as sources of leadership, development and empowerment, contributing to overall participation and change in the society.

In general then, when we talk about linking NGOs from the North and the South, we must recognize this diversity within the fabric of American civic life. On the one hand the image often given to the South of NGOs or voluntary associations in the North reflects a pluralistic and open view of American society, in which issues of power and poverty are not clearly visible. On the other hand, there is another tradition of community-based and nonprofit organizations which is focused upon remedying inequalities within the US – inequalities similar in nature to those faced by many in the South, and addressed by many Southern NGOs.

Unfortunately, many of the Northern NGOs which work in the South are themselves disconnected from grassroots organizations in their own country, many of which work on similar issues to those that they are addressing abroad. As a result, Northern NGOs may project to the South an image of society and civic life in the North which fails to acknowledge the parallels and commonalities which are potentially shared by NGOs and CBOs across the hemispheres. In so doing, they perhaps inadvertently help to perpetuate older divisions between North and South, rather than countering new trends brought on by globalization. New models of linking across borders within the NGO and voluntary sectors must be found.

BUILDING GLOBAL LINKS: CASE EXAMPLES

From 1976–1993, I worked on the staff of the Highlander Research and Education Center, a relatively small but well-known NGO located in the American South. Highlander has a history of over 60 years of carrying out education and training for grassroots communities in Appalachia and the rural south, among the poorest regions in the country. The history is a rich one, spanning work with the labour movement of the 1930s, the civil rights movement of the 1950s and 1960s, the anti-poverty and community action work of the 1970s and environmental and community economic development in the 1980s and 1990s. As staff of this NGO, we developed the view increasingly during the 1980s that our work in the North needed to be linked to and located in the broader work for community development and empowerment conducted across the globe. There were a number of reasons for this.

First, our reading and experience suggested that as a rural region within a wealthy nation, we shared many problems with other poor regions of the world – problems that were perhaps masked by the Northern, wealthy, urban and industrial context in which we were located. In the US, the issues of rural poor people received relatively low levels of attention compared to many other parts of the world. Yet we found parallel issues and movements in the South, especially around such problems as literacy, land reform, rural development and health care.

Second, we increasingly became struck by parallels in methods of working from which we could learn. Many of these grew from working in a context of relatively low literacy levels, strong cultural traditions of rural and ethnic communities, and needs for empowerment and capacity building similar to those found in the South.

Third, and perhaps most importantly, we increasingly found an inter-relationship between the issues upon which we worked, and those of other countries, to the extent that they simply could not be ignored. For instance, one effect of working with communities affected by the toxic poisoning of water was for the plant to close and move to Latin America, simply displacing the problem to others, rather than solving it. Increased globalization meant that communities were affected by economic blackmail which pitted poor regions and workers against one another, with threats of moving jobs elsewhere if community action became too strong.

With these issues in mind, we began to support and foster a series of exchanges attempting to make global connections between the communities with which we worked and other similar community organizations elsewhere, as well as between ourselves as an NGO and other NGOs. The connections took many forms, but mostly involved exchanges from South to North, or North to South, sharing at international workshops and occasionally joint projects.

In the following section, I will describe some of these exchanges by topic area and then turn to lessons learned from them.

EXAMPLE 1 Learning about Methods: Strengthening Grassroots Voices through Participatory Forms of Education and Research

As an NGO, the Highlander Center was known particularly for its methods of using adult non-formal education as a basis for leadership development and capacity building. These methods emphasized peer learning, building on the experiences of the people themselves and linking education to action – all methods which had developed in the South as well.

In the South, many of these ideas grew from the work of Paulo Freire whose particular approach to education as a process of conscientization of the poor spread rapidly across Latin America and parts of Africa and Asia during the 1970s and 1980s. These ideas affected the work of many NGOs and CBOs in their work with poor organizations, for instance in the ways that the methods were used in the Training for Transformation programme in southern Africa.

In the US, Highlander's work had been influenced by differing – yet somewhat similar – traditions, especially the folk school movement of Scandinavia, and the education for citizenship tradition in the US espoused by adult educators such as John Dewey and Edward Lindemann. In the American south, Highlander was perhaps best known for its work using Citizenship Schools as an approach to literacy with African Americans in a way which also contributed to awareness and organization building, much like Freire's work in northeastern Brazil some years later.

In the late 1980s, Myles Horton, the founder of Highlander, and Paulo Freire came together to write a book about their philosophy and practice of using adult education as a force for social change in the North and South

(Horton et al, 1990). In many ways, the book was an important symbol for linking two parallel yet differing traditions. (In some ways, because Freire's work was ironically often better known in the US than Horton's or that of others who represented the internal popular education work, the project helped to give attention to and legitimate a tradition already present in the North.)

In addition to this intellectual exchange, we were also involved in a number of projects during the 1980s designed to share the experiences of popular educators in the South, especially in Latin America, with those in the US and Canada. These projects included an exchange of popular educators from Latin America, the US and Canada with Nicaragua in 1983; an exchange of literacy workers with Nicaragua; and multiple visits of Southern-based educators to the US, to Highlander and to community-based groups. These exchanges were important for a number of reasons. Firstly, concrete methods for literacy work were learned and strengthened. Secondly, especially given the fact that Nicaraguan literacy work was under attack by the US-supported Contras at the time, US grassroots popular educators gained a view of US foreign policy which deepened and developed their grassroots solidarity with other partners in Central America.

A similar transfer of methods from the South to the North is seen in the development and practice of participatory research. The label 'participatory research' was first used by Freire in a conference in Tanzania in the mid-1970s to refer to approaches which involved grassroots people as researchers themselves, rather than as objects of someone else's research. In 1977 in Latin America the first regional conference on participatory research (PR) was held in Cartagena. Under the auspices of the International Council of Adult Education, during the late 1970s and 1980s networks and approaches to participatory research spread rapidly, including to the North. In the US and Canada the development of PR in the South gave strength, both conceptually and practically, to the growth of similar work there. At the Highlander Center, for instance, while we were using similar approaches in our work with poor communities in the Appalachian region, we gained the name, conceptual and methodological understanding, and peer support from links with these Southern networks, through conferences, newsletters, exchanges and partnerships.

In the 1990s, a similar sharing of methods across hemispheres has occurred in the spread of participatory rural appraisal (PRA), now more commonly known as participatory learning and action (PLA), from South to North. First used as a method in India and east Africa in the mid-1980s, these tools have spread rapidly to over 70 countries, and have been used with community development workers in the North. In the UK, for instance, PRA networks have developed in Scotland and in Berkshire and the methods have been used in projects from local planning in Gloucester to assessing health care on housing estates in south London. In one case, PRA practitioners from the South facilitated a community-based planning exercise in Scotland (see resource materials, publications and records at IDS, University of Sussex).

The convergence and sharing of participatory methods between South and North was most recently seen in a conference in Cartagena, Colombia in June 1997. In commemoration of the first Latin American meeting on participatory research held there 20 years before, over 1500 scholars and practitioners representing traditions of PR from both hemispheres came together for a joint congress to share their ideas and experiences.

EXAMPLE 2 Linking Common Issues in Occupational and Environmental Health

While the above exchanges focused on sharing methods of working, especially in participatory education and research, other exchanges have concentrated on linking groups facing common problems, and responding together. At Highlander, one of the areas that became particularly important involved issues of occupational and environmental health, especially those arising from the movement of wastes and toxic produce across the globe.

Appalachia had long experience in this area. As an area with weak enforcement of laws, plenty of land and water, and a relatively (in the North) low-wage, low-literacy workforce, it was a preferred location for the development of more dangerous industries. With globalization of markets and production, as well as increased costs and stronger environmental and occupational regulation in the North, these same industries began during the 1970s and 1980s to expand in Southern countries as well.

In 1984, Juliet Merrifield and John Gaventa from Highlander were invited by the Society for Participatory Research in Asia (PRIA) to go to India to share our work in participatory education and research with Appalachian communities on environmental and occupational health issues. Using videos made with American workers, examples were shown of workers and community groups who had organized around such issues as 'brown lung' in the textile mills, or water contamination from chemical plants. A key workshop was held in Bombay with NGOs and workers for whom this was a relatively new field.

A few months after this workshop, the Bhopal disaster occurred, in which a gas leak from United Carbide's chemical factory killed an estimated 10,000 people and maimed thousands more. Once again there were parallels – the Bhopal plant was modelled after a similar Union Carbide plant that had been built in the relatively poor, primarily black Appalachian community of Charleston, West Virginia.

Because of the links which had been built between Highlander and PRIA, they were able to respond quickly in a number of initiatives to share learning on this issue between North and South. A joint research project, *No Place to Run*, told the story of Union Carbide's record in the US, India and other communities globally. A video tape was made in the US sharing the reactions to similar (though far smaller in scope) industrial accidents in factories in the Institute plant and elsewhere; the tape was for use in India. A delegation of health and worker activists came to the US, sponsored by

PRIA and Highlander, to share the story of Bhopal as well as to learn more about the experience of US NGOs in dealing with occupational and environmental health issues.

Through this effort, learning occurred at a number of levels. While the US media had attempted to portray the accident as the result of the failures of Indian management, the stories from the US helped to show that similar problems occurred there as well. While Union Carbide flew an Indian doctor from its West Virginia plant to Bhopal to assure residents that there would not be significant health problems, groups in the US were able to use freedom of information laws to obtain documents filed in West Virginia by the same doctor declaring the opposite. The visit of the Indian delegation to poor communities in the US also affected by chemical industries heightened the awareness in the North of their common vulnerabilities with communities in other parts of the world.

In India, the impact of the exchange is still being felt. Some 15 years later, Rajesh Tandon of PRIA reflected:

> *These exchanges triggered off a set of activities focusing on worker awareness and occupational health. When our team visited the southern United States in the aftermath of Bhopal, we were impressed by the initiatives of local communities and workers' organizations. The timing of their visit, the sharing of experiences and the support resulted in the establishment of our Centre for Occupational and Environmental Health in PRIA, with fifteen years of experience and a lifetime of commitment (personal interview, August 1997).*

EXAMPLE 3 Who Speaks for the North? The UN Conference on Environment and Development

Through the exchanges and work on Bhopal, as well as through other such incidents, Highlander became increasingly aware of the similarities between issues of environment and development in poor regions of the North and those of other parts of the world. In the early 1990s, with funding from the MacArthur Foundation, Highlander joined with the Institute for Development Research (IDR) and the Program in Conflict Management Alternatives (PCMA) at the University of Michigan to develop a series of exchanges around environment and sustainable development with three Southern partners: the Kenyan Energy and Environment Organization (KENGO); the Movimiento Ambientalista Nicaraguenese (MAN); and the Indonesian Environmental Forum (WALHI).

As an initial part of the three-year exchange, the Southern delegates came to the southern US where they had a chance, in the summer of 1991, to visit rural communities also facing serious environmental issues. They expressed shock at the conditions they saw. At a concluding workshop which brought the international delegates together with representatives of local CBOs and NGOs they had visited, a delegate from Kenya posed the question: 'What will be your position at the UNCED meetings and how are people in your communities feeling about the process?' There were blank stares around the room on the faces of the US activists. 'What is UNCED?' they asked.[1]

The encounter characterized a critical problem of who speaks for the North in the international arena. While many US-based NGOs were of course working to prepare for the United Nations Conference on Environment and Development (UNCED), they on the whole were working with Southern partners, not with grassroots communities in the North. Those speaking for the environment from the North were national governments (in this case the Bush administration) and US-based corporations. US NGOs and CBOs working on issues in the North have, on the whole, not been part of such international fora.

The encounter prompted Highlander, working with other environmental NGOs, to invite grassroots voices from the North to share in the UNCED process. Towards this end, we asked community-based groups in the North to relate their stories of environment and development as part of a report to be released at the Rio conference, co-organized a grassroots people's forum in New York to coincide with the Fourth Preparatory Meeting leading up to the Brazil conference, and organized a delegation of grassroots community leaders to go to Brazil to interact with their counterparts in the Southern hemisphere.

The experience was a powerful one for those involved. The grassroots report gave a very different interpretation of problems of environment and development faced in the North from that provided by the official governmental and non-governmental delegates, who attempted to downplay the problems of environmental degradation at home. Moreover, US activists saw their connections with others around the world. As one young woman from an inner city neighbourhood group dealing with a toxic waste issue wrote:

> *I was surprised to find they deal with many of the same problems as the United States and more ... For me it [the Earth Summit] has underscored the terrible damage we human beings have done to ourselves and our planet. It has revealed the inseparable links between the World Bank, international debt, and unchecked industrial development with poverty, hunger, serious health effects, environmental pollution and world climate change. It has shown the world that these global problems are not simply someone else's concern but a threat to everyone everywhere* (Highlander Reports, 1993: 4).

EXAMPLE 4 Speaking with New Voice to the North: Linking Workers on Jobs and Trade Issues

A final example involves exchanges with workers affected by job loss and by plant closings. Industries which once came to these relatively poor regions of the North looking for low-skill, low-wage labour are now moving on to newly developing parts of the South, where costs are even cheaper. The Appalachian south has been one such region which has been hard hit, as industries flee 'from the mountains to the maquiladoras' (Gaventa, 1990).

At times in such situations, the tendency of Northern workers and community members has been to blame workers elsewhere for 'stealing their jobs', not to assess the corporate and governmental policies in their own country that may have contributed to their job loss. Partly in response to this issue, Highlander worked with the Tennessee Industrial Renewal Network (TIRN), a coalition of unions, churches and CBOs, to organize a study tour so that women who had lost their jobs in the Appalachian region could visit their counterparts who had gained similar jobs in the South – in this case, the maquiladora region of Mexico.

As in other examples given above, the women workers were struck by the parallels they found in the rapidly industrializing parts of Mexico. At the same time, they were shocked by the working and living conditions they saw, conditions promoted by a US corporation and government to which they felt some loyalty. The learning led to new types of action. The US workers, who themselves were primarily unemployed or worked in low-wage jobs, pledged to raise money for a van to be used for a new organization of women workers in Mexico. But more importantly, they began to take action in their own country on government policies which they came to see as part of the reason for their job loss, travelling throughout the state testifying on jobs and trade issues in the context of the North American Free Trade Agreement (NAFTA) debate.

Testifying before a trade policy committee, one of the women, a member of TIRN and of her local union, expressed her learning this way:

> They [the Mexican women] were glad to welcome us because they believed us when we said we would try to come back to this country and tell the American people the truth about life and work in the maquiladoras. They asked us to bring back the word to you about what is happening to those on the bottom in Mexico. Because what is happening ought to be a crime. And it is hurting not only Mexicans, it is a direct threat to the standard of living of American workers.
>
> The multi-national corporations bear much responsibility for what is happening. But it is not just the corporation I blame. I blame the government too. Our government should be insisting on corporate accountability. Instead it rewards irresponsibility. Our government should set some ground rules so companies are not

> *pressured to compete with each other on the basis of how much they can gouge their workers. Instead, it pushes a version of free trade that encourages low wage competition.*
>
> *We must learn from the failures of the maquiladora program and develop a free trade agreement with Mexico that will not repeat the same patterns. We need decent jobs at decent wages for workers on both sides of the border. We need roads and sewers and schools and garbage disposal and health care and retirement plans and parks and safe workplaces and playgrounds on both sides of the border.*
>
> *Any trade deal we reach with Mexico should start with a commitment to a healthy development pattern for both countries (Petty, 1991: 8).*

In this case, the American workers and community groups became vocal organizers, educators and activists at home regarding policy issues affecting trade, human rights and the environment in the South, as well as at home.

CONCLUSION: KEY LESSONS AND THEMES FOR NORTH–SOUTH LEARNING

These are a few examples of learning that have come about through exchanges between Northern and Southern NGOs and communities. What do these examples tell us about the value of such work? Several key principles emerge.

De-mythologizing North and South

First, through these exchanges we have seen that there are numerous examples of participants gaining a recognition of the commonalities between their own situations and those of others in different parts of the globe. This recognition was particularly important because of the ways in which the exchanges worked to de-mythologize the differences between the North and South.

For Southern activists, the image of the US as a land of relative wealth and opportunity serves as a powerful symbol, suggesting that the US model offers a more 'advanced' approach to development. Many participants talked about how important it was for them to see that the North faced similar problems as well. This deconstruction of the symbolic divisions and the recognition of commonalities, as well as differences, became a first necessary step for further learning and action.

For example, following their visit to the US, participants in the worker and occupational health exchange wrote:

> *... we did not believe the under-development we saw in the world's largest capitalist state ... Though the context of that poverty is somewhat different from our situation in India, we were able to understand the growing phenomenon of third world creation within the USA. The powerless and the poor of USA face similar forces as similar groups face in India. This realisation made us keen to learn seriously from the experiences of community groups and workers' associations there (Pandey et al, 1985: 29).*

A Nicaraguan participant in environmental exchanges said:

> *The collaboration has provided enormous learnings for all of us ... We still believed in the U.S. discourse on democracy, on the 'perfect' U.S. model. Through our visit to Highlander, we saw the problems and the links. Our communities and countries serve as the testing ground to see if the North can send us their waste, saying that it promoted jobs. Before the exchange, I would not have seen those relationships. This process has helped us to strengthen the relationships between communities, NGOs and communities and governments. The richness of the experience also contributed to strengthening our capacities for analysis within the diversities of our societies. By building new linkages, opportunities for reflection and communication, we are on the verge of the birth of a new methodology of participation – it's not fully cooked but it's beginning (Covey et al, 1995: 9).*

Equally important for Northern participants was the debunking of received myths about the South. The US educational system and media in particular have tended to limit the understanding and images ordinary people have of the rest of the world. At one level, participants expressed amazement at the knowledge, commitment and sophistication of their Southern counterparts – a reality that did not fit with their received images of 'backward' people. Moreover, they often gained inspiration from the commitment which they saw:

> *I grew up in the civil rights movement so I know about overcoming. I've had personal battles and have made it through but the day-to-day survival scenes I saw in Brazil taught me the meaning of faith, hope and forgiveness. I watched people who possess true power (quoted in* Highlander Reports, *1993: 4).*

Another Northern participant commented:

> *By getting rid of our myths, we create the desire to learn more. Understanding that we have been taught wrong and then looking at the problems and consequences of that misteaching creates enormous*

> *openings. It's like turning a rock into a piece of clay that wants to be*
> *malleable by choice (quoted in Covey et al, 1995: 11).*

For participants from both North and South, seeing similar problems in other parts of the world helped to highlight the universal nature of the problems they were addressing, and to reinforce that they were rooted in larger patterns of development rather than in their own particular circumstance.

The Value of Sharing Methods and Approaches

The case examples have also indicated several examples of where NGOs and CBOs have learned new methods and approaches for their work across North and South – for instance, the use of popular education and PR from the South to the North, or the ways of addressing problems of industrial health, from North to South. There are many other recent examples of transfer of methods in both directions – the use of community or advocacy methods have transferred from the North to the South; the adaptation of Gandhian non-violent methods to the American civil rights movement; the transfer of models of micro-credit and banking from the South to organizations in the US and the UK and so on.

At the same time, the exchanges also pointed to some differences in the types of methods of organizing and action that are possible in different contexts. Some Northern participants expressed shock at the conditions of repression and violence which they saw in other countries, while some Southern delegates learned from the relative openness which they found in the US.

> *Before we went to Brazil, I knew the world was messed up. I knew*
> *about haves and have nots. I knew about the interdependence of the*
> *world's problems stemming from greed and supported by race, class,*
> *and sex division among people. I knew all this by having experi-*
> *enced being a Black, poor, female living in my native Kansas. What*
> *I did not know was that my experiences were similar to those of*
> *many persons from all over the world. What is worse, I was lucky*
> *not to have lived with the daily violence supporting the oppressive*
> *conditions (quoted in* Highlander Reports, *1993: 15).*

While Northern participants learned a great deal about participatory methods from the South, Southern participants reported learning about advocacy and organizing strategies from the North, as well as strategies concerned with freedom of information.

Mutual Learning and Horizontal Relationships

The growing recognition of common issues and of the value of exchanging lessons and experiences can begin to contribute to new models of working together across hemispheres. In the past, relationships between Northern and Southern NGOs have often been somewhat vertical, with the Northern NGOs seen as donors and advisers to the South, and the Southern NGOs seen mainly as recipients and local partners. In the cases examined here, relationships were more horizontal and learning was considered a mutual process. A critical feature of the learning was the fact that people linked based *on their own experiences*. As Rajesh Tandon of PRIA put it, 'when we came together people never talked about other's realities. People talked about their own. It felt like a genuine discussion' (personal interview). The creation of mutual learning and horizontal links also allows the possibility of building the trust and social capital necessary for collaboration across borders.

Towards New Organizational Innovation

To deepen learning and linkages between North and South will itself require new organizational development and innovation. In the cases here, the sharing occurred mainly through isolated exchanges and workshops. A next step, but one which is equally important, is to begin to build North–South alliances and coalitions, or global civil society organizations, which can move from learning to action, and from vertical to horizontal ways of relating.

To do so is not an easy task. To develop and sustain partnerships across borders is logistically and financially difficult, and it also requires the development of new relationships of trust and social capital, new organizational forms, and new commitment to recognize and act upon issues of poverty and power in the North as well as the South. This paper has begun to suggest that such new approaches are possible, especially when they are built upon prior learning that involves de-mythologizing stereotypes of North and South, sharing methods and experiences of work, and mutual, horizontal forms of exchange.

ENDNOTE

1 Drawn from Highlander Center documents and personal observation.

BIBLIOGRAPHY

Bachrach, P and Baratz, M S (1970) *Power and Poverty: Theory and Practice*, Oxford University Press, New York

Boyte, H C (1980) *The Backyard Revolution: Understanding the New Citizen Movement*, Temple University Press, Philadelphia

Boyte, H C, Booth, H and Max, S (1986) *Citizen Action and the New American Populism*, Temple University Press, Philadelphia

Couto, R A (1994) *An American Challenge*, Kendall/Hunt Publishing Company, Dubuque, Iowa

Covey, J, Gaventa, J, Miller, V and Pasmore, W (1995) 'Multinational collaboration in community problem solving: a theoretical perspective', paper presented at the Conference on Organizational Dimensions of Global Change, May 1995' sponsored by Academy of Management and Case Western Reserve University

Delgado, G (1993) *Beyond the Politics of Place: New Directions in Community Organizing in the 1990s*, Applied Research Center, Oakland

de Tocqueville, A (1966, originally written in 1835) *Democracy in America*, volume 2, Collins Fontana Library, London

Gaventa, J (1980) *Power and Powerlessness: Quiescence and Rebellion in an Appalachian Valley*, University of Illinois Press, Urbana and Clarendon Press, Oxford

Gaventa, J (1990) 'From the mountains to the maquiladoras: a case study of capital flight and its impact on workers', in Gaventa, J, Smith, B and Willingham, A (eds) *Communities in Economic Crisis*, Temple University Press, Philadelphia

Gaventa, J (1991) 'Overcoming constraints to ill-health in Appalachia, community-based links with the world', in Morgan, R E Jr and Rau, B (eds) *Global Learning for Health*, National Council for International Health, Washington, DC

Highlander Reports (1993) 'Making the links: the southeast and the southern hemisphere: local community leaders and the United Nations Conference on Environment and Development', Highlander Research and Education Center, Tennessee

Horton, M, Freire, P, Bell, B, Gaventa, J and Peters, J (eds) (1990) *We Make the Road by Walking: Conversations on Education and Social Change*, Temple University Press, Philadelphia

Maxwell, S (1997) *Comparisons, Convergence, and Connections: Development Studies in North and South*, Institute for Development Studies, Sussex

Pandey, G, Thankappan, D, Kanhere, V and Tandon, R (1985) *Worker Activists and Educators Tour: Report of USA and UK*, Society for Participatory Research in Asia, New Delhi

Petty, D (1991) Testimony Prepared for the Trade Staff Policy Committee, Office of the US Trade Representative, Atlanta, Georgia, August 29, Tennessee Industrial Renewal Network, Knoxville, Tennessee

Putnam, R D (1995) 'Bowling alone: America's declining social capital', *Journal of Democracy*, Vol 6, No 1, pp65–78

Verba, G and Nie, N H (1972) *Participation in America: Political Democracy and Social Equality*, Harper and Row, New York

World Bank (1991) *World Development Report 1991*, Table 30, Oxford University Press, New York

2

Social Learning in South–North Coalitions: Constructing Knowledge Systems Across Social Chasms[1]

L David Brown

INTRODUCTION

The construction of knowledge systems involves the development of ideas and conceptual frameworks that inform thinking and practice. Knowledge systems are the product of sustained and iterative inquiry that is shaped, supported, validated and preserved by the social systems in which system creators and users are embedded (Kuhn, 1970). Knowledge construction, in short, involves both intellectual and social processes.

The creation of knowledge systems to guide complex activities may require contributions from quite diverse actors. Developing knowledge systems that enable effective and sustainable local development in an increasingly global world, for example, may require contributions from local activists as well as academic theorists, and from Northern policy makers as well as Southern villagers. So creating some kinds of needed knowledge systems may require spanning social, political, economic and cultural chasms.

But we also know that other things being equal, human beings are most comfortable with others like them. It is not easy to work with or learn from others who are different. Communities with different assumptions may well belittle each other's claims to producing knowledge. Scientists and practitioners often have difficulty understanding each other, just as representatives of different cultures, ideologies or political perspectives may have difficulty in appreciating each other's perspectives.

It is clear that there are sometimes large benefits to be had from joint learning by researchers and practitioners. Participatory action research, for example, is an approach to knowledge creation that brings together activists and researchers to produce outcomes that neither could achieve by themselves (Whyte, 1991; Fals Borda and Rahman, 1991). Actors in this tradition have invested heavily in learning from the differences between activists and researchers.

But even participatory action researchers may have difficulty with the gulfs that separate North and South. While both Northern and Southern investigators practice participatory action research, the two traditions have very little contact with one another (Brown, 1993; Brown and Tandon, 1993) even though they have potentially complementary strengths and weaknesses. The Southern tradition is sophisticated about power inequalities and social transformation; the Northern tradition has useful technologies for organization development and capacity building (Leach, 1994). But participatory researchers from the North and the South have made little effort to learn from one another until very recently.

This chapter is concerned with building knowledge across both the researcher–activist and North–South boundaries. More specifically it focuses on social learning – the emergence of frames and perspectives that can reshape behaviour – in networks that include representatives of both researcher–activist and North–South perspectives. It seeks to identify circumstances in which differences among network members can be combined in ways that promote mutual learning, and proposes to identify patterns of social interaction and organization that enable diverse stakeholders to generate new knowledge systems by examining three experiences with networks of Northern and Southern civil society organizations. Each network was concerned with generating new knowledge about organizing for grassroots development – knowledge relevant to both theory and practice.

BACKGROUND

Social learning that enhances social system capacities to respond to new situations and solve problems has been heralded as a critical capacity for societies and civilizations facing increasing interdependence and accelerating change (Botkin et al, 1979; Milbrath, 1989; Finger and Verlaan, 1995). Social learning can be distinguished from learning by individuals or by organizations in that it alters the capacities of social entities – like interorganizational networks or communities or nations – that include individuals and organizations as sub-units. Social learning may involve learning by individuals or organizations, but its impacts are embodied in more inclusive systems.

The challenge of organizational learning has become a major concern for organizations that face a rapidly changing and increasingly competitive world (eg Argyris and Schon, 1978; Senge, 1990; Swieringa and Wierdsma, 1992). It has been argued that organizational learning involves changes in organizational cognition and awareness, repertoires of potential behaviour, and actual behaviours.

Four processes have been described as contributing to organizational learning:

1) knowledge acquisition;
2) information distribution;
3) information interpretation; and
4) organizational memory.

Knowledge acquisition is the process by which knowledge is obtained: it may include knowledge that the organization has at birth, learning from experience, learning from observation, knowledge acquired by bringing in new members and knowledge acquired by intentional search. Information distribution is the process by which knowledge is shared within the organization. Information interpretation is the process by which distributed information is given one or more common meanings within the organization. Organizational memory refers to the means by which information is stored for future use (Huber, 1991).

We cannot assume that social learning will necessarily be similar to organizational learning. Since there is much less research and theory available on social learning, however, it does seem reasonable to use categories from analysing organizational learning as initial lenses for examining learning in inter-organizational networks. So this analysis will focus in part on how the networks deal with the challenges of knowledge acquisition, distribution, interpretation and retention.

Inter-organizational networks have emerged as important actors in many arenas in the last two decades. For some situations, such as complex activities in competitive and uncertain environments, networks have advantages over the more familiar hierarchy or market forms of organization (Jones et al, 1997; Powell, 1990). They may be particularly useful when rapid learning is necessary, but no one organization has access to all the knowledge required for success (Powell et al, 1996). The creation of knowledge systems for fostering sustainable development must be carried out in notoriously complex and uncertain circumstances with relevant information dispersed among many actors, so network organizations may be important actors in that process.

The rise of network organizations has been particularly visible among organizations in civil society, in part because so many of them are small, narrowly focused and limited in their impacts. Joining like-minded others may be essential in order to carry out larger tasks. The rapid emergence of NGO networks (see Fisher, 1994; Salamon, 1994) as information linkages may herald increased capacity for social learning. But networks that span activist–researcher and South–North differences are much less common.

For our purposes here two aspects of network development will be particularly important: network creation and network decision making. Network creation refers to the ways in which members are selected and network goals and roles are defined, since those decisions have major impacts on how learning can take place. It is clear that the composition of networks and early decisions about member roles have big impacts on their capacity to generate new ideas and perspectives (Gray, 1989). Network decision making refers to the process and patterns by which key choices are made and differences among members are handled. Patterns of decision making create or destroy trust among the members; and frank exchanges that facilitate the synthesizing of new perspectives depend on that trust (Browning et al, 1995; Ring and Van de Ven, 1992).

In the analysis that follows, I will compare experience in three South–North networks of researchers and activists concerned with developing knowledge systems that promote sustainable development. The next section will briefly describe three such networks. The following section examines patterns of network creation and decision making, and processes of knowledge acquisition, distribution, interpretation and retention. The final section explores the implications of those comparisons for network learning in other situations.

SOUTH–NORTH NETWORK EXPERIENCES

The three networks described here all sought to develop new knowledge from the experiences of Southern and Northern civil society organizations. The networks sought to integrate perspectives from North and South and from research and action to generate new knowledge and improved practice. The author's organization, the Institute for Development Research (IDR), was a member of all three networks. All the other organizations are described regionally and functionally: 'US policy organization' refers to a US agency concerned with developing alternative policies; 'Kenya support organization' refers to a Kenyan agency involved in providing training and technical support to grassroots groups. Almost all the network members were support organizations (SOs), in the sense of providing training, consultation, research and advocacy support to non-governmental development organizations. Table 2.1 summarizes briefly the actors, primary concerns and knowledge products of the three networks.

Each of these networks operated over several years, so their members engaged with each other over a relatively long term. Each engaged in initial discussions that created a longer term network that was sometimes larger or smaller than the initial network. In each case, the networks made use of funds from Northern donor agencies interested in the questions under investigation and mobilized grassroots organizations as active partners in the learning process.

Many of the ideas developed in this analysis have emerged from discussions among network members. The author was a participant observer rather than a neutral bystander. Participant observers have access to detailed data about network events – but they also have interests that may colour their observations. The descriptions of the next section and the analysis of the following section have benefited from and been distorted by the participant observation process.

Table 2.1 *South–North Networks*

	Community Problem-Solving Coalition ('Coalition') (1990–94)	*Consortium for Intersectoral Cooperation ('Consortium') (1989–95)*	*Inter-regional Support Organization Alliance ('Alliance') (1994–97)*
Network Actors	**Northern** University Research Group (URG); Institute for Development Research (IDR); US Support Organization (USSO) **Southern** Kenya SO (KSO); Indonesia SO (ISO); Nicaragua SO (NSO)	**Northern** US Policy Organization (USPO); Institute for Development Research (IDR); US Support Organization (USSO) **Southern** African SO 1 (AfSO1); Asian SO (AsSO); Latin American SO (LASO)	**Northern** University Management Development Project (UMDP); Institute for Development Research (IDR) **Southern** Asian SO (AsSO); African SO 2 (AfSO2)
Primary Concerns	Learn and share grassroots strategies for environmental activism in different countries	Learn about cooperative problem-solving among NGOs, government agencies and grassroots groups	Train facilitators and adapt participatory action methodologies for SOs in Asia and Africa
Knowledge Outcomes: Theory and Practice	Problems of the poor are similar across countries; participation and local mobilization is crucial to sustainable change; grassroots activists offer much to global conferences	Cooperation and conflict are key to joint action by diverse groups; NGO bridges and grassroots groups can catalyse joint problem-solving; grassroots organizations can access 'invisible' resources	Northern participatory action methods can be adapted to meet Southern priorities; NGOs need strategic thinking; future searches can find common ground among NGOs and governments

Since this paper seeks to understand patterns of interaction that enabled the development of new knowledge systems, I will briefly summarize some of the key events in each network before discussing patterns that emerged across cases.

Community Problem-Solving Coalition (1990–1994)

The Coalition grew out of an invitation from the University Research Group (URG) to a US grassroots support organization (USSO) and IDR to help design a series of international meetings with support organizations concerned with grassroots environmental activism. With a planning grant from a US foundation, the three sponsors brought together support organizations from Indonesia, Kenya and Nicaragua to explore possibilities for joint learning.

USSO arranged visits to community groups in several Southern states for the visitors, and then convened a three-day workshop on local activism to fight industrial pollution with the visitors and local activists. All the participants agreed that they learned much from their interaction. As a result of discussions about global issues, USSO took the lead to organize participation by US grassroots activists in the environmental summit the following spring.

Discussions after the workshop led to a decision to propose a three-year programme that would involve participatory action research projects in each country as well as a workshop in each of the other three countries at yearly intervals. This planning process was marked by considerable conflict and misunderstanding – some between Southern and Northern participants and some among the Northern sponsors. Planning moved forward after participants agreed that the support organizations (USSO, KSO, ISO, NSO) would define project goals and call on the research organizations (URG, IDR) for support. The support organizations then redefined the programme goals to emphasize capacity building for local action rather than the more theoretical research emphasized in the original agenda.

Resource constraints ultimately further reduced the role of research and prompted URG to withdraw from the project. Over the next three years, participatory action research projects were carried out in each country with local activists, and dozens of activists participated in the workshops held in each country. Over the course of the project, core participants became increasingly ready to engage with each other, to share their perspectives and to be open to learning from others' experience. In the final workshop, for example, the Kenyans actively sought to learn more about how to catalyse the local participation they had observed in other countries and recognized as a critical ingredient to sustained change. The US, Kenyan and Nicaraguan support organizations used the Coalition to build their own capacities. KSO developed a whole new division to pursue the issues raised; NSO revised its long term strategy as a consequence of its participation; USSO developed a thriving international programme.

Consortium for Intersectoral Cooperation (1989–1995)

The Consortium was initially organized by a US policy research NGO (USPO) committed to promoting intersectoral cooperation. It brought together a group of civil society support organizations, including a US grassroots support organization (USSO), regional support organizations from Asia (AsSO), Africa (AfSO1), Latin America (LASO) and IDR, to develop and analyse case studies of successful cooperation among grassroots organizations, development NGOs and government agencies. The project organizer and IDR between them had contacts with all the initial participating agencies (see Figure 2.1, p47).

Consortium members articulated research questions and criteria for case selection. Regional coordinating organizations selected the cases in consultation with the rest of the Consortium. In Asia, IDR and other Consortium members helped train casewriters, gave feedback on initial case drafts and participated in a week-long conference to discuss the cases and draw lessons from their comparison. Several different documents were produced for different audiences: an academic analysis (by IDR and AsSO), a practitioner analysis (by AsSO) and a policy analysis (by USPO). These analyses emphasized the importance of conflict as well as cooperation in making the partnerships work, the different kinds of cooperation possible and the importance of bridging organizations (especially indigenous NGOs) and grassroots organizations in launching and maintaining successful cooperative problem-solving.

In Africa, the process involved more contact among African participants and less contact with other Consortium members. AfSO1 organized a case selection workshop, a training workshop and a conference for presenting and analysing the cases. International Consortium members spent three days with the casewriters discussing the lessons of the cases. So the African process provided less opportunity for contact among Consortium members and African actors than the Asian process. AfSO1 and USPO produced a summary document and coordinated a policy conference with representatives from several African governments and NGO communities.

IDR produced several comparative analyses that considered both the African and Asian cases. The African case comparisons confirmed many of the findings of the Asian case comparisons.

Inter-Regional Support Organization Alliance (1995–1997)

The Alliance brought together four organizations concerned with enhancing the resources of civil society support organizations to facilitate organization and sector capacity building. IDR had been working with the two regional support organizations (AfSO2, AsSO) for several years, while the University Management Development Program (UMDP) had a continuing relationship with IDR. All four parties believed that their different resources could be organized for mutual gains.

The Alliance produced a series of workshops and projects in south Asia and in eastern and southern Africa over the next 18 months. An initial workshop for facilitators from support organizations in both regions produced interest in advanced training in several participatory action methodologies such as strategic thinking, future search conferences and appreciative inquiry. Further workshops in those topics were held in the regions to support participatory action research projects by facilitators to apply the methods to their own civil societies.

Relations among Alliance members, however, were troubled by disputes over resources and decision making. Expectations for regular meetings and joint decision making (especially on the part of UMDP) were frustrated by busy schedules and the high costs of getting together. Concerns about how funds should be managed also produced tensions between UMDP, the holder of most of the financial resources that supported the Alliance, and the other partners. Relations were particularly strained between AfSO2 and UMDP. IDR's efforts as a third party failed to keep relations between UMDP and the other three partners from deteriorating, though they did come to agreement on shared responsibilities and resource use.

A second inter-regional workshop brought together participants from a dozen Asian and African countries to share experiences with using the methodologies and adapting them to fit their own circumstances. Participating support organizations reported on more than 20 applications of the participatory action methodologies carried out with their own resources, and discussed in detail the modifications required to fit the methodologies to local circumstances. Participants agreed that the methodologies were useful and could be modified to fit their concerns. By the end of the workshop, participants had articulated national and regional strategies for developing cadres of facilitators to develop and use participatory action methodologies in their own settings.

DISCUSSION: SOUTH–NORTH LEARNING NETWORKS

Figure 2.1 represents the three networks in graphic terms. Each network is represented in an early form in the left column and in a later form in the right column. The organizations at the top of each figure are located in the North; those on the bottom are from the South. Cooperative links among the actors are represented by connecting lines; where links are missing the parties do not know each other or have become adversaries. The primary source of funding at the beginning is through Northern actors, though in the Alliance case by the end of the project all four actors were mobilizing external funding to support the programme. Note also that the primary links to grassroots groups are through Southern partners, with the exception of

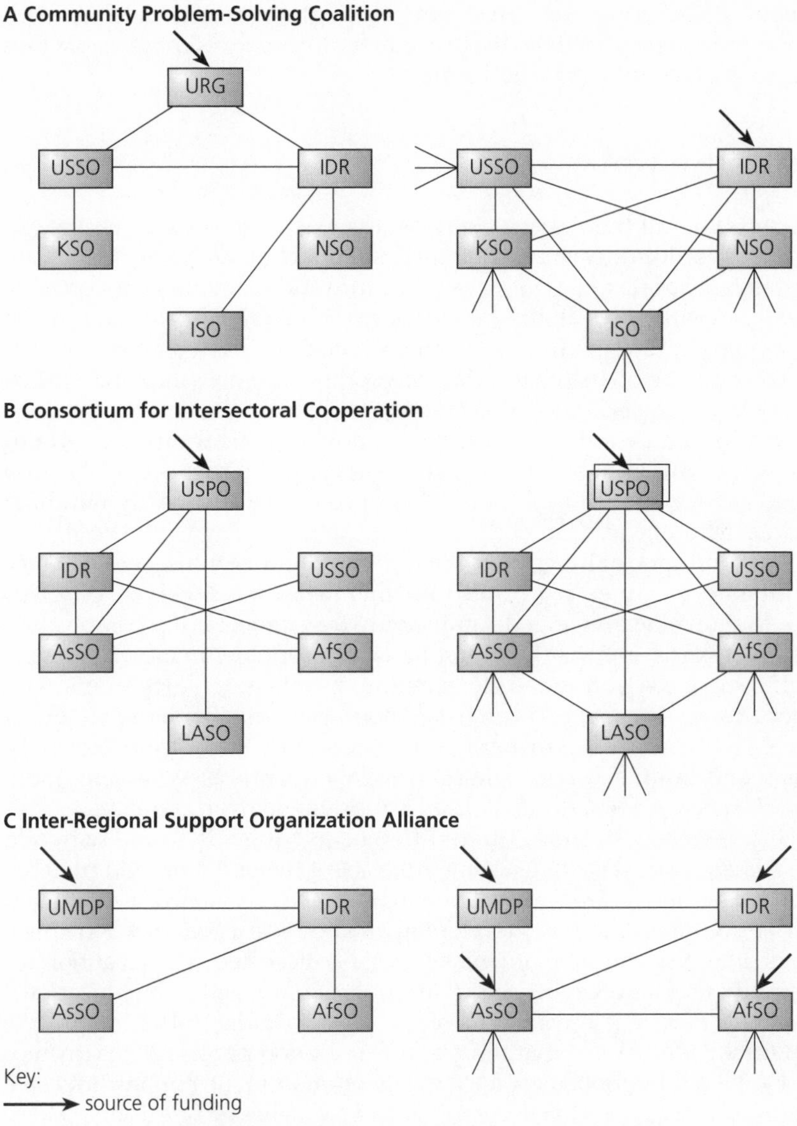

A Community Problem-Solving Coalition

B Consortium for Intersectoral Cooperation

C Inter-Regional Support Organization Alliance

Key:
⟶ source of funding

Figure 2.1 *Early and Late Learning Networks*

USSO in the Coalition (it was recognized as a Southern support organization by other Coalition members). Both funding and links to grassroots actors are critical resources for the learning agendas of all these networks.

What can we learn from these experiences of joint learning by Northern and Southern actors about the construction of shared knowledge systems? Obviously there are many possibilities. I will focus here on issues relevant to acquiring new knowledge, distributing that knowledge across network members, elaborating interpretations through network members and building shared perspectives that will affect future awareness, capacities and actions of the network and its members.

Creating Networks

At the outset of all these cases, no networks existed to provide an institutional basis for joint learning. Potential members of such networks were separated by chasms of power, wealth, culture and many other differences. Indeed, choosing the 'right' members for networks is difficult when network purposes remain unclear. In each of these networks steps were taken by some members to start the network, but membership and participation changed as goals and expectations evolved. In the Coalition the three Northern initiators sought Southern support organizations that would enable work with local environmental activists, and network membership changed as its goals focused more on supporting local capacity building. The Consortium was initiated by three members (two Northern, one Southern) and gradually grew to include different regions. The Alliance was initiated at a meeting of all four members, but levels of different member involvement changed significantly over time. So the composition of these networks and the definition of the appropriate members evolved, though networks continued to include a mix of Northerners and Southerners, researchers and activists. There was some tendency to recruit Southern activists and Northern researchers, but there were Northern activists and Southern researchers in each network as well, and those 'hybrids' – such as USSO – often acted as bridges across differences.

Many members brought quite different initial goals to the network. While all had some stake in learning more about the problems and possibilities of civil society roles in development, they often balanced research and practice priorities differently. Developing a shared set of goals around which network activities could be organized was a critical step. The Coalition for Community Problem-Solving, for example, brought together organizational representatives with relatively little previous contact; their planning process stalled until it was agreed that the grassroots support organizations (including USSO) would define goals for the network and invite support from the research organizations. This reformulation of the network's decision making process change gave primacy to local capacity building over the more academic interests of the research organizations, even though the latter had initiated the network. In the Consortium, arguments over whether to produce knowledge for policy makers, academic researchers or local support institutions were resolved by creating products for all three audiences. Three members of the Alliance were already working together and its proposed goals were very compatible with the programme priorities of UMDP, so the Alliance found network formation and initial goal setting to be relatively easy. For the Alliance the challenges came later, in the implementation of programmes and the use of resources.

A third issue in the formation of these networks was the articulation of member roles, particularly on the dimensions of research and practice. Many Northern participants were academics and consultants, comfortable with being expert resources. But Southern members pressed them to take roles that were less familiar and comfortable. The decision by the Coalition to emphasize local capacity building deprived Northern actors of research roles. Northern experts in the Consortium were challenged by Southern members to be 'friends and supporters, not consultants', and to join in the inquiry about intersectoral cooperation in which research skills were often outweighed by Southern understanding of local realities. Some members of the Alliance were disappointed that interest in participatory action methods was closely tied to immediate problems, and that academic creativity was valued less than easy application to local capacity building. For many Northern researchers participation in these learning processes required significant adaptation from their customary approaches and stances. Joint inquiry required them to 'accompany' their Southern colleagues rather than 'teach' or 'advise' them (Hoyer, 1994). By the same token, participation often asked Southern participants to act as researchers and reflective observers, when many were more comfortable focusing primarily on action-oriented practice. To step back from immediate applications to see many sides of issues and take a 'balanced' view of events seemed 'theoretical' or even in some cases disloyal to their constituents. The most successful joint learning seemed to take place when network members were willing to experiment with unfamiliar roles and respond to others' interests and concerns.

This discussion can be summarized in a tentative proposition that the potential for creating a learning network increases as:

• members are recruited that are appropriate to network learning goals;
• mutually acceptable goals can be articulated and negotiated; and
• member representatives adapt their roles to fit network needs.

Network Decision Making

Networks composed of autonomous organizations must create new processes for decision making, since they do not share a common authority structure. In order to carry out joint activities, all these networks had to develop processes for planning, implementing and assessing learning activities. These initiatives were begun with financial resources held by Northern members. While it is clear that the Southern actors brought critical resources – such as access to and credibility with grassroots groups – access to financial resources contributed to initial perceptions that Northern partners had more power than their Southern colleagues. Although it was not explicit at the outset, Southern members subsequently indicated that their ongoing participation in the network depended on developing a sense of mutual respect and influence across the North–South difference. So convening parties to a North–South learning process often requires managing differences and balancing power in joint decision making processes.

In part, questions about power differences and conflict management were answered by experience. The Coalition brought together Southern participants who had little prior contact with the Northern organizers, so there was considerable ambiguity about how decisions would be made. The decision to have primary goals of the network set by the support organizations rather than the research organizations was critical to establishing some degree of mutual influence. In addition, Southern experience in community visits and the workshop with local activists convinced them that USSO was really a Southern support organization, committed to work with impoverished grassroots communities much like their own constituents. They agreed to participate in the Coalition as long as USSO vouched for it. The same experiences, however, undermined relations among the Northern members, for URG felt that decision making among network initiators violated their expectations about how differences would be handled. The experiences that enabled Southern partners to join the network also set the stage for URG to leave it, largely because of disagreements about how conflicts were to be managed. In short, both the substance of the resolution and the processes by which decisions are made can be critical.

The other networks were more able to draw on existing social capital in making decisions about critical issues. The Consortium for Intersectoral Cooperation built on existing bonds among some of its members; the link between IDR and USPO at the outset made it possible to bring together their partners, and USPO supported a series of meetings to build Consortium relationships and shared perspectives needed for joint inquiry. Many potentially controversial decisions were delegated to the regional partners in Asia and Africa, who held responsibility for choosing cases, training and supporting casewriters and organizing case conferences. A continuing controversy focused on the inevitability of conflict in intersectoral cooperation – an issue that produced so many arguments that it became a standing joke. This issue did not produce North–South polarization because Northerners were major protagonists on both sides, so Southerners acted as mediators rather than primary parties. Decision making processes in the Consortium were initiated by the three network founders, and others were invited to join a network with an existing tradition of mutual influence and delegated decision making.

The Inter-Regional Support Organization Alliance also drew on preexisting links to catalyse joint action. IDR had long standing relationships with all the other actors, and a conference organized by UMDP offered an opportunity for exploring how joint work might advance the goals of all the members. In this case, however, perceived power differences led to continuing conflict: UMDP's efforts to ensure financial accountability were seen as distrust and disrespect by other Southern partners, especially AfSO2. Efforts by IDR and AsSO to mediate these differences were only partially successful. As in the Consortium, however, agreement to delegate responsibility for much activity to regional partners reduced the need for decision making across long distances and contested relationships, so programmatic activity could continue in spite of unresolved differences.

Experience with decision making across power, wealth and cultural differences in these networks suggests that both the continued existence and the quality of network learning may turn on processes and structures that emerge quite early in the network's development. To summarize some of these patterns in a proposition, the potential for network learning is increased as:

- mutual influence replaces initially perceived power differences;
- differences are managed by mutually accepted processes and structures; and
- bridging roles and relationships emerge to mediate conflicts.

Knowledge Acquisition in Networks

Knowledge acquisition in networks involves processes for acquiring new information, learning from past experience or generating new perspectives from existing knowledge. In all of these networks, conferences that brought together members for discussion of key issues were an important part of the knowledge acquisition process; for many, knowledge development also took place in sub-groups authorized to act on the networks' behalf.

The conference process offered opportunities to focus on critical issues, to explore different perspectives on those issues and to generate new ideas and syntheses out of comparisons. Negotiating shared frames and acceptable stances sets the stage for detailed planning of how joint work will be carried out. The organization of joint inquiry includes agreement about how major decisions will be made, the nature of the inquiry process itself and the distribution of responsibilities and resources for carrying out that process.

In the Coalition for Community Problem-Solving, for example, the design and facilitation of annual conferences was the responsibility of national host organizations, rotating each year. Each year the host organization would arrange for teams representing activists associated with other members to visit grassroots projects and then participate in a workshop on grassroots environmental issues current in the host country. Those workshops led to lively discussions and sometimes heated debates on problems like alternative strategies for dealing with local pollution or regenerative agriculture. Host organization and IDR facilitators were charged with fostering synthesis across the different views.

The Consortium on Intersectoral Cooperation, in contrast, focused on the same issue of intersectoral cooperation on different problems and in many regions. This network also used conferences as a major learning tool, though the membership in the primary conferences varied from many outsiders in Asia to mostly Africans in Africa. The regional partner worked with other members to facilitate syntheses across cases and regions, but documenting the resulting learning was delegated to AfSO1 and AsSO for regional practitioner documents, USPO for policy maker summaries and IDR for academic research syntheses.

In the Inter-Regional Support Organization Alliance, the network agreed to focus an initial workshop with facilitators from both regions on a menu of participatory action methods, and then to respond to regional concerns for further developing concepts and tools for local use. Follow-up workshops focused on topics of regional interest, and workshop participants – with support from regional network members – then adapted participatory action methodologies to fit local concerns. A second inter-regional workshop brought facilitators who had undertaken these projects together to share and learn from their experiences. Network members provided facilitation and research assistance in fostering synthesis of more general learning from the specific experiences. In part because of the opportunity for multiple conferences and the encouragement of local experiments, this network was particularly successful in fostering a wide range of innovations.

The patterns of knowledge acquisition and development in these experiences seem quite similar. To summarize, network knowledge acquisition is facilitated as:

- networks focus attention and resources on critical issues;
- differences in information and perspective are recognized, valued and explored; and
- differences are synthesized into new perspectives and knowledge.

Knowledge Distribution in Networks

Social learning in these networks involves more than sharing information with member representatives in conferences or inter-personal communications. For large scale and long term effects, individual learning in conferences must be translated into learning for the organizational members of the network and for some of their constituencies as well. In these networks, the inquiry focus encouraged Southern members to seek the perspectives of their constituents and to distribute knowledge from network deliberations back to them. The processes for disseminating knowledge to constituents of Northern members were often less direct and explicit.

For the Coalition, conferences encouraged grassroots activists (many from the host country and a few from others) to hear other perspectives and share their own, and then to make sure of results in their own work. The emphasis on local capacity building encouraged action at the local level on the basis of network learning. Thus the participation of US grassroots environmental activists in the 'Earth Summit' in Rio in 1992 was a direct result of sharing results from the first conference with USSO's constituents, largely because of the widespread activist antipathy to being represented by 'establishment' environmental organizations. In part because of the decision to emphasize local capacity building over research, however, the Coalition built fewer links to the constituents of the Northern organizations, so relatively little was done to educate donors or Northern actors about learning from the network's experience.

For the Consortium, in contrast, attention was paid to both Northern and Southern constituents as recipients of network learning. The conferences included participants from Southern constituencies, such as organizations involved in the cases, and from Northern constituencies, such as the donors that supported the network. In addition, explicit commitments were made at the outset to develop summaries of Consortium learning to be shared with NGO leaders, development policy makers and academics concerned with intersectoral cooperation. For each constituency, documentation was intentionally couched in appropriate language to make sure that learnings were relatively easy to absorb.

For the Inter-Regional Support Organization Alliance, information was distributed to Southern constituents through a series of conferences, first to facilitators in support organizations in 2 regions and 13 countries, then back to the inter-regional conference, and finally through participants to regional cadres of facilitators. Less attention was paid to influencing Northern constituents, though donors attended parts of the conference at which local projects were shared. Indeed, the donors have actively supported further Alliance activities because they were impressed with its results, and there have been efforts by UMDP and IDR to disseminate the results of some of those experiences.

Experience with distributing information through extended networks suggests that attention to building links to the appropriate constituents and formulating learning in terms relevant to those constituents are both important. In proposition form, network knowledge distribution is facilitated as:

- processes and structures create bridges to key constituents; and
- information is translated in terms relevant to constituents.

Interpreting Knowledge in Networks

Networks of diverse members offer great opportunities for eliciting new interpretations and meanings from complex information, since they represent a wide variety of perspectives and concerns. These networks used conferences to interpret their diverse perspectives. The Coalition for Community Problem-Solving, for example, convened meetings of NGO leaders and grassroots activists concerned with key issues from four countries on four different occasions. The Consortium on Intersectoral Cooperation convened its multinational steering committee on many occasions and organized several conferences that brought together grassroots representatives, NGO leaders, government officials and donor agency representatives to discuss specific cases. The Inter-Regional Support Organization Alliance brought together scores of participants from different regions and countries to examine issues from many perspectives.

While these conferences of diverse actors offer many opportunities for joint learning, they were not all equally successful. Such conferences place a high premium on the capacity of organizers to facilitate meetings to explore the views of potentially adversarial participants. Neither grassroots activists nor academic researchers are famous for their skills in managing conflict to produce constructive dialogue, mutual understanding and creative synthesis. These particular networks were blessed with both Southern and Northern actors skilled at managing differences, and they also continued over periods long enough to develop inter-personal relationships and trust that made it possible to explore and understand each other's perspectives.

The exploration of different perspectives provided a basis for assigning meaning for diverse experiences. Members of the Coalition, for example, after examining grassroots activism on environmental issues across four countries, gradually converged on the idea that building relatively autonomous grassroots organizations is critical to providing sustainable change. The Consortium developed a synthesis of experience with intersectoral cooperation that emphasized the importance of balancing power relations among the parties that emerged from reported examples in many issues and in many countries. The Alliance moved towards regional emphases on capacity building for strategic thinking and organization development through the integration of experiences in many local projects.

A third way in which information was further interpreted was through extensive documentation after conferences in papers or presentations. The Consortium on Intersectoral Cooperation has been very active in engaging a wider audience through public presentations and papers (eg Brown and Ashman, 1996, 1998; Tandon, 1993) for a wide variety of audiences. Although the other networks developed new perspectives among participants, they did not have the resources for such extensive interpretation and dissemination of results.

This discussion can also be summarized in the form of a preliminary proposition that developing interpretations in network social learning is facilitated as:

- participants and constituents explore different perspectives;
- members develop shared meanings to account for experience; and
- resources support elaborating, testing and documenting new perspectives.

Preserving Network Learning

The results of joint inquiry may be various: new perspectives on the issues, basic knowledge about development problems and interventions, applied knowledge of new practices and problem-solving strategies, new capacities for the organizations involved. Some of the results most valued by participants are easily predicted from their initial interests; other outcomes emerge from joint inquiry independent of and beyond initial expectations.

Some of these networks generated results relevant to basic knowledge systems that may be relevant across many situations and regions. The Consortium for Intersectoral Cooperation, for example, generated case studies and comparative analyses of grassroots–NGO–government cooperation from which a variety of general lessons relevant across countries and regions have been extracted (Brown, 1998; Brown and Ashman, 1996, 1998; Schearer, 1993; Tandon, 1993). Some of these ideas are being utilized in settings well beyond the initial network, when pursuing the results in more depth fits the organizational agendas of some members.

Other parties were more interested in constructing practical knowledge systems for action in specific situations. Many of the national and regional support organizations in the networks were particularly interested in enabling grassroots groups to participate more effectively in development processes. Some members of the Coalition for Community Problem-Solving, for example, used the network to develop new action strategies for supporting grassroots initiatives: KSO developed a new department to promote grassroots policy influence and decided to emphasize more participatory approaches; NSO used the Coalition to revamp its strategy for local development. Support organizations that participated in the Inter-Regional Alliance used ideas from the workshops and their own resources to develop participatory action research projects with their own constituencies, and agreed to build cadres of facilitators to use participatory action methodologies in each region in the future.

Some consequences of joint inquiry in these networks were changed perspectives on critical issues. Interaction with other participants can reshape member priorities. IDR became more interested in promoting social learning networks as a consequence of seeing USSO, KSO and NSO use the Coalition to foster strategic learning. AsSO made improving civil society relations with government and business an important programme area after assessing the cases generated by the Consortium. AfSO2 is promoting regional cooperation among governments, businesses and civil society organizations as a consequence of experience with multi-stakeholder planning in the Alliance. The conditions that foster social learning in North–South networks may also lead participants to identify new issues and possibilities. In all these cases, member recognition of network ideas as meaningful and important was critical to their preservation, elaboration and dissemination.

Finally, the extent to which network learning is preserved by member organizations depends on the characteristics of their representatives. When representatives were chief executives or other influential actors, as in the Consortium or the Alliance, new perspectives from the network exerted substantial influence on organization members. Where representatives were less influential – as in the case of some actors in the Alliance and the Coalition – network ideas were less likely to affect organizations or their constituents.

This analysis may be summarized in a final proposition that preservation of network social learning is more likely as:

- learnings are articulated in terms relevant to member concerns (eg research or practice outcomes);
- networks produce novel ideas of high relevance to member organizations; and
- representatives are positioned to influence their organizations.

CONCLUSION

Social learning across research–practice and North–South boundaries is possible – and potentially very fruitful. But learning across such differences is not easy. It requires engagement among actors with very different values, tools and perspectives. Such differences ensure that a rich mix of perspectives, information and intellectual capacities can be brought to bear on the problems, but they also increase the likelihood of diverse interpretations, easy misunderstandings and disagreements that range from mild to fundamental. In short, social learning in these networks often generates conflict.

Conflict can produce many outcomes: withdrawal that reduces conflict at the cost of less engagement; escalation that achieves victory at the cost of undermining future relationships; accommodation that preserves relationships at the cost of ignoring important differences; compromises that build agreements by sharing costs; or syntheses that integrate different views into innovative perspectives (Thomas, 1976). Whether the differences revealed in inter-organizational networks that seek to learn together will produce explosions of conflict, withdrawal, accommodation or some form of joint learning depends in large measure on whether organizational representatives can create a shared institutional base for managing their differences constructively.

Table 2.2 summarizes the propositions generated in this comparison across the three networks discussed in this paper. In its second and third columns, Table 2.2 also suggests implications for Northern and Southern network participants interested in fostering social learning. These implications are based on the assumption that Northern and Southern actors have different perspectives, shaped by their different social, economic and political experiences as well as their different organizational agendas. I have tried to indicate in Table 2.2 action implications relevant to some common differences across Northern and Southern perspectives, though not all organizations will have the same biases. This list is intended to stimulate

Table 2.2 Southern and Northern Actions to Promote Network Learning

	Implications for Northern Members	Implications for Southern Members
Creating Networks		
Invite 'right' members	Seek Southern help to find key actors	Cast a wide net for key actors
Mutually acceptable goals	Negotiate goals for mutual gain	Insist on goals that meet Southern needs
Role flexibility	Explore alternative roles for North	Expand Southern roles to fit resources
Network Decisions		
Balanced power	Assume unbalanced at the start	Insist on mutual influence
Difference management	Jointly devise management process	Expand Northern management process
Bridging roles and trust	Seek credible Southern activists	Seek like-minded Northern researchers
Acquiring Knowledge		
Focus attention on issues	Define Northern inquiry agenda	Define Southern inquiry agenda
Value differences	Respect Southern 'local knowledge'	Emphasize different perspectives
Synthesize shared frame	Integrate Southern views in frame	Integrate Northern views in frame
Distributing Information		
Local translations	Recognize diverse needs	Articulate Southern concerns early
Build needed bridges	Build links to donors, NGOs	Build links to grassroots, SNGOs
Interpreting Information		
Explore differences	Encourage challenges to status quo	Articulate alternatives to Northern views
Build shared meanings	Seek integrated ideas, mutual gains	Seek integrative ideas, mutul gains
Document perspectives	Record agreement and disagreement	Record 'minority reports' if needed
Preserving Learning		
Fit results to constituents	Legitimate diverse learning goals	Establish early what is 'relevant'
Recognize novel ideas	Highlight new possibilities	Test novel ideas on local application
Influential members	Use delegates with organization clout	Use delegates with organization clout

discussion rather than establish a universally relevant set of implications, so it should be treated with some scepticism.

I am convinced that learning that enhances the awareness, capacities and actions of social systems will be ever more essential as societies face rapid changes in an increasingly interdependent world. Civil society organizations can play critical roles in such learning processes, both as the advocates of social values and unheard interests and as sources of social innovation to respond to unmet needs. To fully play such roles, however, civil society organizations must understand and engage many other interests – and become adept in creating institutional arrangements that enable creative and widespread use of diverse viewpoints.

ENDNOTE

1 An earlier version of this paper was presented to the Panel on Civil Society and the Construction of Knowledge Systems at the World Congresses on Participatory Action Research and on Action Research, Action Learning and Process Management in Cartagena, Colombia, June 1–5 1997. The author wishes to express appreciation to the participants in both conferences and to Darcy Ashman, Jane Covey and Aimin Yan for their helpful comments during the revision process.

BIBLIOGRAPHY

Argyris, C and Schon, D (1978) *Organizational Learning: A Theory of Action Perspective*, Addison-Wesley Publishing, Reading, US
Botkin, J W, Emandjra, M and Malitza, M (1979) *No Limits to Learning: Bridging the Human Gap*, Pergamon Press, Oxford
Brown, L D (1993) 'Social change through collective reflection with Asian nongovernmental development organizations', *Human Relations* Vol 46, No 2, pp249–274
Brown, L D (1998) 'Creating social capital: nongovernmental development organizations and intersectoral problem-solving', in Powell, W W and Clemens, E (eds) *Private Action and the Public Good*, Yale University Press, New Haven
Brown, L D and Ashman, D (1996) 'Participation, social capital and intersectoral problem-solving: African and Asian cases', *World Development*, Vol 24, No 9, pp1467–1479
Brown, L D and Ashman, D (1998) 'Social capital, mutual influence and social learning in intersectoral problem-solving', in Cooperrider, D and Dutton, J (eds) *Organizational Dimensions of Global Social Change*, Sage, Beverly Hills
Brown, L D and Tandon, R (1993) *Multiparty Collaboration for Development in Asia*, United Nations Development Programme, New York
Browning, L D, Beyer, J M and Shetler, J C (1995) 'Building cooperation in a competitive industry: Sematech and the semiconductor industry', *Academy of Management Journal*, Vol 38, pp1113–1153
Fals Borda, O and Rahman, A M (1991) *Action and Knowledge: Breaking the Monopoly with Participatory Action Research*, Apex Press, New York

Finger, M and Verlaan, P (1995) 'Learning our way out: a conceptual framework for social-environmental learning', *World Development*, Vol 23, No 3, pp503–515

Fisher, J (1994) 'Is the iron law of oligarchy rusting away in the third world?' *World Development*, Vol 22, No 2, pp129–142

Gray, B (1989) *Collaborating: Finding Common Ground for Multiparty Problems*, Jossey-Bass, San Francisco

Hoyer, H (1994) 'Reflections on partnership and accompaniment', *Institutional Development*, Vol 1, No 1, pp46–51

Huber, G P (1991) 'Organizational learning: the contributing processes and the literatures', *Organizational Science*, Vol 2, No 1, pp88–115

Jones, C, Hesterly, W S and Borgatti, S P (1997) 'A general theory of network governance: exchange conditions and social mechanisms', *Academy of Management Review*, Vol 22, No 4, pp911–945

Kuhn, T S (1970) *The Structure of Scientific Revolutions* (second edition) University of Chicago Press, Chicago

Leach, M (1994) 'Building capacity through action learning', *IDR Reports*, Vol 10, No 5

Milbrath, L (1989) *Envisioning a Sustainable Society: Learning Our Way Out*, State University of New York Press, Albany

Powell, W W (1990) 'Neither market nor hierarchy: network forms of organization', in Cummings, L L and Staw, B M (eds) *Research in Organizational Behavior*, JAI Press, Greenwich, Vol 12, pp295–336

Powell, W W, Koput, K W and Smith-Doerr, L (1996) 'Interorganizational collaboration and the locus of innovation: networks of learning in biotechnology', *Administrative Science Quarterly*, Vol 41, No 1, pp116–145

Ring, P S and Van de Ven, A H (1992) 'Structuring cooperative relationships between organizations', *Strategic Management Journal*, Vol 14, pp483–498

Salamon, L (1994) 'The global associational revolution: the rise of the third sector on the world scene', *Foreign Affairs*, Vol 73, No 4, pp109–122

Schearer, S B (1993) *Building Development Projects in Partnership with Communities and NGOs: An Action Agenda for Policymakers*, UNDP, New York

Senge, P M (1990) *The Fifth Discipline: The Art and Practice of the Learning Organization*, Doubleday, New York

Swieringa, J and Wierdsma, A (1992) *Becoming a Learning Organization: Beyond the Learning Curve*, Addison-Wesley, Reading

Tandon, R (1993) *Holding Together: Partnerships in the Real World*, UNDP, New York

Thomas, K (1976) 'Conflict and conflict management', in Dunnette, M D (ed) *Handbook of Industrial and Organizational Psychology*, Rand-McNally, Chicago

Whyte, W F (1991) *Participatory Action Research*, Sage, Newbury Park, US

3 The Third World's Third Sector in Comparative Perspective

Lester M Salamon and Helmut Anheier

INTRODUCTION

Recent years have witnessed a significant upsurge of organized private, nonprofit activity in the countries of Asia, Africa and Latin America and, with it, a new appreciation of the important role that nonprofit organizations play in the processes of economic and political change (Anheier, 1987; Brown and Korten, 1991; Drabek, 1987; Fisher, 1993; Salamon, 1994). Long recognized as instruments of relief and promoters of human rights, such organizations are now also viewed as critical contributors to economic growth and to the civic infrastructure increasingly seen as a fundamental precondition for markets and representative political institutions to function (Fukuyama, 1995; North, 1990; OECD, 1995; Putnam, 1993; World Bank, 1995). Despite the importance that is increasingly attached to them, however, nonprofit organizations in the developing world remain only dimly understood.[1] This is true, moreover, on three different levels.

In the first place, basic descriptive information on this set of organizations is largely lacking. Though apparently growing in scale and importance, the third sector in the developing world remains a largely uncharted subcontinent on the social landscape of these societies. Even the most basic information about these organizations – their number, size, areas of activity, sources of revenue and the legal and policy framework within which they work – is unavailable in any systematic way.

Behind this descriptive gap lies a significant conceptual one. One reason little is known about the nonprofit or third sector in the developing world is that the concept of such a sector has hardly existed there, or it has existed in a peculiar way. This reflects the extraordinary complexity of the social terrain that lies outside the market and the state in such societies, embracing entities as diverse as village associations, grassroots development organizations, agricultural extension services, self-help cooperatives, religiously-affiliated schools and hospitals, human rights organizations and business and professional associations, to name just a few. Equally important, however, has been the focus in much of the research and discussion of nonprofit organizations in the developing world on what have come to be known as NGOs (Carroll, 1992; Drabek, 1987; Fisher, 1993; Sandberg, 1994; Uvin, 1995; World Bank, 1997).[2] This focus, while quite fruitful, has also been somewhat misleading. For one thing, it has tended to downplay or ignore the presence of large numbers of voluntary organizations that are not normally considered to be NGOs but that would typically be included within the nonprofit sector in most other parts of the world, such as schools, hospitals, social welfare institutions and cultural institutions. In addition, the term 'NGO' often functions as an ideological screen used to differentiate 'good' nonprofits from 'bad' ones along lines that are often not entirely clear. Finally, the concept often includes, within the nonprofit sectors of the developing world overseas, development organizations that really function out of Northern countries. For all of these reasons, the concept of the NGO, far from improving our understanding of third world nonprofit developments, has to some extent impeded it.

Finally, our understanding of the nonprofit sector in the developing world has been constrained by a lack of suitable theory. Much of the available theory on nonprofit institutions emerged in the context of advanced Western societies. It tends to take as given, features that are often lacking in the developing world, such as market economies and democratic political systems (see, for example, Ben-Ner, 1993; Hansmann, 1987; Rose-Ackerman, 1996; Steinberg and Young, 1995; Weisbrod, 1977), or cultural and philosophical traditions associated with Judeo-Christian religions (Lipset, 1995; Payton, 1988). Such theories may be of questionable value, therefore, in developing societies where the market is often poorly developed, authoritarian political regimes are the rule and prevailing religious traditions differ markedly from the Judeo-Christian ones of the West. To come to terms with the reality of the third sector in the third world, therefore, new theory, and not simply new information, may be needed.

PURPOSE AND APPROACH OF THE STUDY

To help fill these gross gaps in knowledge and understanding about the third sector in the third world, we included five developing countries within a broader inquiry into the scope, structure, financing and role of the nonprofit sector carried out in 13 countries around the world.[3] Although it was not possible to undertake as thorough an empirical investigation of the nonprofit sector in the developing countries as in the eight developed ones, it was possible to generate a far more systematic and comprehensive picture than has been available up to now. In the balance of this paper, we outline the overall approach that we used, summarize the major findings that emerged, and, finally, examine the implications our work has for the theory of the nonprofit sector and for the role this sector can be expected to play in the developing world.

Country Selection and Initial Theoretical Considerations

As a first step in carrying out this work, it was necessary to select a set of developing countries that reflected the common features that distinguish the developing world from the more developed areas. Because the goal was analytical as well as descriptive, it was also important to pick countries whose differences corresponded with some of the key factors thought to affect the scope and character of the nonprofit sector. Accordingly, we selected a key country in each of the world's major geographic regions, representing each of the world's major religions (Christianity, Islam, African religions, Hinduism and Buddhism). In particular, we chose Brazil in Latin America, Ghana in Africa, Egypt in the Arab world, India in south-east Asia and Thailand in south Asia.[4]

As reflected in Table 3.1, these five countries have a combination of common features and clear differences of the sort we were seeking.

Low Per Capita Income

In the first place, all five of these countries have per capita incomes that are only 2 to 18 per cent of the average in the more developed countries. Low income implies, of course, tremendous social and economic needs that may be difficult to meet through the market alone. This suggests a great need for non-market mechanisms of the sort that nonprofit institutions represent. But need alone hardly translates into the creation of non-governmental or nonprofit institutions. To the contrary, such institutions themselves require resources – resources of time and organizational skill, if not finances. Indeed, one of the prevailing theories in the field argues that such organizations are most likely to emerge not where resources are uniformly limited, but where heterogeneous needs emerge and some people have the resources to respond to these needs through joint action (Weisbrod, 1977). Far from stimulating nonprofit formation, therefore, low income should impede it.

Small Urban Middle Class

In the second place, all of the countries covered here are still heavily agricultural, with anywhere from four to ten times as large a proportion of the labour force involved in agriculture, fishing and forestry as is common in the more advanced countries. This is significant because it means they lack the sizeable urban middle class elements that have been identified

Table 3.1 *Selected Economic Indicators, by Country, 1990*

Indicator/ Country	Brazil	Ghana	Egypt	India	Thailand	OECD Average
Population (Million)	150	15	52	850	56	–
Per Capita Income ($)	3178	415	837	358	1560	17,410
Tax Revenue as Per Cent of GNP	24.0	31.0	25.0	19.0	26.0	38.0[a] 28.7[b]
Social Welfare Spending as Per Cent of Total Government Outlays	17.3	6.4	12.0	13.7	3.4	36.5[c]
Per Cent of Total Labour Force in Agriculture	31.0	54.7	34.0	67.0	62.0	6.9
Enrolment in Higher Education as Per Cent in Cohort (*cohort*)	11.3 (18–22 years)	1.4 (19–23 years)	17.5 (17–21 years)	7.8 (18–22 years)	12.7 (19–23 years)	16.8 (18–21 years) 12.8 (22–25 years)
Average Growth Rate of GDP (Per Cent):						
1965–1980	9.0	1.3	7.3	3.6	7.3	3.7
1980–1990	2.7	3.0	5.0	5.3	7.6	3.1
Natural Annual Population Growth (Per Cent), 1980–1990	2.2	3.4	2.4	2.1	1.8	0.83
Official Development Assistance (Per Cent of GNP)	<0.1	10.3	15.9	0.6	1.0	–

Key: [a] includes social security; [b] excludes social security; [c] unweighted average
Sources: Population: UN, 1992. Economic: World Bank, 1992; UN, 1995. Education: UN, 1991. OECD countries: OECD, 1996; OECD, 1993. Social welfare spending: Britannica World Data, 1991, pp882–887; Indian data are based on UN national accounts and report social security and welfare spending as a percentage of government final consumption expenditure for 1989. Employment: United States Central Intelligence Agency, *World Factbook*, 1991.

with the growth of nonprofit institutions in the more developed countries (Salamon, 1994; Moore, 1966). Such urban middle class groups typically enjoy a degree of independence vis à vis the landed elite that often dominate pre-modern societies, and they have both the interest and the technical skills to form associations of various sorts.

While the countries covered here have relatively small urban middle classes, however, they also differ somewhat in the extent to which an urban middle class has emerged. This is evident in the relatively high levels of growth in gross domestic product in Brazil, Egypt and Thailand since the mid-1960s, the relatively high proportions of the populations in higher education in these countries, and, at least in the cases of Brazil and Egypt, the relatively lower proportions of the population in agriculture. To the extent that the relationship between the emergence of a commercial and professional urban middle class and the growth of the nonprofit sector holds, we would therefore expect, other things being equal, that nonprofit organizations would be more widespread in Thailand, Brazil and Egypt than in India and Ghana, though the sheer size of India means that the absolute size of the middle class there may be large even though the relative size is much smaller.

Authoritarian Political Regimes

A third feature shared by the countries considered here is a prolonged experience with authoritarianism. In part, this has been the result of colonial domination, which narrowed the realm of freedom left to indigenous populations. But indigenous traditions have also played a role. Thus, of the five countries examined here, only India can look back to a relatively undisturbed political history in safeguarding the right of association. By contrast, Brazil, Thailand and Egypt have all embarked on the process of democratization only in recent years. Ghana stands midway between these extremes, with limited introduction of democratic forms during the colonial era and immediately afterwards, but with periods of military rule since then. While nonprofit organizations exist in autocratic societies, it is generally acknowledged that a meaningful degree of freedom of association is necessary for such organizations to flourish.

Low Levels of Government Social Welfare Spending

This history of authoritarianism may help explain another common feature of the countries examined here; their relatively low levels of government social welfare spending. As Table 3.1 shows, such spending falls below 20 per cent of total government outlays in all of these countries, and is well below the share that is devoted to these purposes in the developed world. This is significant because two of the major theories in the nonprofit sector field relate the size of the nonprofit sector to the scale of government social welfare spending. One of these, the so-called 'market failure/government failure' model, posits an inverse relationship between the scale of government social welfare provision and the size of the nonprofit sector. According to this theory, nonprofit organizations are an alternative provider of public goods when population diversity or other factors make it difficult to mobilize the popular majorities required for government to respond (Weisbrod, 1977; Douglas, 1987). Where government involvement in the provision of needed public goods is low, therefore, this set of theories would lead us to expect a high level of nonprofit activity. The alternative 'voluntary failure' or 'partnership' theory posits a direct relationship between government social welfare spending and the extent of nonprofit activity. According to this theory, government social welfare spending and nonprofit activity are two complementary by-products of the same set of social circumstances (Salamon, 1987, 1995). What is more, there are strong theoretical and practical reasons to expect cooperation between the two since the strengths and weaknesses of the state are the exact opposite of those of the nonprofit sector. The growth of state social welfare spending can therefore be expected to stimulate, not detract from, the growth of nonprofit activity, while limited state involvement in social welfare can reduce the support needed for nonprofit activity.

Religion

The five countries considered here also differ from the developed world, and from each other, in terms of religious traditions. This is significant because past research has established a close connection between religion and nonprofit activity. This has been attributed in part to the role that religiously motivated sentiments of altruism play in stimulating voluntary activity and philanthropic giving (Payton, 1988; Wuthnow, 1991). Also important according to one body of thinking are the incentives religious adherents have to form nonprofit service organizations as a means of attracting adherents to their faith (James, 1987, 1989; Rose-Ackerman, 1996).

Much of the evidence linking the development of nonprofit organizations to religion derives from essentially Western experience and Judeo-Christian traditions, however. The five countries considered here, by contrast, represent significantly different religious traditions and institutions. Thus, Brazil is a heavily Catholic country with a long history of Church involvement in political life, but in ways quite different from what evolved in Europe. Ghana represents a mixture of Christianity and to a lesser extent Islam, superimposed on tribal religions. Egypt is an Islamic country with a significant Coptic Christian minority. In India, Hinduism is the dominant religion, though Islam, Christianity and other religions play important roles. Finally, Thailand is an overwhelmingly Buddhist country, although Christian missionaries introduced Christian beliefs in some quarters.

To what extent might these different religious traditions affect the development of the nonprofit sector? To answer this question, it is necessary to recognize the different facets that religion really represents. In particular, four such facets seem especially relevant to the development of nonprofit organizations:

1) **The basic religious creed.** Some creeds may emphasize the importance of charity, altruism and philanthropy more than others.
2) **The posture towards individualism and individual initiative.** In Gellner's memorable phrase, many religions and cultures are 'non-modular' in orientation, denying, or at least not supporting, the right of adherents to 'combine into specific purpose, *ad hoc* limited associations, without binding [themselves] by some blood ritual' (Gellner, 1995: 42). Such traditions, he argues, are not conducive to the development of intermediary, civil society organizations.
3) **The emphasis on institutionalization.** Religions differ in the emphasis they place on building formal institutional structures for religious worship and other purposes. Religions that place a premium on institutionalization will be likely to contribute more to the development of nonprofit organizations than those that do not.
4) **The degree of autonomy from the state.** Religions differ markedly in the extent to which the institutions they create are perceived to be separate from, or part of, the state. Where religious institutions establish a strong tradition of autonomy, the prospects for nonprofit development are likely to be stronger than where religious institutions come to be perceived, and to operate, as appendages of the state.

In short, religion is a more complex variable than previous accounts have suggested, and it is reasonable to expect that the different religious traditions represented in our target countries will rank differently in terms of these different facets. This is suggested in Table 3.2 on page 67, which ranks the various religions in terms of the four dimensions we have identified. Thus, while every religion seems to place a high or moderate value on philanthropy, altruism and charity (Constantelos, 1987; Hastings, 1908), differences exist in terms of the other facets. In particular, of the religious traditions represented there, we would expect Christianity, particularly its Protestant variants, to be the most conducive to the flowering of nonprofit organizations. This is because of its strong emphasis on individualism, its significant commitment to institution building and its strong commitment to independence from state control (Lipset, 1995; Weber, 1996; Wuthnow, 1997). By contrast, traditional African religions emphasize solidarity over individualism and put little stress on institution building, and certainly institution building independent of the basic tribal political structure (Danquah, 1952; Gerdes, 1975; Little, 1965).

The other religions fall between these extremes. Thus Hinduism shares with Protestantism a deeply individualistic strain but places less emphasis on institution building (Brockington, 1981; Chaudhuri, 1979; Hopkins, 1971). Catholicism is strongly oriented to institution building but is more corporatist and solidaristic in philosophy (Mecham, 1966). Buddhism is individualist and has a strong institution building orientation but has

Table 3.2 *Key Dimensions of Religions with Implications for Nonprofit Development*

Religion	Emphasis on Charity and Philanthropy	Dimension Modularity	Institutional-ization	Autonomy	Hypothesized Encouragement to Nonprofit Formation
Protestantism	high	high	high	high	high
Hinduism	moderate	high	low	high	high
Catholicism	high	low–moderate	moderate	moderate–high	moderate–high
Buddhism	moderate	low–moderate	moderate	low–moderate	moderate–low
Islam	high	low	high	low	moderate low
African religions	moderate	low	low	low	low

tended to accept a high degree of integration with temporal authorities. Islam, finally, is far less modular than most of the other religions and has also stressed integration, rather than separation, between religious and political life (Gomez, 1987; Swearer, 1987: 389). Given these characteristics, we would expect that India and Brazil would have more developed and prominent nonprofit sectors than Egypt, Thailand and Ghana.

Heterogeneity

While religion is important in its own right, moreover, it is also important as one dimension of yet another factor – the degree of heterogeneity in a society. According to some economic theories, as we have seen, the greater the heterogeneity of a population in terms of religion, ethnicity, language and other similar factors, the larger the nonprofit sector is likely to be (James, 1987; Weisbrod, 1988). This is so because heterogeneity makes it more difficult to generate majority support for governmental provision of collective goods. More of the job of producing the collective goods considered important by different population sub-groups consequently falls to nonprofit organizations. In addition, since nonprofit organizations also perform an 'expressive' function, giving organizational voice to particular population groups or perspectives, it follows that the greater the diversity of the population, the greater the number and kind of nonprofit organizations that will be needed.

While it is difficult to develop an overall measure of heterogeneity, Table 3.3 shows that our five countries vary considerably in terms of the number of languages, ethnic groups and major religions. Even without precise indicators of social heterogeneity, we can see that India represents the most heterogeneous country among the five. At the other extreme is

Table 3.3 *Selected Social and Economic Indicators of Heterogeneity by Country, 1990*

Country/ Indicator	Brazil	Ghana	Egypt	India	Thailand
Per Cent of Population in Largest Religion	88 (Catholicism)	38 (African Religions)	90 (Suni-Muslim)	83 (Hinduism)	95 (Buddhism)
Per Cent of Population in Second Largest Religion	6	30	10	11	4
Per Cent of Population in Largest Language Group	97	52	99	39	80
Number of Major Languages	1	5	1	20	2
Per Cent of Population in Largest Ethnic Group	53 (White)	52 (Akan)	99 (Egyptian)	39 (Hindu)	80 (Thai)
Per Cent of Population in Second Largest Ethnic Group	22	16	1	8	12

Source: Britannica World Data, 1991.

Thailand, which appears as the most homogeneous among the countries selected, with Ghana, Brazil and Egypt ranking in between.

Development Assistance

Finally, these countries vary in the extent of development assistance they receive. Such assistance accounts for substantial portions of Ghana's and Egypt's gross national product (GNP), but it is virtually insignificant for the economies of Brazil, India and Thailand (OECD, 1995). Since international aid is viewed as a major stimulator of local nonprofit development, these data would lead us to expect more sizeable nonprofit sectors in Ghana and Egypt than in Brazil, India and Thailand.

Conclusion

In short, the countries selected for analysis here, while sharing certain common features that set them apart from the developed countries, also display a significant range of variation with respect to a variety of other factors that we have reason to expect might affect the scale and character of the nonprofit sectors they contain. Thus, they provide a useful terrain on which to assess some of the central theories in this field.

A Common Definition

In addition to selecting a reasonably representative set of countries, work on this project also required the development of a definition of the nonprofit sector that would permit both the differences and the similarities among these countries to become evident. This turned out to be an especially difficult task given the complex mixture of traditional, modern, indigenous and imported institutions that exist in most countries.

To cope with it, we relied heavily on a network of local associates to formulate a consensus definition. More specifically, for the purposes of this work, we defined the nonprofit sector as the set of institutions in any society that share five key characteristics:[5]

1) They are *organized*, ie they possess some institutional reality.
2) They are *private*, ie institutionally separate from government.
3) They are *nonprofit-distributing*, ie not returning any profits generated to their owners or directors.
4) They are *self-governing*, ie equipped to control their own activities.
5) They are *voluntary*, at least in part, ie they involve some meaningful degree of voluntary participation, either in the actual conduct of the agency's activities or in the management of its affairs.[6]

Quite clearly, this definition of the nonprofit sector goes well beyond the 'NGO' concept in common usage within the developing world. It comes closer to what has more recently come to be referred to as 'civil society organizations', that is organizations that function outside the market and the state (see, for example, Synergos Institute and Overseas Development Council, 1996).

Critical Questions

How extensive is the range of organizations demarcated by this definition in the countries we targeted for examination? To what extent are variations apparent from country to country? What accounts for these variations? More specifically, to what extent do the variations reflect the factors identified in the prevailing theories in this field? What influence do factors such as religion or legal framework have on the scale and operation of the nonprofit sector in these countries? To what extent does a meaningful concept of a 'nonprofit sector' exist in these countries? And what lessons does the experience of these countries hold for general theories of nonprofit action? These are the major questions we sought to answer.

To do so, we drew on a combination of existing data, special surveys, legal and policy analysis, and interviews. Although limitations of time and resources made it impossible to answer these questions definitively, it was possible to shed at least some preliminary light on the answers to them.

MAJOR FINDINGS

In particular, five major conclusions emerged from this work.

The Concept of a Nonprofit Sector

In the first place, in none of the five countries that we examined did a coherent concept of what we here term 'the nonprofit sector' exist either in the scholarly community or among practitioners in the field. The idea of a set of institutions that share crucial features that demarcate them as a sector had not really surfaced forcefully in any of the countries. As a consequence, the task we undertook required that we 'create', at least conceptually, and not simply measure, the reality we were seeking to portray.

Basic Scale

While the concept of a definable nonprofit sector existed in none of the countries covered in this paper, however, the reality of such a sector was nevertheless very much in evidence. Organizations that meet our 'structural–operational' definition turn out to exist in far greater numbers and variety in the five countries examined here than conventional accounts based on the term NGO would suggest.

In India (Sen, 1998), for example, various directories list a total of about 1 million nonprofit organizations including professional associations, social welfare agencies, caste associations and thousands of others. The Gandhian network of 1700 nonprofit organizations alone employs about 600,000 people.

In Brazil (Landim, 1998) the Catholic Church, in close alliance with the state, built a vast network of schools and hospitals, with Protestant denominations setting up competing institutions. At the end of the 19th century, secular voluntary associations such as mutual societies and trade unions emerged as the country developed economically. The upshot is a sizeable and varied set of nonprofit institutions. Federal government registries list over 210,000 nonprofit organizations, including 45,000 in São Paolo alone and another 16,000 in Rio de Janeiro. Most of these organizations are small, with budgets of less than US$30,000, but there are also huge educational institutions and hospitals that are frequently linked to the Catholic Church. Total employment within this sector is at least 1 million, or somewhat less than 2 per cent of total employment. What is more, this sector has been growing in recent years. A survey of nonprofit organizations in São Paolo and Rio de Janeiro revealed that over 90 per cent of the numerous neighbourhood and community organizations that exist in these two cities were formed in the last two decades.

Although nonprofit institutions seem to be somewhat less extensive in Thailand, Egypt and Ghana than in Brazil and India, they are far from nonexistent. In Thailand (Pongsapich, 1998), for example, there are some 15,000 nonprofit organizations, 2200 of them in Bangkok alone. Cremation associations are the most frequent type of such organizations, accounting for 50 per cent of the total. These associations have deep roots in Thai society, handling the all-important burial functions that are so sacred to Buddhism; but they have recently begun assuming modern credit functions as well. In addition to the cremation societies, moreover, numerous social welfare associations also exist, comprising 39 per cent of the registered organizations.

In Ghana (Atingdui et al, 1998), the Department of Social Welfare has identified over 800 nonprofit organizations in the larger urban areas alone. However, only about a quarter of these are officially registered with the government. In addition, there are 114 nonprofit hospitals scattered throughout the country, as well as 242 primary and 229 secondary schools, all typically linked to religious bodies. Moreover, the 800 organizations listed by the Department of Social Welfare do not include the numerous village associations, credit and savings associations and similar types of self-help groups, such as the Susu associations, with roots in village traditions.

Finally, Egypt (Kandil, 1998) boasts some 17,500 nonprofit organizations with an estimated total membership of almost 6 million people out of a total population of over 53 million. This does not include the numerous informal associations among the poor, nor many of the Islamic groups organized around individual mosques. The latter constitutes a vast network of unregistered groups created by popular Islam, providing health, social services and education to populations that the state, with its dwindling resources, is increasingly unable to reach.

Beyond NGOs

Not only is the nonprofit sector in these countries quite large, it also extends well beyond the NGOs that have been the principal focus of attention in the developing world. Thus, for example:

> *In Brazil, nearly one quarter (23 per cent) of the 210,000 nonprofit organizations registered with the federal government are social*

service providers, 20 per cent are sport and recreational clubs, and another 14 per cent are organizations active in the fields of education, research and culture. Based on a survey of nonprofit organizations in the state of Rio de Janeiro, we estimate that the fields of education, health and social services account for over 70 per cent of all nonprofit employment (Landim, 1998).

A survey of the 800 'NGOs' listed with the Department of Social Welfare in Ghana shows that education is in fact the most frequent nonprofit activity in this country, followed by development, environment, health and social services (Atingdui et al, 1998).

In India, a survey in the Varoda-Baroda region shows that education, social services, and culture and recreation account, respectively, for 40 per cent, 19 per cent and 19 per cent of nonprofit activity, and that only 8 per cent of the organizations are engaged in developmental work per se (Sen, 1998).

In Thailand, as we have seen, most nonprofit organizations are traditional cremation societies (Pongsapich, 1998).

Focusing exclusively on NGOs thus gives a distorted picture of the true scale and character of the nonprofit sector in these countries.

Beyond External Funding

Not only does the nonprofit sector in the developing world extend well beyond NGOs, it also receives its funding from sources that go well beyond the traditional development assistance that is often identified with nonprofit organizations in these areas. In India, for example, while some 15,000 nonprofit organizations registered with the government received US$460 million in foreign assistance as of the early 1990s, the majority of revenue actually comes from domestic sources, much of it in the form of fees and charges (Sen, 1998). Similarly, a survey of nonprofit organizations in the state of Rio de Janeiro revealed that fees and charges are more important than funds from abroad in financing nonprofit activity (Landim, 1998). In fact, the really distinctive feature of nonprofit finance in the developing world may not be the relatively higher levels of outside aid so much as the relatively smaller levels of government support. Whether this is a permanent feature or another sign of the stage of development of the sector in these countries is one of the most crucial issues for the future. The significant level of government support to nonprofit organizations in India suggests, however, that the latter may be the case.

Relative Scale

While the nonprofit sectors of the five countries examined here seem to be considerably more extensive than previous analyses limited to NGOs may have suggested, however, they are nevertheless still generally smaller than in the average developed country. Compared to 4 or 5 per cent of the labour force in the developed countries (Salamon and Anheier, 1996a), nonprofit organizations in the developing world generally employ fewer than 2 per cent of the workforce.

What is more, significant variations seem to exist in the scale of nonprofit activity from country to country. Thus the nonprofit sector seems more fully developed in India and Brazil than it does in Thailand, Egypt or Ghana.

EXPLAINING NONPROFIT ACTIVITY IN THE DEVELOPING WORLD

How can we account for these findings? Why has the concept of a nonprofit sector not surfaced in these societies despite the clear presence of sizeable sets of organizations that meet the criteria for such a sector? Why is this set of organizations less fully developed in these countries than in the more developed countries? And what accounts for the interesting variations that seem to exist among countries in the scale and dynamics of nonprofit activity?

Clearly there is no way to answer these questions definitively on the basis of the experience of only five countries. Nevertheless, this experience offers some useful insights into the factors at work.

Authoritarian Political Control

Perhaps the most basic factor accounting for the generally retarded pattern of third sector development in the countries we have examined is the long history of authoritarian rule that seems to have characterized these countries throughout much of their history. The nonprofit sector in Brazil, for example, has taken shape in a historical context characterized by a strong state and a weak civil society. Important factors in this context are the dominant role the Catholic Church historically played as an ally of the state, and Brazil's economic modernization under an authoritarian political system that ended only in the late 1980s after a long period of instability. As Landim (1998: 64) put it, 'In Brazil, the State has always taken on itself the task of "creating" society, whether by arranging groups and individuals hierarchically according to an exclusionary economic order, or by intervening to destroy autonomy.' Coupled with a long history of slavery, the result has been to fix onto Brazilian society a heritage of hierarchical control and patron–client relations. Indeed, even industrialization was managed through a series of agreements among dominant elites, producing a pattern that has come to be known as 'conservative modernization' (Schwartzman, 1982).

Strong state control also figured prominently in the histories of Egypt and Thailand. First under the Ottoman Empire, and later under British colonial rule, Egypt was ruled by a succession of authoritarian leaders with only limited opportunity for effective democratic involvement. In Thailand as well, a centralized monarchy took shape in the 13th century that fused secular and religious power and held effective sway for the subsequent 700 years. Under the prevailing 'Devaraja' concept of Brahminism, the king was seen as a god-like creature to be revered and followed without question (Pongsapich, 1998).

Authoritarian traditions were somewhat more muted in Ghana and India, but still very much present. The precolonial societies in what became Ghana were organized in traditional tribal form, with local chieftains exercising dominant control and villages adhering to generally accepted traditions of proper behaviour. India's history is a rich tapestry of successive empires that rose to power, flourished and then went into decline. Through it all, the dominant form of social organization was hierarchical, with limited opportunity for social organization outside of the control of the state and its supportive religious orders.

Given this pattern of authoritarianism, little room was left for a truly independent third sector in these societies. What charitable institutions emerged therefore had to fit within the prevailing structures of political and social power and avoid posing a serious challenge to the dominant political authorities. Passivity and dependence rather than empowerment and autonomy thus became the early watchwords of nonprofit sector activity.

Although these features have moderated considerably in more recent times, moreover, authoritarian political control did not end in these countries with independence. Rather, with the possible exception of India, it persisted. The upshot has been a persistent atmosphere of distrust between the nonprofit sector and the state in many of these countries. The state remains highly watchful of its power and too easily interprets the emergence of nonprofit organizations as a challenge to its very legitimacy. In Egypt, for example, this distrust is currently fuelled by the antagonism between a strong secular state and Islamic fundamentalist groups that are using nonprofit institutions as a way to strengthen their links with the urban poor. In Brazil, state distrust is a residue of a recent authoritarian past and a social and economic policy that seeks to build up the private business sector and still views the citizen sector as an antagonist. In Thailand and India, a stronger tradition of partnership is emerging, though not without deep-seated reservations about the bonds that have formed between indigenous nonprofit institutions and their foreign supporters.

Conflicting Values and Organizational Self-Perception

This tension helps to explain the absence of a clear concept of a 'nonprofit sector' in these countries. The emergence in recent years of a class of nonprofit institutions willing to challenge the prevailing powers-that-be has brought with it a desire to differentiate these newer organizations from those that came before. The use of a single term to refer to these different types of entities has therefore had political and social costs that those involved have simply been unwilling to pay. To be part of the associative sector in Brazil, for example, is to be in opposition to the state and to the prevailing political and economic elites, something those engaged in charitable organizations have historically not wanted to convey. By contrast, 'philanthropy' and 'assistance' are perceived within the citizen movements to be props of a repressive old order. Those engaged in the new 'development NGOs' therefore have a strong need to distinguish themselves from these older, presumably more conservative, and to some extent discredited, institutions. Lumping all of these organizations into a single entity called the 'nonprofit sector' thus blurs distinctions that many have a strong interest in preserving. Definitional coherence has therefore taken a back seat to political ideology and organizational expediency in the conceptualization of the social space that lies outside the market and the state in these societies.

Religion

That political authoritarianism survived so effectively in these countries is, in turn, due in part to the nature of the religious traditions that took shape there. The record of the five countries examined here gives ample support, in fact, to the hypotheses outlined earlier about the multiple impacts of religion on the development of the nonprofit sector. In addition to the basic creed and the support it gives to acts of charity, other crucial facets of religion's impact need to be taken into account – its posture towards individualism, its commitment to institution building; and its relationship with state authorities. As the evidence examined here makes clear, religions can share a positive orientation towards philanthropy yet still not be highly supportive of the emergence of private nonprofit institutions.

So far as basic religious creed is concerned, virtually all of the religions in our target countries provide strong support for philanthropic activity and charitable giving. Thus, for example, in Brazil the Catholic Church stressed the importance of charity and help to the poor as a basic requirement of a religious life. Islam, like Christianity, makes charitable giving a central element of its creed. The paying of *zakat* to support religious institutions and care for the needy is thus one of the 'Five Pillars' of Islamic practice (Rahman, 1987: 309), and strong religious incentives exist as well to establish *al waqf*, or charitable endowments. In India, the notion of voluntarism found early inspiration in the Rig Vedas; while in Ghana, tribal religious and social ceremonies reinforced patterns of mutual help and assistance.

Despite this generally positive influence of religious doctrine in nurturing charitable traditions in these countries, however, the influence of religion on the development of nonprofit organizations was still considerably less pronounced in most of these countries than it was in western Europe and North America. This is so because certain of the other facets of religious activity were less supportive of such institutions. Although both Islam and Buddhism emphasize the importance of philanthropy, for example, the limited development of nonprofit institutions in Egypt and Thailand can still be attributed in important part to facets of the religious traditions of these countries that we identified earlier. Thus both Islam in Egypt and Buddhism in Thailand tend to stress the submersion of individual initiative into a larger whole rather than its forthright expression through organized nonprofit activity or other means. In addition, both have favoured close working relationships between religion and the state rather than the establishment of separate religious institutions outside of, and in opposition to, the state. In the terms introduced earlier, both are thus less modular in their outlook than was the case of Protestantism in western Europe. Islam, in fact, is one of the least modular of religions, stressing the integration of the individual into a larger social and religious order rather than the existence of a separate social space for the exercise of individual initiative. Islam, as one author has put it, is not simply a religion but rather 'the name of a total way of life' that regulates far more than an individual's personal relationship with God (Rahman, 1987: 305). Indeed, Islam recognizes little separation between the religious and the political spheres (Laroui, 1987).

Buddhism places somewhat greater emphasis than Islam on individual action and self-discovery as the path to redemption, a feature it shares with Christianity. However, the institutions built by Buddhism had a more narrowly religious function than the comparable Christian or Catholic institutions, reflecting Buddhism's stress on providing places of escape where monks could achieve inner peace (Gomez, 1987). What is more, at least in its southeast Asian variants evident in Thailand, Buddhism developed a highly symbiotic relationship with the prevailing structures of political authority that made it far less congenial to the establishment of a sphere of organized, private action outside the state. Buddhism provided, as one writer has put it, 'a cosmology in which the king was accorded the central place and a view of society in which the human community was dependent on the role of the king' (Swearer, 1987: 389). Thus neither Buddhism in Thailand nor Islam in Egypt offered much stimulus for the establishment of an independent nonprofit sector.

The role of Hinduism in the development of the nonprofit sector in India was more complex. Like Protestantism and Buddhism, Hinduism places great emphasis on individualism and individual initiative in its stress on personal spiritual devotion as the path towards inner peace (Brockington, 1981; Chaudhuri, 1979; Hopkins, 1971). In addition, a complex system of deity structures and worship practices encouraged a sense of pluralism. At the same time, however, unlike Christianity,

Hinduism places much less emphasis on the development of complex organizational structures of the sort that characterized Protestantism and Catholicism. It has therefore done little to foster formal organizational networks through which individuals could act. What is more, the caste system sanctioned by Hinduism further segmented the population into a complex arrangement of hierarchical clusters, inhibiting the ability of people to form and re-form along interest and professional lines. Thus, while including three components associated positively with nonprofit sector development, ie a creed that stresses charity, modularity and autonomy, Hinduism lacked the institution-building tendency of Christianity. It was not until the Gandhian movement, and later the independent Indian state, provided this missing element, therefore, that Hinduism's facilitation of nonprofit sector development really came into its own.

Even those religions most supportive of the development of autonomous nonprofit institutions in their basic creed and organizational dynamics operated rather differently in the developing world than they did in the developed. This was the case, for example, with Catholicism in Brazil. Far from being a force for liberation and independent action based on conscience, the Church in Brazil functioned historically to reinforce secular authority and a monolithic system of social and cultural control, thereby sharply reducing the opportunities for developing an independent nonprofit sector. Indeed, the Jesuit order was banished from the Spanish Empire in Latin America because of what was perceived to be its excessive independence from secular authorities, and Portuguese authorities in Brazil were careful to minimize independent impulses within the Church in Brazil. While the Catholic Church was active in creating networks of health, education and social service institutions in Brazil, these largely restricted their attention to providing 'assistance' and pointedly refrained from challenging the social and economic systems that made such assistance necessary. On the contrary, until the rise of liberation theology in the 1960s, Church authorities were generally supportive of the authoritarian regimes that dominated the region. As a consequence, Catholicism in Brazil provided far less space for the blossoming of an independent nonprofit sector than it did in its European manifestations. Indeed, as one student of Brazilian history has noted: '… the Church administration was so meshed with the administrative machine of civil government that it would be hard to see it as an autonomous power and not a department of the State' (Hollanda, 1985: 57, quoted in Landim, 1998). Not until the rise of liberation theology did the Church emerge as a stimulator of independent nonprofit action in Brazil and elsewhere in Latin America.

In short, based on the evidence from our case studies, it appears that the particular character of religious practice in the developing world is partly responsible for the generally limited development of a vibrant, independent, nonprofit sector in these countries. What is more, religion was a more significant retarding influence in Egypt, Brazil and Thailand than it was in India and, to a lesser extent, Ghana.

Colonialism

A fourth factor that helps to explain the generally retarded pattern of third sector development in the third world is the recent history of colonial control. Like religion, however, colonialism's impact on third sector development has been multi-dimensional. What is more, it has varied somewhat depending on the national traditions and values of the colonial power. Thus, on the one hand, colonialism has tended to undermine the independence of local social classes that might have provided the rallying point for private, nonprofit institutions. This was particularly true of the Spanish and Portuguese colonial traditions, which fixed especially authoritarian political and social structures on their respective colonies. In much of Latin America, colonialism created a highly inhospitable environment for the emergence of truly autonomous nonprofit institutions that might have challenged the monopolistic power of the colonial regime and its local allies.

At the same time, colonialism also affected the legal systems and political traditions of the colonies, and these impacts often served to encourage nonprofit development. This was the case, for example, of the British impact on both India and Ghana. In both, legal systems were put in place that actually facilitated the rise of legally protected nonprofit organizations. In addition, both countries absorbed from the colonial power a long standing tradition of voluntary organization and oppositional politics that contributed in its own way to legitimizing nonprofit activity. This may help explain why nonprofit institutions seem to be so much more numerous and highly developed in India than in Brazil, and why the atmosphere of hostility between these two sectors is far less evident in the former than in the latter.

Low Income and Constrained Social Development

Perhaps the most important impact of colonialism on the countries where it held sway, however, was the constraint it exercised on social development. One of the principal consequences of the colonial experience, in fact, was to limit the space that indigenous middle class elements could occupy in the developing world. This was so because the colonial administration handled many governmental and commercial functions that might otherwise have been performed by an indigenous bourgeoisie, and restricted middle class professional opportunities as well. What middle class cadre emerged in these countries thus tended to be tightly bound to the colonial administrations and therefore lacked the independence characteristic of the urban commercial and professional middle class elements that emerged in western Europe during the dawn of the industrial era.

This situation persisted well into the post-World War II period, moreover, because of the general poverty and lack of development characteristic of these countries. As growth has gathered momentum in at least some regions, however, this situation has changed considerably. In Brazil,

Thailand and Egypt, where economic growth has been especially robust, for example, extensive, urban middle classes have emerged. Not surprisingly, moreover, the growth of the nonprofit sector in these countries has followed suit. Indeed, the significant upsurge of nonprofit activity in Brazil over the past two decades can be attributed in important part to the emergence of a sizeable new urban middle class as a result of recent economic growth.

Legal Treatment

A further factor impeding the development of the nonprofit sector in the five countries considered here has been the legal environment within which nonprofits must operate. Certainly in civil law countries such as Brazil, Thailand and Egypt, where no basic right to organize is automatically recognized, and where the formation of legal entities is a privilege that must be explicitly recognized in law, formal law can shape the environment for nonprofit action rather fundamentally. Reflecting the generally authoritarian politics that have characterized at least four of these five countries during much of their recent history, it should therefore come as no surprise to learn that the legal structures for nonprofit activity have been quite restrictive. For example, the Religious Bodies Registration Act of 1981 in Ghana revoked the legal status of all religious nonprofit organizations and required them to reapply through a highly restrictive registration procedure. In Brazil, Law 91 of 1935, regulating the public utility status of nonprofit organizations, was used as a means of political control and favouritism. In Egypt, Law 32 of 1964 establishes de facto governmental control of large segments of the nonprofit sector; and in Thailand, the Cremation Welfare Act of 1974 was passed by the military government to pre-empt feared infiltration by communists. The Act required all existing local cremation and related communal welfare societies to register with the central authorities in Bangkok, and to submit to state supervision.

In many respects, however, the formal legal framework for nonprofit activity in the countries we have examined is far less restrictive than their long histories of authoritarianism might suggest. This is so because the legal provisions have often been transplanted from the colonial power regardless of whether they suit local circumstances or have otherwise been copied from other nations during periods of liberalization. Thus, for example, the basic legal provisions affecting nonprofit organizations in India and Ghana were borrowed from those in force in late 19th and early 20th century Britain through a system of legal ordinances. Similarly, the basic law on associations in Brazil was adopted during a period of liberal control in the early part of the 19th century. The legal environment for nonprofit organizations in these countries therefore appears quite open. To get around these general legal provisions, governments have had to add various restrictions to limit their general thrust, something that is a bit more cumbersome, though hardly impossible, to do. Thus, for example, notwithstanding the supportive general provisions for organizing nonprofit organizations in Ghana, Law 221 of 1981 established de facto state superiority over the nonprofit sector. Moreover, tax laws and related legislation often establish significant obstacles to the operation of nonprofit organizations, as the example of Brazil and the Indian system of government supervision of international funding to nonprofit organizations show. What this makes clear is that establishing an enabling legal environment for nonprofit action is only a first step towards opening the way for a viable nonprofit sector. A variety of other obstacles can easily frustrate the intent of even the most supportive legal provisions. In the cases of Brazil, Egypt and Thailand in particular, it seems likely that the growth of the nonprofit sector has been impeded by legal restrictions even though the overall legal environment seems supportive.

The State and Development Ideology

One final factor helping to explain the historically constrained pattern of third sector development in the third world, as well as the recent growth of such institutions, is the changing fashion in development policy and development ideology. During the 1950s and 1960s, development thinking emphasized the importance of a strong state as the principal agent of modernizing reforms. As a consequence, considerable effort went into differentiating a sphere of state action outside the pre-modern structures of tribe or community, and into creating modern, secular administrative structures that could effectively operate in this sphere. The conceptual maps that guided this project of state construction included a sphere of business in addition to that of government, but it downplayed, if not excluded, nonprofit organizations, local communities, civil society and voluntary groups, all of which were viewed, to one degree or another, as holdovers from a prior era of traditional social organization.

Nor did the shift to structural adjustment in the 1980s change this fundamentally. On the contrary, the structural adjustment paradigm of development merely replaced government with the private business community as the deus ex machina of development. In the process, however, it reinforced an essentially two-sector model of society that left little room for a vibrant private, nonprofit sector. That a coherent notion of such a sector did not arise is thus understandable given the mental maps that guided the central policy debate.

Even during the period of state-centred development, however, important nonprofit institution building occurred. For the most part, this took the form of top-down efforts designed to extend the reach of state-sponsored modernizing reforms (and often national political leadership) into the countryside. The Nasser Bank in Egypt, the network of Gandhian associations in India, and the socialist mass associations created in Ghana under Nkrumah are all examples of such efforts. Though hardly independent entities, these organizations nevertheless contributed in important ways to the ultimate development of third sector institutions in many of these countries. The substantial nonprofit presence in India can be attributed in important part, in fact, to such policies.

Even more significant, however, were the efforts of a variety of external actors, in cooperation with indigenous elements, to create independent mechanisms through which to pursue alternative approaches to development outside the official channels. Included here are the efforts of a number of Northern foundations and private voluntary organizations as well as the Catholic Church and other religious bodies (Salamon, 1994; Smith, 1990). Beginning with the Second Vatican Council in the mid-1960s, the Catholic Church, for example, shifted its allegiance to a marked extent in Brazil and other Latin American countries from the prevailing powers that be to grassroots communities, creating vast networks of 'Church base communities'. In Brazil alone, 80,000 such communities were created in the 1970s and 1980s, each representing a locus for community problem-solving and organization (Krischke, 1991). During the same period, Northern voluntary organizations began to shift markedly from a 'relief' perspective to an 'empowerment' focus in their work, encouraging the formation and expansion of indigenous organizations promoting self-help activities at the grassroots level and often managing to tap official aid funds in the process (Anheier, 1987; Brodhead, 1987; Drabek, 1987). As disaffection with state-centred development has spread, moreover, the official bilateral and multinational aid agencies have moved in a similar direction, increasing the assistance provided to development-oriented nonprofit organizations operating in the developing world. The upshot has been an important stimulus not only to the expansion of Northern private voluntary organizations operating in the South, but to the creation and growth of a new tier of development-oriented indigenous organizations. Indeed, public and private development agencies are increasingly conditioning their aid on the active engagement of such indigenous nonprofit institutions in externally funded development projects, or at least on the existence of a supportive environment for the operation of Northern nonprofit organizations. This has caused even countries with little homegrown interest in nonprofit organizations to foster, or at least stop discouraging, them. Local political elites have sometimes welcomed this development. In other places, however, they have responded coolly, as the cases of Egypt, Ghana prior to 1990 and to some extent even India, attest. The result is a certain tension and distrust between this internationally-oriented nonprofit sector and the state in these countries. What is more, tensions also exist between this NGO segment of the nonprofit sector and the rich networks of other third sector organizations that also often exist (Bratton, 1989; Cernea, 1987; Fisher, 1993; Lewis, 1987; Qureshi, 1988; Ritchey-Vance, 1991).

Summary

In short, the development of the third sector seems to have been inhibited in the countries examined here by a long history of authoritarianism; by a colonial heritage and a history of limited economic growth that restricted the growth of an independent urban middle class; by religious traditions that placed less emphasis on modularity and the fostering of independent institutional structures; by legal structures that often placed impediments in the way of nonprofit formation; and by development policies that stressed the creation of a modernizing state and later the fostering of private enterprise rather than the promotion of independent institutions outside the confines of the market and the state. At the same time, these factors hardly operated to the same extent everywhere; and they often encountered opposite tendencies more conducive to third sector growth. Thus, for example, authoritarianism was especially pronounced in Brazil, yet a sizeable array of Church-related nonprofit institutions nevertheless took shape to handle the vast social welfare business that a repressive social system left in its wake. This vast institutional structure was then available at a later date to serve as a rallying point for more citizen-based initiatives. In India, religious traditions played a far less active role in creating nonprofit organizations but nevertheless fostered the atmosphere in which such organizations could ultimately flourish when state policy actively encouraged them. While middle class elements have played a meagre role historically in most of these countries, moreover, economic growth in the post-World War II period in both Brazil and Egypt has stimulated significant middle class growth, and with it the same kind of extensive third sector development that accompanied the rise of the bourgeoisie in much of western Europe. Finally, the 'discovery' of the nonprofit sector by international development agencies in more recent years has injected a new dynamic into the picture, stimulating the growth of a particular class of grassroots development organizations as alternatives to an increasingly discredited state.

Taken together, these factors thus help us explain both why third sector development has been relatively stunted in the five countries examined here, and why it is more advanced in India and Brazil than in Egypt, Ghana and Thailand. They also help us to understand why the concept of a coherent third sector has failed to take hold in these countries. Such a concept is difficult to square with the considerable diversity that characterizes the local third sector scene. It also runs counter to the political and institutional interests that many in the sector still have in differentiating themselves from other third sector institutions which may have developed in different eras and served very different purposes. As the sector's presence becomes 'normalized', however, we can expect these divisions to subside.

THEORETICAL IMPLICATIONS

From the discussion here, it should be clear that the path of third sector development in the third world differs considerably from that in the so-called 'first world'. To what extent, therefore, does this have implications for our theoretical understanding of this sector? To what extent do prevailing theories of the nonprofit sector help us explain third sector developments in the countries we have examined, and to what extent does the experience of these countries require us to refine or re-interpret some of these theories?

While it is obviously difficult to answer these questions definitively on the basis of five cases, certain tentative theoretical implications do flow from the discussion here. Five of these in particular deserve special mention.

Ubiquity of the Third Sector

Perhaps the most basic theoretical point that emerges is the challenge that the record briefly examined here poses to prevailing assumptions about the essentially Western character of nonprofit institutions. What the discussion here makes clear is that nonprofit type institutions exist in widely divergent cultural and social settings in virtually every part of the world. What is more, they are not recent creations imported into these societies from the outside; indeed they have deep indigenous histories and roots. This is not to say that the embodiments of the nonprofit sector are identical from place to place. On the contrary, they often differ markedly. Thus Thailand's cremation societies are different in both concept and form from the caste associations common in India, let alone the friendly societies of 19th century Britain. What is more, the nature of these organizations has changed over time. The village associations of west Africa and Brazil are thus significantly different from the Church-based assistance agencies that developed in these areas in the 19th century. And these are different in turn from the empowerment-oriented urban squatters' associations and development organizations, as well as the middle class professional associations, that have emerged in the past 20 years. Nevertheless, these organizations share certain common features that make it meaningful to think of them as parts of a single sector, and to group them together conceptually with comparable organizations sharing these same basic features in the more developed North. Armed with a broader concept of the nonprofit sector, in short, a far richer institutional tapestry comes into view in many of these countries than is often assumed, and one that seems to coexist with a variety of social and economic structures.

Market Failure Theories

This ubiquity and variety of nonprofit organizations in the developing world poses a particular challenge to the 'market failure/government failure' theory that has been the dominant explanation of the nonprofit sector in academic circles in the West. This theory ascribes the existence of nonprofit organizations to the presence of demands for public goods that are left unsatisfied in a market economy by either the market or the state (Weisbrod, 1977). According to this theory, the more diverse a society in religious or ethnic terms, and therefore the more diverse the conceptions of the good life and the desirable bundle of collective goods that must be supplied, the larger the nonprofit sector that is likely to exist. This is so because, with a democratic political system, government, which is the principal vehicle for supplying collective goods, will respond only to those demands for collective goods that enjoy majority support, leaving unsatisfied those demands pressed by sub-groups of the population. The result is a significant residue of unsatisfied demands for collective goods that nonprofit organizations are especially suited to meet.

The evidence reviewed here lends some credence to this theory even in the context of the developing world. This is most clearly evident in the case of India, perhaps the most heterogeneous society in the world, and also a society in which nonprofit institutions exist in profusion. Similarly, a major stimulus for the development of nonprofit organizations in Thailand was the arrival of numerous Chinese immigrants who formed language societies to preserve their cultural heritage (Pongsapich, 1998).

At the same time, the experience reviewed here also points out the limitations of this theory. A fundamental premise of this market failure/government failure theory is that both a market system and a democratic political structure exist. Only in such a context is it meaningful to expect that consensus about the desirable bundle of public goods will lead to action by the state, leaving nonprofit organizations to handle only those public goods demanded by various minority interests. In the developing world, however, as we have seen, political systems are more likely to be authoritarian than democratic, and the reach of market relations is also quite constrained. Under these circumstances, even majority needs are rarely translated into public response. The relatively low levels of government social welfare spending in Thailand and Egypt despite the considerable population homogeneity that exists in these two countries is one indication of this. Minority demands, by contrast, are rarely even given voice. Thus, in Brazil and Ghana authoritarian political structures effectively obstructed the emergence of sizeable nonprofit sectors despite the considerable population heterogeneity that existed.

These observations do not, of course, disprove these demand side economic theories. On the contrary, the theories acknowledge the presence of a functioning market and a democratic political system as boundary conditions for their applicability. What the experience examined here suggests, rather, is that these theories are not so much wrong as of limited relevance to the kinds of circumstances that exist in much of the developing world. To understand the role of the nonprofit sector in these circumstances, therefore, it is necessary to look elsewhere for theoretical help.

Supply Side Theories

One such potential alternative line of theoretical insight is the set of theories that locates the principal explanation for the emergence of nonprofit institutions not so much on the demand for nonprofit services as on the supply of entrepreneurs with a commitment to establish nonprofit institutions to meet such demand. According to these theories, one of the most likely sources of such supply is religious institutions, particularly in circumstances where religious competition exists (James, 1987). In this view, the formation of nonprofit institutions to meet human needs is one way that religious zealots can win adherents to their cause. In desperate need of the education, health care or other basic necessities that religious entrepreneurs offer through nonprofit institutions, disadvantaged people come to accept the creed that sponsors the provision of such basic services. The creation of nonprofit assistance agencies is thus not wholly altruistic in motivation; it also has the instrumental function, implicitly if not explicitly, of attracting religious adherents.

The record of the countries examined here lends some credence to this line of thought as well. The Catholic Church in Brazil and the Protestant missionary societies in Ghana and India certainly extended their reach in important part by offering social welfare assistance to the impoverished peasants and villagers of these countries. In more recent years, the Moslem Brotherhood and the Islamic mosques have pursued a similar course in Egypt, organizing health clinics within the mosques as a way to entice poor urban dwellers away from adherence to a secular state. The rise of liberation theology in Latin America can also be understood within this framework. The Church's commitment to the creation of Christian 'base' communities in Latin America in the 1960s was certainly motivated in important part by fears over the spread of communism among the rural and urban masses in the wake of the Cuban revolution and a desire to organize vehicles that could compete with communist guerilla movements in winning the hearts and minds of the poor.

While religious entrepreneurs have played an important role in the founding of nonprofit institutions, however, the sources of such entrepreneurship have broadened considerably in more recent years, as we have seen, to include Northern relief and development organizations. Constrained from providing assistance through governmental bodies, such agencies have had to stimulate the formation of local nonprofit organizations in order to operate. These needs on the part of international development agencies have meshed nicely, moreover, with the desires of many middle class professionals in the developing world for more fulfilling ways to contribute to the development of their countries than are afforded by positions in the governmental bureaucracy or local businesses. The result is a powerful new supply side drive for the formation of nonprofit organizations in the developing world (Salamon, 1994).

In short, the experience of the developing countries reviewed here provides significant support for the supply side explanation of the emergence of nonprofit organizations, though this theory must be reinterpreted somewhat to accommodate the particular sources of nonprofit entrepreneurship recently evident in the developing world.

Partnership Theory

A third body of theory on which the experience of the developing countries might shed useful light is the 'voluntary failure' or 'partnership' theory developed by Salamon (1987). According to this line of thinking, the competitive, almost conflictual, relationship between the nonprofit sector and the state posited in the market failure/government failure theory outlined above is seriously overstated. The nonprofit sector is not, as this prior theory suggested, simply an alternative to the state in the provision of public goods that can be expected to grow only where state provision of such goods is constrained. Rather, there are strong theoretical reasons to expect the state and the nonprofit sector to grow in parallel, and even in cooperation with each other. This is so because both are responses to the same set of social pressures for expanded public goods, and each brings to the response to these pressures unique attributes that the other lacks – the ability to generate resources on the side of the state and the ability to deliver services at the local level on the side of the nonprofit sector. Far from operating in conflict, therefore, we might expect these two sectors to work hand in hand.

The experience of the developing countries examined here provides mixed, but still significant, support to this line of thinking. Throughout much of their histories, the conflictual elements of the relationship between the nonprofit sector and the state were clearly in the ascendance in these countries. Authoritarian governments generally discouraged the emergence of nonprofit institutions, fearing the challenge they might pose to elite control. In more recent times, however, the partnership model seems to be gaining ground, and for many of the reasons this model predicts. In particular, governments are coming to recognize the contribution that nonprofit organizations can make to the processes of social and economic development and are joining forces with nonprofit organizations to help promote the development process. Such cooperation has long been a central part of development thinking in India, where the Gandhian village associations were incorporated into government development planning from the outset. Similar patterns have recently gained prominence as well in Thailand, Ghana and Brazil, where government support for nonprofit organizations has recently grown considerably. Indeed, it might fairly be said that the single most important factor shaping the size and durability of the nonprofit sector in the developing world is the extent to which a modus vivendi has been established between the nonprofit sector and the state.

To be sure, this relationship raises as many challenges as it solves. While benefiting from state financial aid, nonprofit organizations must be careful not to be crushed in the state's embrace. Some degree of private funding is therefore essential to allow nonprofits to retain a meaningful degree of independence of state control. Nevertheless, the recent history of the countries we have examined provides significant confirmation of the line of development that the partnership theory predicts.

The Social Origins Approach

Finally, the data reported here lend considerable support to what we have elsewhere termed the 'social origins' approach to understanding the development of the nonprofit sector (Salamon and Anheier, 1996b). The central argument of this approach is that the nonprofit sector is deeply embedded in the social, economic and political dynamics of different societies. As such, its evolution cannot be attributed to any single factor, such as unsatisfied demand for public goods or the supply of nonprofit entrepreneurs. Rather, the emergence of nonprofit institutions is rooted in the broader structure of class and social groupings in a society. In particular, vibrant nonprofit organizations are likely to emerge where the hold of traditional landed elites is effectively challenged by middle class elements, or where traditional elites turn to such institutions as a way to forestall more radical demands from below, often in alliance with conservative religious forces. Limited state provision of social welfare services therefore does not automatically lead to the emergence of extensive nonprofit activity as the market failure/government failure theory seems to imply. Rather, where traditional elites remain in control and utilize authoritarian methods, it is quite possible that both sectors will remain underdeveloped. All of this suggests four models of nonprofit activity, each characterized by a particular constellation of social forces: first, a statist model characterized by limited state activity and a weak nonprofit sector; second, a liberal model characterized by limited state activity but a strong nonprofit sector; third, a social democratic model characterized by expanded state involvement in social welfare activity and limited nonprofit involvement; and fourth, a corporatist or partnership model in which both the state and the nonprofit sector are actively involved in societal problem-solving, often in cooperation with each other.

Without elaborating fully the social conditions hypothesized to account for each of these alternatives, there is ample evidence that the record of nonprofit development in the countries examined here provides important support to this theory. In particular, the developing countries we have examined seem, historically at least, to have been archetypes of what we have termed the statist model of nonprofit development. This model is characterized by low levels of both nonprofit development and government social welfare spending, and it is predicted to occur in situations where traditional social and political elites maintain authoritarian control, and where effective challenges either from urban middle class elements or urban or rural masses are limited or nonexistent. This is consistent with several key features of the social circumstances we have identified in these countries – an authoritarian political structure; dominant urban elites holding power in alliance with a colonial administration and, subsequently, its local middle class elements; a religious apparatus firmly allied with the conservative elites or those holding governmental power; and limited or nonexistent working class power or peasant mobilization.

The recent history of several of these countries also lends support to this social origins approach. One of the most salient features of this recent history has been the emergence of newly emboldened educated middle class elements seeking greater economic and political opportunities. In some countries, political elites have resisted the resulting pressures and sought to dampen the civic activism and nonprofit development to which it has given rise. This was the case, for example, during the military regime in Brazil, in the Nasser era in Egypt and during the latter Nkrumah and early Rawlings periods in Ghana. Elsewhere, however, traditional elites have sought to encourage civic involvement through grassroots nonprofit institutions and to search for a modus vivendi under which the state and the nonprofit sector can cooperate to promote development. The result is what the social origins approach would characterize as a corporatist model featuring significant expansion of both government and the nonprofit sector to address development needs. Elements of such a model have long been evident in India and Brazil, and may be emerging as well in Thailand and Ghana, though in these latter countries a heavier residue of distrust between the civic sector and the state still persists.

CONCLUSION

From the evidence reported here, it should be clear that the nonprofit sector is a significant presence in the developing world. What is more, the manifestations of this sector in these societies go well beyond the collection of organizations known in the development literature as NGOs. Side by side with NGOs are a host of associations with roots in traditional religious and cultural life, others that emerged during the period of colonial expansion and missionary activism, and still others that represent the growing assertiveness of middle class professionals and commercial elites. The result is a rich mosaic of organizational types and purposes that nevertheless share certain common features by virtue of their nonprofit-seeking character and essentially private structure. Analyses of the developing world that ignore this rich network of organizations, or that focus exclusively on one type – whether this be NGOs or village associations – will consequently overlook an increasingly important facet of the social, political and economic life of these countries. In this sense, the invention of the concept of the nonprofit sector illuminates a facet of social reality in the developing world that has long been quite important, but that has nevertheless remained largely invisible heretofore.

At the same time, the experience of the developing world sheds useful light on the theories and concepts being used to understand the nonprofit sector elsewhere. As we have seen, some of the prevailing theories in this field turn out to be of limited value in explaining the patterns of nonprofit development in the third world because they have boundary conditions that many third world countries do not meet. In other cases, the experience of the developing world can help enrich and refine existing theories. This is the case, for example, with our understanding of the relationship between religion and the nonprofit sector, which turns out to be somewhat more complex than previous accounts have assumed, involving not only issues of religious creed, but also the religion's posture towards individualism, its orientation towards institution building and its relationship with the state.

Obviously, however, no analysis of five countries, and certainly not the somewhat limited one that we have been able to undertake here, can fully exhaust all of these issues or provide a complete explanation of the way the nonprofit sector operates in the developing world. Our goal, therefore, has not been to offer the last word on these issues but to broaden the discussion, to bring the developing world more explicitly, and more fully, into the worldwide assessment that is now underway of the character and role of the nonprofit sector, and, perhaps most importantly, to stimulate even broader, and more systematic, analysis of this sector in this part of the world.[7]

ENDNOTES

1 We use the terms 'third sector' and 'nonprofit sector' interchangeably.
2 On recent literature on NGOs, see the special issue of the *Third World Quarterly* edited by Gordenker and Weiss (1995), and the case studies in the *Non-Governmental Organizations Series* coordinated by the Overseas Development Institute (ODI) in London (Bebbington and Thiele, 1993; Farrington and Bebbington, 1993; Farrington and Lewis, 1993 and Wellard and Copestake, 1993). Other terms widely used in the literature are 'grassroots organizations', 'private voluntary organizations' and, more recently, 'civil society organizations'. For a recent treatment of NGOs in rural development, see contributions in the Special Section of *World Development* on 'State, market and civil organizations' by de Janvry et al, 1996; and for a more critical assessment of NGO performance see Edwards and Hulme, 1995.
3 In addition to the five developing countries, this work focused on the US, the UK, France, Germany, Italy, Sweden, Hungary and Japan. For a discussion of this broader project, see Salamon and Anheier, 1996a.
4 In each of the developing countries, we pursued a common research approach guided by a common concept of the nonprofit sector. At the same time, to

guarantee sensitivity to local realities and adapt common concerns to local circumstances, we relied on local associates in each country to carry out the data gathering and analysis. For more complete summaries, see Landim, Kandil, Atingdui, Pongsapich and Sen in Anheier and Salomon, 1998.

5   For further elaboration of these features, see Salomon and Anheier, 1997.

6   To keep the empirical work manageable, we further restricted our attention to only a sub-set of all the organizations that fitted this definition. In particular, we decided to exclude two principal types: a) churches, synagogues, mosques and similar entities principally devoted to religious worship; and b) political parties primarily engaged in putting candidates into political office. Thus we excluded, for example, the sacramental activities and related administrative functions performed within the Catholic Church, yet included Church-related schools, hospitals, clinics and social service organizations. Moreover, we excluded political parties, but included party-related organizations such as cultural and political clubs, or vacation facilities and research institutes linked to political parties. Since little of the empirical work was carried out in the countries covered here, these exclusions are not as germane to the discussion.

7   This chapter draws on the introductory and concluding chapters of a forthcoming book that reports in greater detail on the material presented here. The book includes the five country studies that form the background for much of the analysis: Brazil (by Leilah Landim), Ghana (by Lawrence Atingdui et al), Egypt (by Amani Kandil), India (by Siddhartha Sen) and Thailand (by Amara Pongsapich). See Anheier, H and Salomon, L M (eds) *The Nonprofit Sector in the Developing World*, Manchester University Press, Manchester, 1998.

BIBLIOGRAPHY

Anheier, H K (1987) 'Indigenous voluntary associations, nonprofits, and development in Africa', in Powell, W W (ed) *The Nonprofit Sector: A Research Handbook*, Yale University Press, New Haven

Anheier, H K and Salomon, L M (1998) *The Nonprofit Sector in the Developing World*, Manchester University Press, Manchester

Atingdui, L, Anheier, H K, Sokolowski, S W and Laryea, E (1998) 'The nonprofit sector in Ghana', in Anheier, H K and Salomon, L M (eds) *The Nonprofit Sector in the Developing World*, Manchester University Press, Manchester

Bebbington, A and Thiele, G (eds) with Davies, P, Prager, M and Riveros, H (1993) *NGOs and the State in Latin America: Rethinking Roles in Sustainable Agricultural Development*, Routledge, London

Ben-Ner, A (1993) *The Nonprofit Sector in the Mixed Economy*, University of Michigan Press, Ann Arbor

Bratton, M (1989) 'Beyond the state: civil society and associational life in Africa', *World Politics*, Vol 41 (April), pp407–30

Britannica World Data (1991) *Comparative National Statistics*, Encyclopedia Britannica, Chicago

Brockington, J L (1981) *The Sacred Thread and Hinduism in its Continuity and Diversity*, Edinburgh University Press, Edinburgh

Brodhead, T (1987) 'NGOs: in one year out the other?' *World Development* Vol 15, supplement (August), pp2–5

Brown, L D and Korten, D C (1991) 'The role of voluntary organizations in development', *IDR Reports*, Vol 8, No 1, pp1–60

Carroll, T F (1992) *Intermediary NGOs: The Supporting Link in Grassroots Development*, Kumarian Press, Connecticut

Cernea, M (1987) 'Farmer organizations and institution building for sustainable development', *Regional Development Dialogue*, Vol 8, No 2 (summer), pp1–19

Chaudhuri, N (1979) *Hinduism*, Chatto and Windus, London

Constantelos, D J (1987) 'Charity' in Eliade, M (ed) *The Encyclopedia of Religion*, Macmillan, New York

Danquah, J B (1952) 'The culture of the Akan', *Africa*, Vol 22, No 4

de Janvry, A, Sadoulet, E and Thorbecke, E (1996) 'Introduction: special section on state, market and civil organizations: new theories, new practices, and their implications for rural development', *World Development*, Vol 21, No 4, pp565–576

Douglas, J (1987) 'Political theories of nonprofit organization', in Powell, W W (ed) *The Nonprofit Sector: A Research Handbook*, Yale University Press, New Haven

Drabek, A G (1987) 'Development alternatives: the challenge for NGOs – an overview of issues', *World Development* 15, supplement (August): ppix–xv

Edwards, M and Hulme, D (eds) (1995) *Beyond the Magic Bullet: NGO Performance and Accountability in the Post-Cold War World*, Kumarian Press, Connecticut

Farrington, J and Bebbington, A with Wells, K and Lewis, D (1993) *Reluctant Partners? NGOs, the State and Sustainable Agricultural Development*, Routledge, London

Farrington, J and Lewis, D (eds) with Satish, S and Miclat-Teves, A (1993) *NGOs and the State in Asia: Rethinking Roles in Sustainable Agricultural Development*, Routledge, London

Fisher, J (1993) *The Road from Rio: Sustainable Development and the Non-Governmental Movement in the Third World*, Praeger Press, Connecticut

Fukuyama, F (1995) *Trust: The Social Virtues and the Creation of Prosperity*, The Free Press, New York

Gellner, E (1995) 'The importance of being modular,' in Hall, J A (ed), *Civil Society: Theory, History, Comparison*, Polity Press, Cambridge, UK

Gerdes, V (1975) 'Precursors of modern social security systems in indigenous African institutions', *Journal of Modern African Studies*, Vol 13, No 2, pp209–228

Gomez, L (1987) 'Buddhism', in Eliade, M (ed) *The Encyclopedia of Religion*, Macmillan, New York

Gordenker, L and Weiss, T G (1995) 'Pluralizing global governance: analytical approaches and dimensions', *The Third World Quarterly, Special Issue: NGOs, The UN and Global Governance*, Vol 16, No 3, pp357–388

Hansmann, H (1987) 'Economic theories of nonprofit organizations', in Powell, W W (ed) *The Nonprofit Sector: A Research Handbook*, Yale University Press, New Haven

Hastings, J (1908) *Encyclopedia of Religion and Ethics*, Charles Scribner's Sons, Edinburgh and New York

Hopkins, T J (1971) *The Hindu Religious Tradition*, Dickenson Publishing Co, California

James, E (1987) 'The nonprofit sector in comparative perspective', in Powell, W W (ed) *The Nonprofit Sector: A Research Handbook*, Yale University Press, New Haven

James, E (1989) *The Nonprofit Sector in International Perspective: Studies in Comparative Culture and Policy*, Oxford University Press, New York

Kandil, A (1998) 'The nonprofit sector in Egypt', in Anheier, H K and Salamon, L M (eds) *The Nonprofit Sector in the Developing World*, Manchester University Press, Manchester

Krischke, P J (1991) 'Church base communities and democratic change in Brazilian society', *Comparative Political Studies*, Vol 24, No 2 (July), pp189–192

Landim, L (1998) 'The nonprofit sector in Brazil', in Anheier, H K and Salamon, L M (eds) *The Nonprofit Sector in the Developing World*, Manchester University Press, Manchester

Laroui, A (1987) 'Islam in North Africa', in Eliade, M (ed) *The Encyclopedia of Religion*, Macmillan, New York

Lewis, J P (ed) (1987) *Strengthening the Poor: What Have We Learned?* Transaction Books, New Brunswick

Lipset, S M (1995) *American Exceptionalism*, Norton, New York

Little, K (1965) *West African Urbanization: A Study of Voluntary Associations in Social Change*, Cambridge University Press, Cambridge

Mecham, L J (1966) *Church and State in Latin America*, University of North Carolina Press, Chapel Hill

Moore, B Jr (1966) *Social Origins of Dictatorship and Democracy: Lord and Peasant in the Making of the Modern World*, Beacon Press, Boston

North, D (1990) *Institutes, Institutional Change and Economic Performance*, Cambridge University Press, New York

OECD (1993) *National Accounts Detailed Tables*, OECD, Paris

OECD (1995) *Development Cooperation: Efforts and Policies of the Members of the Development Assistance Committee*, Chairman's Report, 1994, OECD, Paris

OECD (1996) *Education at a Glance*, OECD Indicators, OECD, Paris

Payton, R (1988) *Philanthropy: Voluntary Action for the Public Good*, Macmillan, New York

Pongsapich, A (1998) 'The nonprofit sector in Thailand', in Anheier, H K and Salamon, L M (eds) *The Nonprofit Sector in the Developing World*, Manchester University Press, Manchester

Putnam, R (1993) *Making Democracy Work*, Princeton University Press, Princeton

Qureshi, M A (1988) 'The World Bank and NGOs: new approaches', paper delivered at the Washington Chapter of the Society for International Development Conference on 'Learning from the Grassroots', Washington, DC, April 23

Rahman, F (1987) 'Islam', in Eliade, M (ed) *The Encyclopedia of Religion*, Macmillan, New York

Ritchey-Vance, M (1991) *The Art of Association: NGOs and Civil Society in Colombia*, Interamerican Foundation, Virginia

Rose-Ackerman, S (1996) 'Altruism, nonprofits and economic theory', *Journal of Economic Literature*, Vol 34, No 2, pp701–726

Salamon, L M (1987) 'Partners in public service: the scope and theory of government–nonprofit relations', in Powell, W W (ed) *The Nonprofit Sector: A Research Handbook*, Yale University Press, New Haven

Salamon, L M (1994) 'The rise of the nonprofit sector', *Foreign Affairs*, July/August

Salamon, L M (1995) *Partners in Public Service: Government–Nonprofit Relations in the Modern Welfare State*, The Johns Hopkins University Press, Baltimore

Salamon, L M and Anheier, H K (1996a) *The Emerging Nonprofit Sector*, Manchester University Press, Manchester

Salamon, L M and Anheier, H K (1996b) 'Social origins of civil society', *Working Papers of the Johns Hopkins Comparative Nonprofit Sector Project*, No 22, The Johns Hopkins Institute for Policy Studies, Baltimore

Salamon, L M and Anheier, H K (eds) (1997) *Defining the Nonprofit Sector: A Cross-National Analysis*, Manchester University Press, Manchester

Sandberg, E N (1994) *The Changing Politics of Non-Governmental Organizations and African States*, Praeger Publications, Connecticut

Schwartzman, S (1982) *Bases do Autoritarismo Brasileiro* [Bases for Brazilian Authoritarianism], Campus, Rio de Janeiro

Sen, S (1998) 'The nonprofit sector in India', in Anheier, H K and Salamon, L M (eds) *The Nonprofit Sector in the Developing World*, Manchester University Press, Manchester

Smith, B (1990) *More than Altruism: The Politics of Private Foreign Aid*, Princeton University Press, Princeton

Steinberg, R and Young, D (1995) *Economics for Nonprofit Managers*, Foundation Center, New York

Swearer, D (1987) 'Buddhism in Southeast Asia', in Eliade, M (ed) *The Encyclopedia of Religion*, Macmillan, New York

Synergos Institute and Overseas Development Council (1996) *Strengthening Civil Society's Contribution to Development: The Role of Official Development Assistance*, Synergos Institute, New York

United Nations (1991) *UNESCO Statistical Yearbook*, United Nations, New York

United Nations (1992) *United Nations Population Statistics*, United Nations, New York

United Nations (1993) *System of National Accounts*, United Nations, New York

United Nations (1995) *United Nations Statistical Yearbook*, 41st edition, United Nations, New York

United States Central Intelligence Agency (1991) *World Factbook*, Central Intelligence Agency, Washington, DC

Uvin, P (1995) 'Scaling up the grassroots and scaling down the summit: the relations between third world nongovernmental organizations and the United Nations', *Third World Quarterly*, Vol 16, No 3, pp495–512

Weber, M (1996) *The Protestant Ethic and the Spirit of Capitalism*, Roxbury Publishing Co, Los Angeles

Weisbrod, B (1977) *The Voluntary Nonprofit Sector*, Lexington Books, Lexington, Massachusetts

Weisbrod, B (1988) *The Nonprofit Economy*, Harvard University Press, Cambridge, Massachusetts

Wellard, K and Copestake, J (eds) (1993) *NGOs and the State in Africa: Rethinking Roles in Sustainable Agricultural Development*, Routledge, London

World Bank (1992) *The World Development Report*, World Bank and Oxford Press, Washington, DC

World Bank (1995) *Working with NGOs: A Practical Guide to Operational Collaboration Between the World Bank and Non-Governmental Organizations*, World Bank, Washington, DC

World Bank (1997) *Handbook on Good Practices of NGO Law*, World Bank, Washington, DC

Wuthnow, R (1991) *Between States and Markets: The Voluntary Sector in Comparative Perspective*, Princeton University Press, Princeton

Wuthnow, R (1997) *Poor Richard's Principle*, Basic, New York

Part 2
Contrasts and Complementarities

4

Voluntary Sector Governance – Problems in Practice and Theory in the United Kingdom and North America

Margaret Harris

INTRODUCTION

This chapter focuses on issues surrounding governance in third sector organizations – voluntary agencies, nonprofits and NGOs. It takes the term 'governance' as referring to the ongoing process in institutions by which guidelines for action are developed and adherence to them is monitored. The concept of governance is taken to include ideas about moral and legal accountability and organizational legitimacy and it is assumed that the governance structure of an institution can usually be distinguished from its executive work system (Rowbottom and Billis, 1987; Selznick, 1992).

In both the UK and North America there is growing recognition that the governance of third sector organizations (generally referred to in the constituent countries as 'voluntary agencies' or 'nonprofits') is an important public policy issue. The third sector is increasingly looked to as an instrument for the delivery of social welfare services and as a key element in the development and maintenance of civil society. But the accountability, effectiveness, credibility and viability of third sector organizations cannot be taken for granted; the extent to which those qualities are attained is closely linked to the way in which the governance function is performed within individual agencies (Ashby, 1997; Ben-Ner and Van Hoomissen, 1994).

The governance function in third sector organizations is generally regarded as being the responsibility of voluntary boards. Thus, collectively and as individuals, board members face high expectations in the changing public policy climate. As commentators on the spate of scandals which recently hit the sector in the US have observed, 'If nonprofits, personified in the board of directors, do not "clean up their act" ... public skepticism will continue to grow...' (Gibelman et al, 1997: 36).

Concern amongst policy makers and practitioners about third sector governance has been reflected to some extent in the work of researchers. Since the mid-1980s, numerous scholars – some British and several North American – have attempted to describe and analyse the work of third sector boards. As a result we now have a substantial body of research literature on the topic which can be said to be relatively mature within the broader field of third sector studies.

This chapter, then, draws on the accumulated literature to review briefly the key issues surrounding the implementation of voluntary sector[1] governance as experienced by those who work in the sector and those who study it. It goes on to consider theories and concepts which researchers, including the present author, have offered as explanations of the issues faced in practice.[2] It concludes by identifying some remaining gaps in knowledge and understanding of voluntary sector governance.

The term 'board' is used throughout the chapter to refer to the group within a voluntary agency which carries 'ultimate responsibility for what the organisation does' (Dartington, 1994: 208). Although this definition is rooted in a legal conceptualization, I should point out that the role of boards and the concept of governance are topics which have an importance well beyond legal niceties. In addition to ensuring legal accountability, voluntary sector governance is concerned with establishing and maintaining an agency's mission and with achieving legitimacy with an agency's internal and external 'constituencies' or 'stakeholders' (Stone and Wood, 1997).

In fact, from an organizational point of view, boards constitute the very heart of a voluntary agency. Voluntary agencies may, or may not, involve volunteers in their operational work; they may, or may not, have voluntary members; and they may, or may not, benefit from voluntary donations of money. But if they do not have a (largely) volunteer governing body then they are missing a key qualification for being included in the third sector. Likewise, if an agency has a board whose independence is in doubt – say because members can be appointed or removed at the will of a powerful governmental or commercial stakeholder – then its claim to be part of the third sector must also be in doubt (Billis, 1993b; Salamon and Anheier, 1992). In fact, anybody who is questioning whether a particular organization is classifiable as part of the voluntary sector can probably make a decision by examining the composition of the governing body and the degree of autonomy it enjoys.

ISSUES IN VOLUNTARY SECTOR GOVERNANCE

The British and North American research literatures suggest that the issues experienced within voluntary agencies in relation to governance are of two main types. First, there are problems about who should be in a governance role and what that role entails; problems which tend to be interpreted within voluntary agencies themselves as being related to the composition of the board – to a feeling that in some way the 'right' people have not been found or recruited.

Often there are complaints about what board members – as individuals or as a collectivity – are failing to do. Perhaps they are attending meetings infrequently or erratically, or not engaging in debate, or not being seen to be supporting and managing the paid staff who are officially their employees. Again, staff may complain that their board members do not identify with the agency's mission or understand the nature of the work it does. In the UK, boards may be reluctant to embrace the more entrepreneurial culture created by recent changes in public policy and unwilling to take the risks demanded by a competitive environment (Harris, 1996a).

Sometimes, on the other hand, there are complaints about what members of boards *are* doing. Representatives of funders on boards, for example, can intimidate colleagues such that open discussion is curtailed. Professionals and others with expert knowledge can dominate those who are amateurs or users of the agency's services. Commentators have voiced concerns about boards which advance the views of only specific sections of society or specific interests and fail to acknowledge the wider constituencies – women, users, ethnic minorities, those with disabilities – affected by their agencies' work (Hardina, 1993).

The second broad category of problems evident in the research literature concerns the relationship between the governance and the executive work system within voluntary agencies; that is, between boards and staff. Voluntary sector staff seem rarely to be satisfied with their boards. Some complain that their board members are insufficiently interested in their work, do not understand it and do not put sufficient effort into trying to understand it. The staff say that, as a result, they feel that they, rather than the board, are in practice carrying responsibility for their agency's continuity and very survival. But staff in other agencies say the very opposite; that their board members try to 'micro manage' and do not leave the paid and volunteer staff enough space to get on with the day to day work.

Board members themselves, on the other hand, often complain of feeling powerless and excluded, unable to control the staff or to understand the work they do. Often board members feel that their staff are so professional that the board is redundant, serving only a ceremonial function. In both the US and the UK, researchers have frequently found that, notwithstanding the theories of governance referred to at the beginning of this chapter, voluntary boards are in practice dominated by staff and reduced to a passive, reactive role within individual agencies (Gouldner, 1969; Harris, 1989; Middleton, 1987).

In such a context, where both boards and staff are dissatisfied with their mutual relationship, numerous practical questions are raised about the power to be allowed to staff. Should staff be members of governing bodies for example?[3] If so, should they have a vote or should they be restricted to an advisory and observer role? If they can vote, should they be able to out-vote other categories of board member? Is it the job of staff to support and develop board members – even though those board members are officially their employers? Should staff be permitted to form themselves into a collective and, if they do so, is there still a role for a separate governing body? And finally, whose job is it to make policy?

Several prescriptive handbooks (for example, Carver, 1990; Hind, 1995; Houle, 1989) are unequivocal on this latter point; boards, they say, should make policy and leave their staff to implement it. This reflects widely promulgated views about the governance of the governmental and commercial sectors. (See for example, Osborne and Gaebler, 1992 who famously refer to 'steering not rowing' as the essence of good governance.) Yet research has shown repeatedly that this is usually not what happens in practice – at least in the US and UK third sectors (Harris, 1991; Herman and Tulipana, 1989; Kramer, 1981).

In sum, the practical implementation of the governance function in voluntary agencies is experienced as being fraught with difficulties. Despite the proliferation of prescriptive guides which offer solutions and urge clarification of roles, problems persist in practice and researchers continue to try to tease out the complexities of what has been termed 'an abiding source of confusion and ambiguity' (Batsleer et al, 1992: 134).

How, then, can these practical problems surrounding the implementation of board roles be explained? If we can begin to understand the circumstances which give rise to the many problems which manifest themselves in the implementation of voluntary sector governance, we might be able to move towards organizational responses – responses which might be more helpful, perhaps, than the quick fixes and formulae offered in the prescriptive handbooks. In the remainder of this paper, then, I will review some of the main concepts and theories which have been developed by researchers in the UK and North America in relation to the practical challenges of voluntary sector governance.

DILEMMAS OF BOARD COMPOSITION

In analysing the first set of problems – those generally attributed to failures in board composition – three key dilemmas which face voluntary agencies can be distinguished:

1) Can we have a mix of people and also develop corporate identity?
2) How do we reconcile the needs of the organization with the needs of volunteer board members?
3) What kind of governing body do we need?

Mix Versus Corporate Identity

Most of the prescriptive literature recommends that voluntary agencies aim to have a board whose membership represents a range of interests, experiences and skills. The assumption behind this recommendation is that such a board will be able to offer resources to the organization and will also be able to represent and respond to the multiple constituencies which are characteristic of third sector organizations (Leat, 1988; Middleton, 1987). External pressures – such as an increasingly competitive environment, exhortations to be business like, a proliferation of stakeholders and drives to implement equal opportunities policies – have led many voluntary agencies to believe that the pick and mix approach to board recruitment is plain common sense. But this approach does not take into account some key findings in the research literature which point in a different direction.

For the more a voluntary agency mixes its board, the more difficult it may become for that governing body to develop a sense of collective identity and loyalty to the aims and purposes of the agency. And in so far as the members do not have a corporate identity, the trust needed for open debate and to make major decisions is likely to be absent too. The accumulated body of research on voluntary boards points to at least two important concepts to be taken into account: 'representative members' and 'welfare ideologies'.

It is common practice for boards to include a number of people who are appointed as representatives of other organizations, perhaps other voluntary agencies working in the same area or field, or governmental or commercial organizations which provide important resources. This practice reflects the idea mentioned in the introduction to this chapter – that responding to organizational stakeholders or constituencies is a key aspect of third sector governance. Yet such representative members (as distinct from those elected or appointed in their own right) are inevitably subject to conflicts of institutional loyalty. They cannot be expected to identify fully with the aims of the voluntary agency on whose board they sit, nor can they be expected to make impartial decisions without thinking too about the implications of those decisions for their own agency. Indeed, research has shown (Harris, 1989; Leat, 1988) that representative members of boards often act as spies, using the information they obtain at board meetings for the benefit of their home agency.

With the advent of the contract culture this has become a matter of particular concern in the UK. Where representatives of purchaser organizations are sitting on the boards of potential service providers, the market assumptions underpinning tendering and contracting are severely undermined (Harris, 1997). Recently, some governmental agencies in the UK have started to question the appropriateness of having their representatives on voluntary agency boards. However, their misgivings seem to be more to do with concern about the legal liabilities of charity trustees than with qualms about obtaining an unfair advantage in market-like transactions with the voluntary agencies concerned.

In addition to representative membership, the concept of 'welfare ideologies' (Billis, 1993a; Kramer, 1965) provides another clue to understanding the complexities of board composition. In a voluntary agency which has sought variety of composition, the board is likely to contain people with fundamentally different approaches to responding to the particular issues that the agency was set up to deal with: professionals alongside consumers of services; those with a bureaucratic, legal, accounting or business background alongside community activists or those with collectivist ideologies; and those who value empowerment and participation alongside those with a philanthropic approach to solving social problems.

The more the members of a board are varied as to their social background and experiences, the more they are likely to differ in their understanding about human motivations and behaviour, the causes of social problems and how best to respond to those problems. And the more board members differ in this way in their welfare ideologies, the greater the difficulties the board as a whole will experience in reaching consensus or decisions on key issues (Billis et al, 1994). Work in both the US and the UK suggests that the problems of differing welfare ideologies coexisting within boards is aggravated by voluntary sector norms which discourage value differences from being made explicit (Hall, 1992; Harris, 1989). The practical outcome of pick and mix recruitment to boards may be a group of people with 'opposing welfare ideologies' who are nevertheless 'structurally and functionally bound together in the policy-making process of the voluntary agency' (Kramer, 1965: 107).

Needs of the Organization Versus Needs of Board Members

Board members are volunteers and the accumulated body of research literature on volunteering indicates that volunteers are rarely motivated by altruism alone; they bring to their volunteering their own personal needs, anything from training for paid work to filling time and countering loneliness (Sargant and Kirkland, 1995; Widmer, 1989). As with the involvement of other kinds of volunteers, the challenge for voluntary agencies is to find ways of meeting the personal needs of volunteers whilst at the same time meeting the organizational needs of the agency.

Making this match is not always straightforward and often voluntary agencies will have to make difficult compromises in order to secure the services of board members. For example, they may have to turn a blind eye to instrumental motives of those who undertake board membership in order to enhance their status in the community or to gain access to privileged information. Or they may have to accept inept or incompetent performance from board members whose presence, support or expertise is deemed essential to the agency's future. Thus, Brophy (1994) has written about local play groups whose governmental funding was conditional upon them having parent governing bodies. Parents generally did not want to be governors and the groups were thus forced to accept any parent who could be persuaded to serve, irrespective of competence or commitment. The result was described by one of Brophy's interviewees, a paid play leader: 'For parents it's a learning experience but they are our employers yet they're unaware of their responsibilities and they're often not equipped to do it' (178).

In the UK, these difficulties of matching individual and organizational needs and of negotiating satisfactory exchanges and compromises seem to have been aggravated by recent tendencies to emphasize the legal and financial responsibilities of charity trustees (members of boards of voluntary agencies registered as charities) (NCVO/Charity Commission, 1992). In this climate, people are becoming concerned about the nature of the commitment that they are undertaking in joining a voluntary sector board (Harris, 1996a). There are also indications that those who have specialist skills and who are, therefore, in high demand to sit on voluntary boards, do not necessarily want to exercise those skills in their leisure time (Marsden, 1996).

What Kind of Governing Body?

Problems in recruitment and composition of voluntary governing bodies may be attributable to a more fundamental dilemma: doubts about what functions are to be carried by the board. As the management slogan suggests, 'form follows function'. So if voluntary agencies are not sure about the job of boards, difficulties in deciding what kind of board is needed and therefore who should be recruited, are a likely concomitant.

Here the research literature to date offers little help. Despite the accumulated body of descriptive data about what boards *do*, there has been little academic attention paid to analysing the broad concept of voluntary sector governance or to the functions attributed to boards. From the legal point of view, boards in North America and the UK constitute the core of a voluntary organization or association. From an organizational point of view, the research literature suggests five key functions (broad duties) which are attributed officially to voluntary sector boards. I have described these in detail elsewhere (Harris, 1996b) but they can be briefly restated here as follows.

1) **Being the point of final accountability.** The board is accountable for the conduct of paid and voluntary staff and for the management of agency resources. External groups including funders, donors, clients, purchasers of services, journalists and regulatory authorities look to the board to answer for the agency's conduct.
2) **Being the employer.** As the employer of any paid staff, the board may be involved in performing a range of tasks including hiring and firing, discipline, monitoring of work, promotion and payment. In larger voluntary agencies many of these tasks may be delegated for day to day purposes to paid staff.
3) **Formulating policy** – determining how the mission, purposes and goals of the voluntary agency are set. The tasks involved in carrying out this function may include setting priorities, developing plans,

monitoring and evaluating staff activities and maintaining an awareness of need and demand in the agency's field.

4) **Securing resources** – not only money but also premises, staff and
equipment. Responsibility for the continuity and very survival of a
voluntary agency is thus placed with its governing body.

5) **Acting as a 'boundary spanner'** – providing a link and a buffer
between a voluntary agency and its environment. On the one hand, a
board represents the agency's activities and policies *to* the outside
world; and on the other, it bring in knowledge, pressures and
opinions *from* the outside world.

Since the official functions allocated to boards are both multiple and
onerous (Widmer, 1993), voluntary agencies in practice have to choose
what emphasis they wish to place on each one of the possible functions
and what the balance of priorities is to be. Without paying explicit attention to this question of relative priorities, decisions about appropriate
recruitment to the board will be difficult to make. In these circumstances
the pick and mix approach emerges as the easy, but not necessarily the
most appropriate, solution. It may provide a spread of interests and expertise across the range of functions but insufficient weight to enable any one
function to be performed competently.

The difficulty of deciding on what the board should be expected to do
as a priority is further compounded by the fact that there are so many
possible models of voluntary governance to choose from. A scan of the
descriptive and prescriptive literature suggests a number of possibilities.
Some literature assumes that voluntary sector boards are the result of
democratic elections by members and are delegates or representatives of
members' interests. Some draws little distinction between voluntary sector
boards and the boards of the corporate sector in which executive and non-
executive members are routinely mixed together and in which the
executive members are generally expected to take a leading role in
responding to the market (Hodgkin, 1993). In some voluntary agencies,
there is a working assumption that, whatever the official statements may
say, the board has a ceremonial purpose only and should confine itself to
advice-giving rather than policy setting or decision making. Many paid
staff in smaller and local voluntary agencies seem to assume that the prime
purpose of the board is to manage them (an assumption reflected in the
common use of the term 'management committee' in the UK). Finally, there
is a growing body of prescriptive literature which urges increased, if not
dominant, user involvement in voluntary sector governance.

The fact that there is more than one available model of voluntary sector
governance, as well as a range of possible functions which voluntary
boards can perform, is rarely made explicit or openly discussed within
voluntary agencies. Like the existence of competing welfare ideologies
within the board membership, the fact that people are holding different
working assumptions is often not acknowledged and the distaste for
confrontation in the voluntary sector generally militates against what

Middleton (1987) has termed 'noisy' boards (that is, those which openly debate and disagree amongst themselves).

DILEMMAS OF BOARD–STAFF RELATIONSHIPS

Just as the problems surrounding the composition of boards can be seen to have a number of explanations, so too the research literature offers several explanations for the perennial problems surrounding board–staff relationships in the voluntary sector.

Interdependence

The prescriptive handbooks consistently urge voluntary organizations to respond to the problems which surround board and staff roles in the voluntary sector by clarifying the respective roles of each and keeping them separate (eg Carver, 1990; Hind, 1995). This advice seems to reflect ideas about the distinction between the governance structures and executive work systems of organizations referred to at the start of this chapter. But it also flies in the face of numerous studies in recent years that show that in practice the roles of boards and staff are interdependent and open to negotiation; that is, that the exercise of governance functions is not in practice confined to board members alone.

Thus, authors such as Gouldner (1969) and Kramer (1965) described the relationship between the two groupings as one of 'reciprocal dependence', with staff needing boards to give credibility and legitimacy to their work and boards craving the power, influence, opportunities and status in the community which come from being acknowledged by paid staff. Similarly, several authors have pointed out the interactive nature of the relationship (Harris, 1989; Heimovics and Herman, 1990; Herman and Tulipana, 1989; Zald, 1969.) The relationship is conceptualized as one which has to be constantly negotiated and renegotiated as circumstances and personalities change (Harris, 1993; Wood, 1992).

There is a debate within the literature which draws on these insights about the interdependent nature of the board–staff relationship; a debate which is essentially about the extent to which the relationship is appropriately conceptualized as a 'partnership'. Here again, research-based studies reveal a rather more complex situation than the one suggested by the prescriptive literature. In general, they suggest that the partnership metaphor is inappropriate (Herman, 1989). The two groups may be interdependent in implementing their roles but they are not equals. As Kramer (1985) says, there are different and changing power balances between the two. 'Difference and dissensus' is just as likely to occur as collaboration. Similarly Middleton (1987: 152), reviewing US empirical research, says that the assumption of partnership is misleading as the relationship is paradoxical. 'For many important decisions, the board is the final authority. Yet it must depend on the executive for most of its information and for policy articulation and implementation.'

Acceptance of the idea of board and staff roles as ones which are, in practice, contingent, interdependent and interactive, opens the door to developing practical tools for use by voluntary organizations. One such tool is 'total activities analysis' (TAA) which I developed as a means of working collaboratively with staff and board members of voluntary agencies (Harris, 1991; 1993). Instead of trying to pull out the elements of the different roles as is recommended in training handbooks, I concentrate in the first place on the tasks involved in running a voluntary agency; tasks which are acknowledged as needing to be done by somebody or some group. This enables boards and staff to focus on their common ground and to move from there into an analysis of how those tasks are currently being shared between them and how they think they should be shared. The emphasis is on sharing rather than on differences and clarification. TAA has now been used in numerous organizations and its success reflects the fact that in voluntary agencies there are few, if any, functions which in practice belong unequivocally, or on a long term basis, to either board or staff. It also reflects the fact that there can be a great discrepancy between formal statements and what happens in practice in voluntary agencies (Fink, 1989; Harris, 1989).

The lessons from the accumulated research then, are that tensions between boards and staff are best resolved by approaches which acknowledge the negotiated and dynamic nature of governance in a voluntary sector context and do not imply that there is a best or correct way of allocating tasks and functions. Thus rather than seeking to separate and polarize the roles of staff and governing bodies, voluntary agencies can accept their essentially interdependent nature and allow for negotiation, and periodic renegotiation, of 'who is responsible for what' and 'who does what'.

Power

Another insight about board–staff relationships is provided by research on the power of boards in relation to their staff. Using concepts developed originally by Max Weber (1964), boards in the UK and North America can be seen as having 'authority'; they are, as mentioned earlier, the legal essence of their agencies and the people who collectively carry ultimate responsibility. Yet it is clear that in practice their ability to get others, especially their staff, to do what they want them to do, can be very limited. In other words, and again using Weberian concepts, the 'power' of boards in relation to staff appears in practice to be limited (Kramer 1985; Murray et al, 1992).

An interesting solution to this problem was proposed in an article by Ben-Ner and Van Hoomissen (1994) which attracted much scholarly interest. They suggested that legal regulations should be changed in such a way that nonprofit organizations would be obliged to reflect the key stakeholders on their boards. The assumption of the authors seemed to be that changing the law and prescribing the composition of boards could in some way ensure that stakeholders retain power and control. My own work on the power of boards in service-providing voluntary agencies (Harris, 1994; 1996b) suggests that this too may be rather simplistic. In many cases the inability of boards to exercise power over their paid staff is traceable to organizational structural factors rather than to a failure in constitutional or legal frameworks. My own understanding of variations in board power rests on a distinction between four key groups: clients or users; staff; the board; and a fourth group which I have called 'guardians'. This latter group is rarely mentioned in other voluntary sector research but it is implicitly recognized by practitioners. It comprises the people who have a positive concern for the long term survival of the agency and its purposes. It may include founders, funders, former members or former clients. My argument is that the power that boards are able to exercise in relation to their staff depends on the way in which the relationships between these four key groups are structured in a particular voluntary agency.

In the traditional, philanthropic model of voluntary agencies there is a straightforward linear relationship; guardians appoint the board who employ the staff who deliver a service to beneficiaries – or people who are experiencing some kind of problem which the guardians and the board want to respond to. In this kind of linear relationship boards do indeed generally have the power to control their staff and ensure that services are delivered according to guidelines that they set. Behind the board stand the guardians who give credibility and support to the board itself and therefore empower it relative to staff.

However, problems can arise because many voluntary agencies were not set up according to this linear model and their functioning does not reflect the model either. Self-help groups and membership organizations, for example, operate according to a circular model in which staff deliver services to users who are also guardians, rather than distant third parties experiencing a problem or a social need. Paid staff may resent the threat to their professionalism posed by a situation in which their clients are so close to their employers and managers. Alternatively, the close day to day contacts between staff and guardians can result in the board being bypassed or marginalized.

There is a third possible combination of relationships between the four key groups which I have termed the 'entrepreneur' model. In this model the guardians establish and maintain a board in the expectation that the board will then employ the guardians themselves to deliver services. This model is becoming increasingly common as job opportunities shrink whilst at the same time there are state schemes which offer funding for the development of social projects so long as they conform to governmental policy priorities. Enterprising people seize the opportunities to deliver worthwhile services and earn a living at the same time (Leadbeater, 1997). But while public policy ends may be well served in this way, such entrepreneurship may also lead to the growth of essentially ungovernable voluntary agencies. For how can a board control its paid staff if that board owes its very existence and continuity to those same paid staff who are also the agency's guardians?

Communication Links

In seeking research-based explanations for the problems that arise in the board–staff relationship, a third possible area to focus on is that of the point of communication between chairs (or presidents) of boards and their chief executive officers (CEOs) or directors. It seems that the relationship between these two individual roles is crucial for the effective functioning of voluntary agencies (Kearns, 1995). If problems in the broader board–staff relationship are to be avoided, a trusting and open relationship between chair and CEO is required and both of them have to be willing to discuss and negotiate their relative roles and duties (Dowsett and Harris, 1996). The role of good communication in maintaining working systems is widely accepted in organizational and managerial literature. But there are special features of voluntary agencies which make communication between CEOs and chairs especially important and also especially complex.

As McLaughlin (1986) has argued, the governance and work systems of voluntary agencies can be conceptualized as an hourglass, with the board in one section and the staff in the other. The two systems touch through the roles of the chair and the director who are positioned adjacent to each other at opposite ends of the hourglass neck. Jointly and severally, CEO and chair thus act as gatekeepers between the governance and work systems. If they fail to communicate with each other, or if one of them fails to pass on information communicated by the other, the links between board and staff are broken. The two systems are then left free floating or, equally problematic in organizational terms, those positioned in one or other cup have to bypass the chair and CEO in order to communicate with one another.

In the event of the communication bottleneck being broken, questions of accountability are also raised. For the legal structure and the constitution of most voluntary agencies place paid staff in a position where they are accountable to the board which, in turn, is ultimately and collectively accountable for the quality of work and proper conduct of the agency (Harris, 1996b). In practice, the collective accountability of the board is usually exercised through the chair or president (Dowsett and Harris, 1996). The director provides the point of accountability for the staffing structure of a voluntary agency and in turn accounts to the chair. Thus it is the chair who provides the point at which the authority of the board in relation to staff is exercised. In this scenario, the neck of the hourglass is not just a communication channel. It is also the place at which a total overview of the agency's work can be achieved and internal accountability can be assured.

DISCUSSION – GAPS IN KNOWLEDGE AND CHALLENGES FOR THE FUTURE

The study of voluntary agencies as organizations is still a relatively new academic field in the UK and North America so the study of voluntary sector governing structures is a sub-field of a field which is itself only partially explored. All the same, as this review has demonstrated, there is now a substantial body of accumulated research literature on boards which has already yielded a number of explanations for the problems that are experienced as surrounding the implementation of voluntary sector governance.

Yet major gaps in understanding remain. For example, the question of how to involve users and other stakeholders in voluntary sector governance has received relatively little attention from researchers. This is despite the fact that there is increasing pressure from funders and politicians for voluntary agencies to demonstrate commitment to democratic structures and user involvement whilst, at the same time, research indicates how difficult this is to achieve in practice (Hardina, 1993; Robson et al, 1995).

More work is also needed on the role of voluntary governing bodies as instruments of internal and external accountability. Here too there are rising expectations of boards from funders and policy makers; expectations which are hard to reconcile with the fact that board members are essentially volunteers who carry out their functions in what would otherwise be their leisure time (Harris, 1996a; Russell and Scott, 1997).

Another neglected topic is that of governance at different organizational levels within the third sector. The relationship between local branches of a voluntary agency and the regional, national and international offices has received some attention from researchers in the US (for example, Young, 1992; Young et al, 1996; Zald, 1970). But the focus has been on staff and staffing relationships. The composition of, and relationships between, boards at different levels of an organization has barely been touched on.

In addition to filling some of these gaps in existing organizational knowledge, a second challenge which emerges from this paper is that of making better links between researchers and practitioners. Prescriptive handbooks and introductory texts about the organization and management of the voluntary sector are proliferating now in the UK as well as in North America. Many of these publications give advice and rules about the work and role of boards which fly in the face of research findings about how boards work in practice and the problems they face day to day.

Part of the responsibility for this discrepancy between research findings and advice must lie with researchers themselves. We need to ensure that we publish our findings not only in academic journals but also in the places where they will be seen by board members and by those consultants who write popular texts. And we also need to give more thought to how theoretical insights can be translated into usable organizational tools. The development of TAA as a practical application of theories about board–staff interdependence (Harris, 1991) provides an example of how this can be done when researchers work in collaboration with practitioners.

Beyond the twin challenges of filling gaps in organizational knowledge and disseminating research findings lies a third, broader challenge; the challenge of responding to the implications of changing public policy expectations. The worldwide renewal of interest in the non-state, non-market public space – variously referred to as 'civil society', the 'third sector' or 'associative democracy' – raises major theoretical and practical questions about how that space is governed, how it should be governed and about the right of states and commercial sectors to be involved in setting the rules by which third sectors are run.

The governance of the public (governmental) sectors and the corporate sectors are subjects which have both attracted substantial attention from researchers (see, for example, Charkham, 1994; Ferlie et al, 1996; Kooiman, 1993). In contrast, the broad public policy theme of voluntary sector governance (as distinct from research on the behaviour of voluntary boards and research on voluntary sector management) has been relatively neglected.

In these circumstances there is a danger that if researchers do not enquire into the distinctive features of third sector governance, models developed to explain and prescribe corporate or public sector governance will be imposed on the voluntary sector along with inappropriate expectations about such matters as public accountability, efficiency and effectiveness. A trend in this direction is already evident in the UK where the Nolan Committee on Standards in Public Life has chosen to encompass a range of organizations which are currently on the boundary of the public and voluntary sectors including higher and further education colleges, training and enterprise councils (TECs) and housing associations (Meikle, 1997). Housing associations, ironically, have also been under pressure to adopt corporate sector models of governance and accountability (National Federation of Housing Associations, 1995).

In order to address the pressing public policy questions about the actual and requisite nature of third sector governance, we will also need to tackle the even broader and more challenging questions about the nature and purposes of third sectors themselves; about the extent to which they serve distinctive purposes and the extent to which their constituent groupings have distinctive organizational features (Billis and Harris, 1996; Najam, 1996). If, for example, third sector organizations are seen as essentially public interest organizations, the implications for their governance are very different from the ones which would apply if they are seen as essentially private interest groups. Similarly, questions about matters such as accountability, user involvement, representativeness and appropriate roles of boards will be answered differently according to whether one sees third sectors as being principally about social change, philanthropy, the accumulation of social capital or the provision of needed public services.

As indicated earlier, Ben-Ner and Van Hoomissen (1994) have provided a starting point for a debate about the essential and distinctive elements and purposes of specifically third sector governance, building on the concept of 'constituencies'. And further insights are provided by Jeavons (1994) and Smith (1992) who draw attention to the moral principles under-pinning nonprofit governance. These contributions resonate with a recent commentary by Selznick (1992: 290) which, although it is not focused specifically on the third sector, draws attention to both the moral and the constituency-serving aspects of governance and the way in which moral leadership and the representation of multiple interests are inextricably linked. This provides a helpful indication of how a theory of third sector governance might be developed:

> *To govern is to accept responsibility for the whole life of the insti-tution. This is a burden quite different from the rational coordination of specialized activities [ie management]. Governance takes account of all the interests that affect the viability, competence, and moral character of an enterprise. The strategies of governance are basically political. They have to do with forming public opinion, accommodating interests, and determining what ends should be chosen and by what means those ends should be pursued.*

If robust theory of governance in civil society or the third sector is to be developed, collaboration and debate on an international level will be essential. This is a topic which is of concern well beyond the specific contexts of individual countries. Moreover, work by Tandon (1995) on the governance and accountability of NGOs suggests that many of the challenges facing third sector boards in the south Asia context are very similar to those experienced in the North: for example, responding to multiple stakeholders; developing and maintaining a shared vision; involving beneficiaries; and distinguishing between board and staff responsibilities. His work also provides some initial indicators of gover-nance-related problems which are perhaps more likely to arise in the South than in the North: for example 'family boards' which become inappropriate as organizations experience growth and change; and meeting the accountability demands of chains of funders.

There are clearly opportunities here for collaborative and comparative knowledge building. Researchers in the UK and North America seeking to plug the gaps in their understanding of boards and the distinctive charac-teristics of third sector governance will no doubt be eager to share data and theory derived from the experiences of NGOs in the South.

ENDNOTES

1 In this chapter I use the terms 'voluntary sector' and 'voluntary agencies' according to common usage in the UK to refer broadly to that sphere of societal activity which is also termed elsewhere 'the third sector', 'nongovern-mental organizations', 'the independent sector' and 'the nonprofit sector'. The

use of the terms 'voluntary sector' and 'voluntary agencies' does not imply any particular viewpoint about the definition of the various terms.

2   The general approach of this paper, which aims to provide theory-based explanations of practical problems, reflects the mission of the Centre for Voluntary Organisation at the London School of Economics which seeks to develop 'usable' theory, to bridge the traditional gap between academics and practitioners and to explicate issues of policy implementation (Billis and Harris, 1996).

3   Organizations which are registered as charities in England and Wales are subject to rules which severely restrict the number of paid staff who may be members of their governing bodies. This reflects ideas about the distinction between governance and executive work systems mentioned in the introduction to this chapter.

BIBLIOGRAPHY

Ashby, J (1997) *Towards Voluntary Sector Codes of Practice*, Joseph Rowntree Foundation, York

Batsleer, J, Cornforth, C and Paton, R (1992) *Issues in Voluntary and Non-Profit Management*, Addison-Wesley, Wokingham

Ben-Ner, A and Van Hoomissen, T (1994) 'The governance of nonprofit organizations: law and public policy', *Nonprofit Management and Leadership*, Vol 4, No 4, pp393–414

Billis, D (1993a) *Sliding into Change*, Working Paper 14, Centre for Voluntary Organisation, LSE, London

Billis, D (1993b) 'Sector blurring and nonprofit centres', *Nonprofit and Voluntary Sector Quarterly*, Vol 22, No 3, pp241–258

Billis, D, Ashby, J, Ewart, A and Rochester, C (1994) *Taking Stock: Exploring the Shifting Foundations of Governance and Strategy in Housing Associations*, Report of the Centre for Voluntary Organisation, LSE, London

Billis, D and Harris, M (1996) 'Introduction: enduring challenges of research and practice', in Billis, D and Harris, M (eds) *Voluntary Agencies: Challenges of Organisation and Management*, Macmillan, London

Brophy, J (1994) 'Parent management committees and pre-school playgroups: the partnership model and future management policy', *Journal of Social Policy*, Vol 23, No 2, pp 161–194

Carver, J (1990) *Boards that Make a Difference*, Jossey Bass, San Francisco

Charkham, J (1994) *Keeping Good Company: A Study of Corporate Governance in Five Countries*, Oxford University Press, Oxford

Dartington, T (1994) 'Trustees, committees and boards', in Davis Smith, J, Rochester, C and Hedley, R (eds) *An Introduction to the Voluntary Sector*, Routledge, London

Dowsett, J and Harris, M (1996) *Trusting and Talking: The Relationship between Directors and Chairs of Voluntary Agencies*, Working Paper 18, Centre for Voluntary Organisation, LSE, London

Ferlie, E, Asburner, L, Fitzgerald, L and Pettigrew, A (1996) *The New Public Management in Action*, Oxford University Press, Oxford

Fink, J (1989) 'Community agency boards of directors: viability and vestigiality, substance and symbol', in Herman, R and Van Til, J (eds) *Nonprofit Boards of Directors*, Transaction, New York

Gibelman, M, Gelman, S and Pollack, D (1997) 'The credibility of nonprofit boards: a view from the 1990s and beyond', *Administration in Social Work*, Vol 21, No 2, pp21–40

Gouldner, A (1969) 'The secrets of organizations', in Kramer, R and Specht, H (eds) *Readings in Community Organization Practice*, Prentice Hall, New Jersey

Hall, Peter Dobkin (1992) 'Cultures of trusteeship in the United States', in Hall, Peter Dobkin (ed) *Inventing the Nonprofit Sector and Other Essays on Philanthropy, Voluntarism and Nonprofit Organizations*, Johns Hopkins University Press, Baltimore

Hardina, D (1993) 'The impact of funding sources and board representation on consumer control of service delivery in organizations serving low-income communities', *Nonprofit Management and Leadership*, Vol 4, No 1, pp69–84

Harris, M (1989) 'The governing body role: problems and perceptions in implementation', *Nonprofit and Voluntary Sector Quarterly*, Vol 18, No 4, pp317–323

Harris, M (1991) *Exploring the Role of Voluntary Management Committees: A New Approach*, Working Paper 10, Centre for Voluntary Organisation, LSE, London

Harris, M (1993) 'Exploring the role of boards using total activities analysis', *Nonprofit Management and Leadership*, Vol 3, No 3, pp269–282

Harris, M (1994) 'The power of boards in service providing agencies: three models', *Administration in Social Work*, Vol 18, No 2, pp1–15

Harris, M (1996a) 'Tough going: voluntary boards and the impact of public policies', paper presented to the Annual Meeting of Association for Research on Nonprofit Organizations and Voluntary Action (ARNOVA), New York City, November 1996

Harris, M (1996b) 'Do we need governing bodies?', in Billis, D and Harris, M (eds) *Voluntary Agencies: Challenges of Organisation and Management*, Macmillan, London

Harris, M (1997) 'Voluntary management committees: the impact of contracting in the UK', in 6, P and Kendall, J (eds) *The Contract Culture in Public Service*, Arena, Aldershot

Heimovics, R and Herman, R (1990) 'Responsibility for critical events in nonprofit organizations', *Nonprofit and Voluntary Sector Quarterly*, Vol 19, No 1, pp59–72

Herman, R (1989) 'Board function and board–staff relations in nonprofit organizations: an introduction', in Herman, R and Van Til, J (eds) *Nonprofit Boards of Directors: Analyses and Applications*, Transaction, New Jersey

Herman, R and Tulipana, F P (1989) 'Board staff relations and perceived effectiveness in nonprofit organizations', in Herman, R and Van Til, J (eds) *Nonprofit Boards of Directors: Analyses and Applications*, Transaction, New Jersey

Hind, A (1995) *The Governance and Management of Charities*, The Voluntary Sector Press, Barnet

Hodgkin, C (1993) 'Policy and paper clips: rejecting the lure of the corporate model', *Nonprofit Management and Leadership*, Vol 3, No 4, pp415–428

Houle, C (1989) *Governing Boards*, Jossey Bass, San Francisco

Jeavons, T (1994) 'Stewardship revisited: secular and sacred views of governance and management', *Nonprofit and Voluntary Sector Quarterly*, Vol 23, No 2, pp107–122

Kearns, K P (1995) 'Effective nonprofit board members as seen by executives and board chairs', *Nonprofit Management and Leadership*, Vol 5, No 4, pp337–358

Kooiman, J (ed) (1993) *Modern Governance: New Government–Societal Interactions*, Sage, London

Kramer, R (1965) 'Ideology, status and power in board–executive relationships', *Social Work*, October, pp107–114

Kramer, R (1981) *Voluntary Agencies in the Welfare State*, University of California Press, California

Kramer, R (1985) 'Towards a contingency model of board–executive relations', *Administration in Social Work*, Vol 9,No 3, pp15–33

Leadbeater, C (1997) *The Rise of the Social Entrepreneur*, Demos, London

Leat, D (1988) *Voluntary Organisations and Accountability*, National Council for Voluntary Organisations, London

McLaughlin, C (1986) *The Management of NonProfit Organizations*, Wiley, New York

Marsden, Z (1996) *A Beneficial Experience: A Study of Business People on Voluntary Management Committees*, Working Paper 17, Centre for Voluntary Organisation, LSE, London

Meikle, J (1997) 'Nolan plans catch-all law', *The Guardian*, September 9, p4

Middleton, M (1987) 'Nonprofit boards of directors: beyond the governance function', in Powell, W W (ed) *The Nonprofit Sector: A Research Handbook*, Yale University Press, New Haven

Murray, V, Bradshaw, P and Wolpin, J (1992) 'Power in and around nonprofit boards: a neglected dimension of governance', *Nonprofit Management and Leadership*, Vol 3, No 2, pp165–182

Najam, A (1996) 'Understanding the third sector: revisiting the prince, the merchant and the citizen', *Nonprofit Management and Leadership*, Vol 7, No 2, pp203–220

National Federation of Housing Associations (1995) *Competence and Accountability: The Report of the Inquiry into Housing Association Governance*, NFHA, London

NCVO/Charity Commission (1992) *On Trust: Increasing the Effectiveness of Charity Trustees and Management Committees*, National Council for Voluntary Organisations, London

Osborne, D and Gaebler, T (1992) *Reinventing Government*, Addison-Wesley, Reading, Massachusetts

Robson, P, Locke, M and Dawson, J (1995) *User Involvement in the Control of Voluntary Organisations*, Report to the Joseph Rowntree Foundation, Centre for Institutional Studies, University of East London, London

Rowbottom, R and Billis, D (1987) *Organisational Design: The Work Levels Approach*, Gower, London

Russell, L and Scott, D (1997) *Very Active Citizens? The Impact of Contracts on Volunteers*, Department of Social Policy, University of Manchester, Manchester

Salamon, L and Anheier, H (1992) *In Search of the Nonprofit Sector I: The Question of Definitions*, Working Paper 2, The Johns Hopkins Comparative Nonprofit Sector Project, Baltimore

Sargant, N and Kirkland, K (1995) *Building on Trust*, National Council for Voluntary Organisations, London

Selznick, P (1992) *The Moral Commonwealth: Social Theory and the Promise of Community*, University of California Press, Berkeley

Smith, David H (1992) 'Moral responsibilities of trustees: some first thoughts', *Nonprofit Management and Leadership*, Vol 2, No 4, pp351–362

Stone, M and Wood, M (1997) 'Governance and the small, religiously affiliated social service provider', *Nonprofit and Voluntary Sector Quarterly*, No 26, ppS44–S61

Tandon, R (1995) 'Board games: governance and accountability in NGOs', in Edwards, M and Hulme, D (eds) *Non-Governmental Organisations: Performance and Accountability*, Earthscan, London

Weber, M (1964) *The Theory of Social and Economic Organization*, Free Press, Toronto

Widmer, C (1989) 'Why board members participate', in Herman, R and Van Til, J (eds) *Nonprofit Boards of Directors: Analyses and Applications*, Transaction, New Jersey

Widmer, C (1993) 'Role conflict, role ambiguity and role overload on boards of directors of nonprofit human service organizations', *Nonprofit and Voluntary Sector Quarterly*, Vol 22, No 4, pp339–357

Wood, M (1992) 'Is governing board behavior cyclical?', *Nonprofit Management and Leadership*, Vol 3, No 2, pp139–163

Young, D (1992) 'Organising principles for international advocacy associations', *Voluntas*, Vol 3, No 1, pp1–28

Young, D, Bania, N and Bailey, D (1996) 'Structure and accountability: a study of national nonprofit associations', *Nonprofit Management and Leadership*, Vol 6, No 4, pp347–365

Zald, M (1969) 'The power and functions of boards of directors: a theoretical synthesis', *American Journal of Sociology*, No 75, pp97–111

Zald, M (1970) *Organizational Change: The Political Economy of the YMCA*, Chicago University Press, Chicago

5 NGO Governing Bodies and Beyond: A Southern Perspective on Third Sector Governance Issues

Qadeer Baig

INTRODUCTION

Governance, defined as the overall guidance, direction and supervision of an organization, is an area in which differences in emphasis between the nonprofit research literature and the development NGO literature are apparent. In recent years researchers working on nonprofit organizations have explored in some detail the distinctive issues of governance relating to the third sector in rich countries (see Harris, this volume), but the NGO literature has with a few notable exceptions paid surprisingly little attention to the subject. While the nonprofit literature has addressed governance mainly in terms of an organization's governing body, the subject of an NGO's own governance has been a neglected aspect of the NGO literature and is only occasionally referred to as part of wider discussions about NGO accountability (Edwards and Hulme, 1995).

As Harris (this volume) shows, there is now a substantial body of research on voluntary sector governance which has been generated during the past decade by scholars in the UK and the US, focusing mainly on the work of voluntary boards. Harris shows that research on governing bodies in the North has focused broadly on problems relating to what such groups either do or do not do within their wider organizations, along with common problems which may emerge in the ways in which governing bodies relate to the staff of the organization.

Since third sector organizations all over the world share at least some common organizational features it would be reasonable to assume that many similar problems to those described in the UK and US contexts will also be found to occur within the governing bodies of NGOs in 'developing' countries. This is largely borne out by Tandon's (1995) study of Indian NGOs, which stands as one of the few items of NGO literature dealing with this topic in explicit terms.

Tandon first characterizes different types of board scenarios drawn from south Asia and presents a range of observed behaviour which he terms 'board games':

1) 'family boards' (in which the NGO founder's family members are recruited and the board takes on an informal, closed character);
2) 'invisible boards' (in which the founder convenes a token board from time to time with little real function);
3) 'staff boards' (in which the staff themselves form the board with the result that wider governance becomes indistinguishable from day to day management); and
4) 'professional boards' (individual board members are recruited for their special professional skills or contacts but may not cohere or sit easily with the overall mission of the organization).

These ideas, though independently researched, resonate strikingly with findings that Harris (this volume) and other Northern scholars present in their work on the UK and US.

Moving beyond the governing body itself, Harris (this volume) points out that the governance issues for voluntary and nonprofit agencies are not only dependent on the structure and relations within an organization but are also conditioned by the wider legal and regulatory contextual framework. This is of particular relevance to development organizations in the South. The second part of the present chapter expands on this wider aspect of governance by drawing attention to particular problems for NGOs in the South in relation to their operating environment. The political and legal regulatory framework in which NGOs operate in many developing countries (such as the Pakistan case discussed below) poses special problems for NGO governance in the South. The context tends to be resource-scarce, politically volatile and littered with a colonial legacy of inappropriate or confusing legislation.

THE GOVERNING BODY IN THE NGO CONTEXT

The main exceptions to the general absence of research and documentation on governing bodies in the NGO literature are recent works by Tandon (1995) and Fowler (1997). In the development literature, governance is often subsumed within larger debates about NGO accountability.[1] Edwards and Hulme (1995), in keeping with writers in nonprofit literature, stress the idea of NGOs' 'multiple accountabilities' upwards to donors and governance structures as well as 'downwards' to beneficiaries and staff, and emphasize the problems of maintaining a balance between all these different stakeholders. These authors point out that in practice NGOs are frequently biased towards donors and other resource providers and are less responsive in governance terms to the wishes of clients, users or beneficiaries.

Tandon (1995: 42) defines governance as 'the totality of functions that are required to be carried out in relation to the internal functioning and external relations of the organisation' and distinguishes it from 'management' which he views as 'the issues of day-to-day implementation of programmes'. In Tandon's view (48), sound governance structures are central to the functioning of an NGO:

> *An effective system of governance enables an NGO to formulate, review and reformulate its mission in a changing context ... [it] ensures that programmes follow the requirements of the NGO's mission; promotes a performance orientation and accountability in the institution; and requires that the values (integrity, participation, professionalism, quality, commitment), statutes (reporting and legal standards and procedures) and norms of socially concerned civic institutions are articulated, practiced and promoted. An effective structure and process of governance in an NGO is absolutely critical for ensuring accountability in this wider sense.*

Fowler (1997: 37) conceptualizes governance issues for NGOs in terms of power and identity. Fowler shows how different groups exercise power differently; the formal owners of the organization as recognized by law can be contrasted with the organization's social base and the staff. Fowler points out that a common model of NGO governance in Latin America is one which he terms a 'self-regulated governing structure':

> *The civic code under which NGDOs register creates a governing body composed of staff representatives, which can be expanded to include outsiders but this does not have to occur. In this sense, the staff who make up the organization also own it; in effect, they own themselves and lack a social constituency with formal power.*

This is contrasted with the more familiar governing board structure, which Fowler terms a 'self-selected oligarchy'. A third model identified is that of the constituency-governed NGO in which an organization relates strongly to an identifiable political or economic group in the community.

These observations on the internal issues of governance tend therefore to mirror many of the concerns of the Western nonprofit literature. However, the wider context in which Southern NGOs (SNGOs) operate brings some distinctive challenges. A specific problem faced by SNGOs is in their relations with international aid donors (either government or NGO) which seek accountability or control over the use of their funds and which may bring a specific ideology of development (which may include the promotion of participation for instance). Both of these factors bring important implications for SNGO governance. For example, some donors have been pushing SNGOs for greater beneficiary participation in governance and have urged representation on the board to ensure accountability to their clientele (personal observation). This is a complex situation. Some

NGOs have provided for beneficiary representation on their boards (such as the Grameen Bank in Bangladesh), but the participation of these representatives in board matters has yet to be evaluated.

Another important dimension for SNGO governance lies in the transnational dimensions of inter-NGO relationships. Northern NGOs (NNGOs) have in recent years worked with SNGO partners in developing countries or have established local offices. For NNGOs wishing to indigenize their relationships with SNGOs or their country offices, continuing access to governance structures may remain a priority even when the rhetoric is one of autonomy and decentralization. The current preoccupation with capacity building of SNGOs by NNGOs often includes attempts to strengthen governance structures within SNGOs (Sahley, 1995).

A second and related dimension is that of the asymmetrical relationships which are formed between SNGOs and foreign government donors. To increase accountability to the donors, an argument is sometimes put forward by the donors to include donor representatives on the governing body. This may have the consequence of limiting open discussion, pushing their own agenda and moving away from downward accountability to the beneficiaries (personal observation). NGOs have experimented with creative solutions to such demands of donors and government. In Pakistan, two NGOs initially started as a project of Northern NGOs were converted into local NGOs. But still the NNGOs are sitting on their governing bodies in order to exert some control. It may be a supportive act with the intention of supporting the process of indigenization but it raises important issues for the relative autonomy of a SNGO.

BEYOND THE GOVERNING BODY: EFFORTS AT IMPROVING THE REGULATORY FRAMEWORK FOR NGOS IN PAKISTAN

While far more research is needed to address the special problems of governing bodies in SNGOs, this section widens the discussion in order to examine the legal and political framework within which NGOs operate in Pakistan. The following case study describes joint action by NGOs and government to improve the environment in which NGOs operate in Pakistan. At the time of writing these efforts have been only partially successful.

Pakistan is the ninth most populated country in the world with an estimated 128 million people and an annual population growth rate of 2.9 per cent. Two-thirds of the population are based in rural areas and almost one-half is below the age of 15. Multi-ethnic and multi-linguistic, Pakistan has a per capita GNP of US$440 (the highest in south Asia) with a public debt liability of around US$20 million. In the United Nations Human Development Index, Pakistan ranks 132nd in the world and 45 per cent of the population are considered to be below the poverty line (Khan, 1991).

Pakistan is in many ways a feudal society in which the established order remains one of welfare and patronage from above (Morgan, 1992).

NGOs have been active in Pakistan since its formation in 1947, principally providing rehabilitation and social welfare for the poor and marginalized (Kamal, 1997). The modern NGO sector in Pakistan has grown rapidly in the past two decades and an estimated 10–30,000 NGOs are now believed to exist (Kamal, 1997). There is little available information about many of these organizations, many of which are small and have limited capacity. They face a range of problems, for example lack of sustainability and a dependence on donor funding, a middle class bias in their staffing and management, a lack of trust between NGOs and government and the lack of an adequate legal framework within which to operate (Baig, 1997). However, there is also a growing recognition that NGOs have played an important role in creating awareness of issues such as environment, human rights, the status of women and population planning as well as providing basic services such as water, sanitation and health care to poorer sections of the population (Kamal, 1997).

NGO governance in Pakistan is systematically undermined by the lack of a clear legal structure (which is still reliant on old welfare laws dating from the colonial period) and from an absence of recognized guidelines for NGO codes of conduct. In Pakistan, the term 'NGO' has not been defined in any statute and is used to refer to all types of organizations, foreign and local, involved in a wide range of activities. Since they emerged over a long period of time (since 1860) the laws use varying terminologies and concepts, and have been added to such that NGOs can now be registered under different laws.

There are several statutes in Pakistan that deal with the formation, regulation or recognition of different types of organizations in the third sector. The 1860 Societies' Registration Act (SRA) registers voluntary societies, while the Voluntary Social Welfare Agencies (Registration and Control) Ordinance of 1961 is reserved for social welfare agencies. Nonprofit companies are registered under the Companies Ordinance of 1984 and public charitable trusts under the Trust Act of 1882.

The 1860 Act fails to reflect adequately the diversity in definition, scope and function of the NGOs (VANI, 1997). Significantly, the origin of the SRA is related to the revolt of 1857 in the subcontinent. After the rebellion was crushed, an analysis of its origins led to the discovery by the British government that 'the intellectual underpinnings of the rebellion came from the numerous arts and cultural societies that had sprung up in the subcontinent in the middle of the nineteenth century' (Devi, 1997: 57). As a result, two years later the SRA was promulgated – a provision that required all associations of seven or more people to be formally registered with the government. As such the governance mechanisms provided by these laws were designed to control rather than facilitate the activities of third sector organizations and arguably do not match with the needs of the contemporary development-oriented NGO sector.

The existence of these laws means that there are many NGOs which are not registered at all, and the partial records which do exist make it difficult to monitor the work of NGOs around the country. NGOs complain that the government has draconian powers to interfere with the governance of NGOs. For example, under the 1961 Ordinance the Department of Social Welfare is authorized to suspend the governing body of the NGO without any right of appeal. At the same time, an NGO cannot amend its constitution, rules or by-laws or dissolve itself without the approval of the Department of Social Welfare (Baig, 1997).

There are also strange inconsistencies in the rules. In Pakistan, organizations registered under the 1860 Societies Act are required to have seven members on the management committee while 'not for profit companies' registered under the 1984 Act are required to have 11 members on their boards (NGORC, 1991). The small size creates problems such as limiting group discussion, opening up possibilities for interference from staff and sometimes dictatorship by a few.

Another criticism made by NGOs is that there is too much administrative discretion in the application of the laws which are not uniformly applied. For example, an NGO with good connections can be registered in a matter of hours, while another can take several years to complete the process. The ambiguity is illustrated by the example of a lawyers' NGO which has had its application pending for the past two years as it is passed between the Corporate Law Authority and the Bar Council (Baig, 1997).

Many NGOs have therefore regarded recent efforts by government to reform the system as an attempt to control NGOs further. In 1994 the government initiated attempts to rationalize the situation by proposing a new Social Welfare Agencies (Registration and Regulation) Act as the sole law with which to register and regulate all NGOs. At the same time, there was a press campaign attacking NGOs in the country as organizations securing large amounts of resources without public accountability; and of corruption, with NGO leaders accused of making personal fortunes from what is sometimes termed the 'NGO business'.

The 1994 draft Bill gave the government new powers to check and dissolve fraudulent NGOs, to control foreign NGOs in Pakistan, to control the flow of funds to religious NGOs which might undertake anti-government activities, and to monitor the flow of international funding to NGOs. Fearing the growth of government control rather than facilitation, NGOs organized themselves to try to influence the drafting of the new law and a dialogue was eventually established with government about the draft Bill. But the new 1995 draft which resulted was regarded as a betrayal by NGOs as it did not reflect points which had been agreed. The following year, after a period of communication breakdown, the activation of strong personal contacts between an NGO activist and a key senator went some way towards restoring relations between government and NGOs. A new 'Consensus Draft 1997' was prepared, which remains to be passed into law. Political instability in Pakistan has consistently thwarted progress on these issues.

CONCLUSION

This chapter has briefly sketched a range of issues concerning problems of NGO governance from a Southern perspective. It has suggested that there is far more attention devoted to organizational governance issues in the nonprofit literature than in the research literature on development NGOs in the South. Much of relevance to Southern organizations can therefore be learned from ongoing research work on governing bodies in the UK and US contexts. However, the argument has been put forward here that for many SNGOs it is necessary to go beyond a focus on the governing body structure in order to concentrate on governance problems relating to the uncertain regulatory framework for NGOs which exists in a country such as Pakistan. For many NGOs, governance issues are complicated by the nature of local regulatory contexts and by the asymmetrical relationships which emerge with other development actors at the international level, such as NNGOs and official aid donors.

NGOs in developing countries may in many cases have weaker governing bodies than many of their Western nonprofit counterparts. Some may adopt completely different models of governance. We can expect all the problems which exist in nonprofit boards in the North to feature in many developing country organizations, but there are a range of other factors which complicate the picture still further:

- Resource scarcity can skew accountability very strongly towards donors and resource providers at the expense of beneficiaries and other stakeholders.
- The lack of resources also creates opportunistic incentives for NGOs to be created or used instrumentally by elites for private purposes, with negative implications for governance.
- Incomplete or inappropriate legal frameworks (often inherited from the colonial period) may hinder the operation of NGOs and lend them to manipulation by predatory states.
- Unstable political structures may predispose governments to seek to control NGOs rather than provide an enabling environment, as the case of Pakistan shows.

These issues constitute a future research agenda for NGO governance. As Tandon (1995: 49) points out, '... it is of crucial importance that NGOs, their supporters and their donors begin to understand the meaning and significance of effective governance and its contribution to NGO account-ability'. The nonprofit literature on governing bodies represents a substantial point of entry on these issues for NGO researchers.

ENDNOTE

1   A separate, though related, strand in the development literature concerns the international aid donor discourse of 'good governance' which forms part of the post-Cold War international new policy agenda which emphasizes market liberalization and liberal democratic political structures and processes in developing countries (Robinson, 1993).

BIBLIOGRAPHY

Baig, Q (1997) *The Legal Framework in which NGOs Operate: Control or Facilitation?* unpublished MSc dissertation, London School of Economics

Dartington, T (1994) 'Trustees, committees and boards', in Davis Smith, J, Rochester, C and Hedley, R (eds) *An Introduction to the Voluntary Sector*, Routledge, London

Devi, U (1997) 'Laws and regulations for the voluntary sector and South Asia: the Indian scenario', in VANI (1997), below

Edwards, M and Hulme, D (1995) (eds) *Non-Governmental Organisations: Performance and Accountability*, Earthscan, London

Fowler, A (1997) *Striking A Balance: A Guide to Enhancing the Effectiveness of Non-Governmental Organisations in International Development*, Earthscan, London

Kamal, S (1997) *A Study of NGOs in Asian DMCs: Pakistan Country Paper*, International Development Support Services (Australia)/Asian Development Bank

Khan, A H (1991) 'Work without contractors and bondage', in Wignaraja, P (ed) *Participatory Development: Learning From South Asia*, Oxford University Press, Karachi

Morgan, P (1992) *Pakistan Social Institutional Development Programme*, Report of the Feasibility/Design Mission, CIDA/Aga Khan Foundation, Canada

NGORC (1991) *NGO Registration Study Volume 1*, Policy Research Report, NGO Resource Centre, Aga Khan Foundation, Karachi

Robinson, M (1993) 'Governance, democracy and conditionality: NGOs and the new policy agenda', in Clayton, A (ed) *Governance, Democracy and Conditionality: What Role for NGOs?* INTRAC, Oxford

Sahley, C (1995) *Strengthening the Capacity of NGOs: Cases of Small Enterprise Development Agencies in Africa*, INTRAC Management and Policy Series No 4

Tandon, R (1995) 'Board games: governance and accountability in NGOs', in Edwards, M and Hulme, D (eds) *Non-Governmental Organisations: Performance and Accountability*, Earthscan, London

VANI (Voluntary Agencies Network of India) (1997) *Laws, Rules and Regulations for the Voluntary Sector*, Report of the South Asian Conference, March 6–10 1996, New Delhi

6

Building NGO Legitimacy in Bangladesh: The Contested Domain

Syed Hashemi and Mirza Hassan

BACKGROUND

On the eve of Bangladesh's independence one could identify at least three institutional actors (state, political parties and traditional civil society organizations) that had historically played a role in the contest to provide leadership on economic and social changes.[1] The state, throughout the 1960s, projected itself as the principal agent of development, through promoting industrialization and building rural institutions. The opposition political parties had campaigned against such state intervention, claiming that it led to severe regional disparity, income inequality and impoverishment. Civil society organizations had essentially aligned themselves with political parties and projected the vision of nationalism, secularism and democracy.

By early 1972, however, it was clear that although the bureaucracy had remained intact from the period when Pakistan and Bangladesh were one country, the old institutions of the state were hopelessly inadequate in coping with the problems of massive reconstruction of the economy and rehabilitation of millions of refugees. Organizations on the left of the political spectrum, which had strong peasant bases, were on the defensive in the face of indiscriminate state violence. Civil society organizations proved to have only a very narrow constituency amongst the urban educated middle class. It was in this context that NGO activities for providing relief, for rehabilitating those who had suffered in the war and for income earning activities amongst the rural poor, took on significance (Hashemi, 1989). Since then NGOs have been struggling to establish and consolidate their legitimacy.

This chapter analyses NGO actions in the establishment and consolidation of legitimacy in Bangladesh; legitimacy perceived in terms of building institutions that are sensitive to poor people's needs, facilitating access to resources for poor people and in providing democratic space for them to assert their legal and basic human rights. In such activities, NGOs are contesting the functions of the state as well as political parties and traditional civil society organizations that have historically claimed to play such a role. In fact NGOs claim that to a great extent such traditional organizations actually reproduce and strengthen the prevailing structure of inequity and subordination. This chapter explores NGO activities in three specific areas:

1) in building institutional alternatives to provide resources and services;
2) in their capacity to mobilize the rural poor and women against local elites and the local power structure; and
3) in their struggle for greater democratic participation in the ongoing transition to pluralist democracy at the national level.

NGOs and Service Delivery

The historic failure of state institutions in providing the rural poor with access to resources, coupled with market imperfections that ensure the dominance of a few actors, have set the stage for NGO programmes. The Grameen Bank, and later NGOs, have created a successful micro-credit model for ensuring that poor people receive access to credit. Non-formal education programmes have ensured that thousands of children of the rural poor who were not part of the formal education system would at least receive some schooling. In the health field, NGOs have interacted closely with the government to ensure high contraceptive use and increased immunization rates. NGOs have also come forward to ensure delivery of relief goods to people in distress. This success has led to a recognition of NGOs (even by the state) as legitimate institutions for ensuring service provisions for the poor.

The NGO service delivery model was, however, seriously contested by the fundamentalist groups who saw, in NGO schools and in NGO work amongst women, a challenge to their ideological control of rural society. This coalesced into a major backlash against NGOs in 1994 which was successfully combined with national-level fundamentalist political concerns. The failure to sustain this opposition probably stems from the inability to mobilize the local elites effectively, and in the strong NGO support from donors and the state. Local elites do not necessarily see service delivery (as opposed to conscientizing activities) as potentially threatening. Often they see such interventions as fulfilling a legitimate patriarchal duty to help the poor.

NGOs AND CONSCIENTIZATION

From the mid-1970s onwards many NGOs, led by the Bangladesh Rural Advancement Committee (BRAC) and followed very closely by Gono Shahajjo Sangstha (GSS) and Nijera Kori, adopted conscientizing (based on the pedagogical approach of Paulo Freire) as the integral principle of organizing the poor (Hashemi, 1995). The essential analytical premise underlying such a strategy suggests that poverty is sustained by the prevailing inequality in the structure of power and access to resources and that this can be rectified only through effective challenges to the system. Such challenges can, however, be effective only if and when the poor are mobilized, and only when actions are organized collectively by the poor. While this strategy does not reject outright provisions of credit and economic resources to members, they do not see such access leading to the weakening of structures that contribute to the reproduction of poverty. In fact there is an underlying fear that individual access to economic resources could actually have a negative impact on the collective consciousness of the poor by promoting individualistic, competitive, profit-maximizing behaviour.

NGOs' conscientizing activities led to collective actions against local injustices. Members mobilized against corrupt local government officials, against local landlords who forcibly took over land and against local elites which intimidated poor people. NGOs also organized against shrimp culti-vators who were linked to the highest echelons of state power. NGO members even ran for local government elections. Such NGO participation in the transformation of local power structures was perceived by the state as a challenge to state power, subversive of institutional order. State reprisal was swift; violence, arrests and intimidation took place. There were threats of revoking NGO licences.

The choice facing conscientizing NGOs was twofold. If they wanted to continue in their path of confrontation they would lose state licencing and foreign funds. If they wanted to continue receiving foreign funds they could not expand on their conscientizing activities. The path that GSS (probably the most vocal conscientizing NGO) followed is symptomatic of the end of such models of organization.

GSS went through a radical restructuring. Their new strategy involves working with civil society rather then setting up independent organiza-tions of the poor. The model of class harmony has replaced their previous model of class struggle. GSS economic activities are now replacing their previous political activities. This has, interestingly, paid off well in terms of the flow of foreign funds. The GSS budget, supported by Western governmental aid agencies, has increased to make GSS one of the top ten NGOs in Bangladesh. The strategic shift in GSS is reflected in several organizational and programmatic changes in the past few years. Staff recruitment, which used to favour political activists, now introduces staff with higher university degrees and greater professional competency. Applicants with formal writing skills, articulate in expression, conversant in English, and presentable to donors, get preference over rural-based political activists of the left (those who formed the core of the GSS cadre during its more political phase). Management too has changed from being decentralized, where local political issues determined actions to be undertaken, to a situation now of centralization where specific programmes (such as education, legal aid and so on) are pursued by the local staff with directives from the centre rather than from collective decisions made at the local level. Targets, quotas, action plans and reports to reflect progress receive greater emphasis, since these are what donors demand.

A major issue reflecting the shift in GSS philosophy is that of sustainability. In its earlier phase GSS would make a strong categorical distinction between itself (the NGO, the organization of middle class 'do-gooders', the conduit for foreign funds), and the *Gonoshongothon* (the organization of the poor, of the dispossessed). It was strongly argued that the imperative of GSS was to strengthen the *Gonoshongothon* and make it sustainable. It was argued that NGOs were incapable of transforming society. The responsibility for change rested with the poor themselves. It was only the organization of the poor that could bring about a transformation in the structure of power (Wood, 1993). In fact every phase in the strengthening of the *Gonoshongothon* would be matched by a concomitant weakening of GSS. As the *Gonoshongothon* emerged as an independent entity, GSS itself withered away. Current organizational and managerial efforts at the GSS are, however, focused on making it sustainable through an increased flow of foreign funds and greater management proficiency introduced by professional managers.

GSS's strategic shift is even more concrete in terms of the civil society model it now professes to pursue. GSS has, for the last three to four years, been strongly advocating change through involvement in civil society. Groups within civil society have therefore received primacy over the poor as change agents. Rather than the poor organizing themselves against prevailing structures of power, now groups within civil society, such as lawyers and journalists, university teachers and artists, are targeted to lead the movement for change. At best the poor form one such group within civil society. The paradigmatic implication for this is profound. GSS had initially provided an analytical picture of society where the poor were pitted antagonistically against other groups in society (in a model of disharmony and conflict). Currently, however, the revised version suggests that the poor can be in a harmonious relationship with other groups in society. More importantly it suggests that the poor can be successful only through aligning themselves, or even following, other groups in society. Objectives too have therefore undergone serious revision. While the earlier version was promoting a movement for an exploitation-free society through a restructuring of society and dismantling of the state, the current version stipulates its objective as promoting human rights, and increasing democratic participation. While these represent positive objectives that can possibly be achieved only through struggles, it nevertheless represents a retreat from what GSS had set out as its raison d'être. While these may represent more feasible objectives guided by pragmatic appraisals of objective conditions, it nevertheless implies a shift in the GSS paradigm.

Under the new paradigm donors are appeased; the state is not threatened. Direct confrontations by mobilized groups are discouraged. In fact within groups wealthier households are freely incorporated. In the changed objective of better management and better record keeping, the more educated and better-off members become group leaders. Under these conditions GSS is now initiating credit programmes. The improvement in the conditions of the poor is being sought through access to economic resources. The conscientization model has come full circle to resemble the credit and service delivery model.

NGOS AND THE TRANSITION TO PLURALIST DEMOCRACY

Historically the process of transition to democracy in Bangladesh involved a contest between the bureaucratic authoritarian state and the political society. In this essentially urban-based transition, societal actors from the non-urban sphere played a passive role. In recent years we have witnessed a strategic institutional attempt on the part of NGOs to increase democratic participation, especially of the rural poor, through strengthening civil society. This involves civic education emphasizing the need to register and vote, especially for women, and educating electoral groups regarding their legal rights, building opposition to the use of money and intimidation during elections and so on. Training is also provided to local government officials as well as ensuring greater accountability of local government. Election monitoring, to ensure free and fair elections, is an integral aspect of this training. The purpose is to have a more aware electorate so that elections can truly reflect people's needs and aspirations. A corollary of this awareness is ensuring better governance at the local level by making government institutions more accountable to people. A major advantage of NGOs in conducting such civil society interventions stems from their seemingly non-partisan identity, their institutional access to the grassroots and, probably most of all, strong donor support (both moral and financial).

Civil society interventions have also taken place in national election monitoring, in the framing of electoral rules and in creating greater awareness of electoral transparency. While this seems to increase NGO legitimacy in expanding the space for democratic participation, it needs to be pointed out that state attempts at ensuring greater electoral participation are still far more important and far more visible. A sample survey of 2000 randomly selected men and women in ten parliamentary constituencies during the general election of 1996 indicated that the overwhelming majority of voters had received positive messages from state agencies (primarily the electoral commission) for participation in the election. In fact for many of them it was such messages that encouraged them to vote. Only a small fraction of voters had received such messages from NGOs.

Interestingly, NGO electoral messages even included calls for building opposition to fundamentalists and corrupt and oppressive traditional leadership. This is interesting because political parties (except for those on the left) do not encourage any sustained attacks on 'black' money (loan defaulters, corrupt businessmen) or the use of violence in elections. In fact many of the dominant political party candidates have dubious financial and moral backgrounds. While NGOs have been ineffective in combating specific power structures, they do seem to have the potential to initiate a moral critique of the prevailing political practice.

NGO attempts at seeking legitimacy as independent civil society actors in the transition to pluralist democracy have recently suffered some serious setbacks. In 1996 strong civil society opposition had built up against the Bangladesh Nationalist Party (BNP) government for its failure to protect the democratic rights of citizens and its increasingly authoritarian method of governing the country. While this opposition benefited the Awami League (the primary opposition political party) many civil society organizations strongly emphasized their non-partisan identity in their opposition to the government. However the Association of Development Agencies in Bangladesh (ADAB, the coordinating council of the NGOs) led by Proshika, Nijera Kori and the Participatory Rural Initiatives Project (PRIP), opted strongly for the Awami League, even going to the extent of making formal speeches from the Awami League platform. ADAB's identification with the Awami League was challenged from within. The struggle for control created a situation where the director of ADAB (who was opposed to this party alignment) had to resign. This is reminiscent of the conflict within ADAB in 1990 when Gono Shashthya Kendra, the foremost health NGO in Bangladesh, was forced out of ADAB. Proshika and other NGOs even asked their membership to vote for the Awami League. They used ADAB's grassroots organization (Trinomool) to drum up support in their favour. This has led to a new form of political clientelism influencing the current evolution of government organization–non-government organization (GO–NGO) relations. Anecdotal evidence indicates some kind of selective embeddedness between the current regime and the politically aligned NGOs leading to patronage distribution from the state. Questions have been recently raised in the media regarding the lack of transparency in the offering of construction contracts to specific NGOs.

NGO factional politics also influence the current GO–NGO relationships. In this context it is pertinent to mention the nature of factional politics surrounding ADAB. Such conflicts have little to do with ideological principles; rather, individual conflicts and the nature of a particular regime's relationship to the leadership of ADAB play a critical role in the formation of factional identities.

One needs to be clear in realizing that there is no monolithic NGO vision in terms of civil society action. In fact what ADAB and Proshika are pursuing is a strategy of alignment and accommodation with the government. BRAC, GSS and others are purporting to build a strong civil society independent of narrow political party influences. To what extent this can be successful remains to be seen. NGOs have had a long tradition of acquiescing with the state, even to the extent of forming unholy alliances with military dictatorships. The NGO task in maintaining independence while building a strong civil society therefore remains a challenge.

NGO intervention as a major civil society actor must be understood in the context of traditional civil society organizations. Such traditional organizations (students, workers, peasants, lawyers, journalists, university teachers, intellectuals, poets, writers and cultural activists) have historically played a monumental role in the struggle for Bengali nationalism, for building a secular society and for democratic rights. In fact the movement against the military dictatorships of Ayub Khan and H M Ershad, and even the war of independence, were often led by civil society organizations rather than narrow political parties. However, such organizations may be losing their independent moral leadership due to the increasing political polarization and colonization of these organizations by the dominant political parties. The decline in status and power of traditional civil society organizations, coupled with the financial strength of NGOs, have enabled NGOs to move in and increase their role in civil society. Two specific areas where NGOs have recently gained considerable legitimacy in providing leadership are promoting human rights, and the rights of women. Although their leadership may be contested for some time to come, NGOs are definitely acknowledged as legitimate actors in these specific domains of social mobilization.

NGO intervention in rural Bangladesh had to confront two different but widely prevalent social visions. The first was the vision of the political left, of class struggle and radical populism, the vision of social transformation. The second was the fundamentalist vision of theocracy, which was packaged in terms of equity and justice and submission to a higher order. The NGO starting point essentially upheld the vision of the political left, but with the necessary caveat that the leftist organizational form was inadequate, and that left wing political parties were unable to deliver. NGOs strongly identified the left line as hierarchical, top-down, elitist, and alienated from the everyday problems of the poor. The reactions of both the political left and right to this ideological challenge were vicious. Parties on the left accused NGOs of receiving donor patronage, of being agents of international capital, of stopping the revolution by pretending to be a revolutionary force. The right saw in NGO actions, especially in their work amongst women, an intrusion of Western modernity, a Christian attack on Islamic values. While neither the left nor the right has much electoral power, they do have extensive leverage in shaping middle class world views. The intellectual community, for example, is mostly anti-NGO; adopting a clear pro-NGO position is still considered a liability. However it will not be an exaggeration to claim that, in terms of building and consolidating moral leadership, NGOs have, so far successfully, met the challenge posed by both left and right ideological discourses.

CONCLUSION

This chapter demonstrates that NGO legitimacy is being constructed in Bangladesh through an ongoing contest between the state, political parties and traditional civil society organizations. The success of NGOs in providing alternative resource delivery mechanisms has contributed greatly to their legitimacy as development agents. However there has been a major retreat from the NGO vision of transforming structures of power. In this the specific lesson has been the contradiction in challenging the precise establishment (the state) that provides its licencing lifeline. NGOs have, however, learnt that state accommodation can be achieved through donor support. This has created a situation where old conscientizing visions of radical transformations have given way to new donor-supported/ sponsored liberal-pluralist visions of making the prevailing system more accountable. NGOs have proved themselves legitimate actors in the transition to electoral democracy and are now struggling to assert and consolidate their leadership vis à vis traditional civil society.

ENDNOTE

1 By 'state' we refer to the state apparatus and the regime in power; traditional civil society organizations are not foreign aid development organizations.

BIBLIOGRAPHY

Hashemi, S M (1989) *NGOs in Bangladesh: Development Alternative or Alternative Rhetoric?*, mimeo, Dhaka
Hashemi, S M (1995) 'NGO accountability in Bangladesh: beneficiaries, donors and the State', in Edwards, M and Hulme, D *NGOs: Performance and Accountability*, Earthscan, London
Wood, G D (1993) *Seeking Power in the Society: An NGO's Approach to Social Mobilisation and Legal Rights in Bangladesh*, Working Paper 02/93, Centre for Development Studies, University of Bath

7 The Trouble with Values

Rob Paton

INTRODUCTION: THE CENTRALITY OF VALUES

The amorphous field of voluntary and nonprofit research contains a wealth of historical, political and sociological – as well as organizational – studies. This literature has long recognized that the values and commitments expressed by voluntary organizations – and by those who found and work in them – are one of their most significant features. For example, the association between philanthropic activity and religious commitment has been well documented (James, 1989). Likewise, it is well understood that many nonprofit organizations are formed as the practical expressions of the concerns that are seen in historical perspective as social or political movements – the labour movement and trade unionism, the cooperative movement, pacifism, feminism, environmentalism and so on. Not surprisingly, therefore, as voluntary organizations and their management have become a discrete area of reflection and research, writers have affirmed the importance of values in understanding the role and functioning of voluntary organizations:

> *Voluntary activity is essentially value based (Gerard, 1983: 34).*

> *... These latter organizations are the heartland of the social economy. Since they are marked by a distinctive value system and a more intense involvement by members, they will be referred to as value-based organizations (Paton, 1992: 6).*

> *What should, in my view, distinguish the voluntary sector from the commercial sector is the system of values by which charities can bind together people from different backgrounds and provide a*

> conduit by which they can all work together towards a common goal
> (Hind, 1995: 35).

Both the broader nonprofit literature and the more purely organizational writing now frequently discuss the different sorts of values expressed in and by voluntary and nonprofit organizations, and by the conflicts, divisions and complications associated with organizing on the basis of commitments which may be variously interpreted and prioritized by those involved. But it has not always been thus. The Report of the Wolfenden Committee (Wolfenden, 1978), for example, makes no such references – indeed, neither values, nor substitute terms (commitments, ideals, etc) appear in the index – whereas the authors of the Report of the Commission on the Future of the Voluntary Sector see them as central:

> *The value base of voluntary organisations is one of their defining characteristics (CFVS, 1996: 113).*

This emphasis on values has been enthusiastically taken up by those who write more prescriptively about voluntary organizations and who have, over the last decade, provided a 'how to do it' literature for managers in a sector that has not just grown considerably, but which appears to have become more self-confident and self-aware (6 and Leat, 1997).

The primary aim of this chapter is to provide a review of the main themes in this more popular writing. It does so in the form of an argument: that in the shift away from complex description and analysis aimed at understanding, towards far simpler principles and prescriptions intended to guide action, a great deal is being lost – and some worrying currents are emerging.

A MANAGERIAL MANIFESTO

The burgeoning professionally-oriented literature on voluntary sector management is unanimous in affirming the important and pervasive implications for managers of an organization's value base.

- Mission and strategy must be based on and express the organization's core values and commitments. For example, a self-help guide to strategic planning for voluntary organizations approaches the definition of an organization's purpose in terms of its values, mission and vision (in that order) and offers methods for developing statements of each (Barnard and Walker, 1994). Likewise, under the heading 'what is mission?' one of the most influential writers and consultants writes, 'The first element of mission is the common values held by people in the organization' (Hudson, 1995).
- Marketing and fundraising must be ingrained with and promote the organization's values. For example, for charities Ian Bruce adds

another 'P', for philosophy, to the famous lists of elements in the marketing mix, saying, 'By philosophy is meant an explicit recognition of the value-laden approach to be taken or encouraged in the product, be it a physical good, a service or an idea aimed at the beneficiary, supporter, stakeholder or regular markets' (Bruce, 1994: 100).

* Internal policies, standards and procedures must all be consistent with the organization's declared commitments. For example, 'It is these values – effectively or otherwise summed up in a mission statement or statement of aims – which underlie the conduct of the organization. These values have to be represented in every document issued, every policy and procedure followed, every part of every service delivered' (Gann, 1996: 56). Or more succinctly in the Report of the Commission on the Future of the Voluntary Sector, 'Mechanisms must be put in place that ensure organizations practice what they preach' (CFVS, 1996: 114).

This emphasis on values should not be seen simply as idealistic, though it may be so on occasions. For some organizations it can be justified on very hard-headed, commercial terms. As several commentators have pointed out (for example Rose-Ackerman, 1997), a strong value base is an attraction for the customers of many human services (*vide* the popularity of Montessori and church schools) even if they do not themselves subscribe to the beliefs and commitments in question. And more generally, this can be seen as a variant of the strategy of building a particular corporate culture – an approach that has been much in vogue in the private sector over the last decade for very pragmatic reasons (essentially it has been seen as offering a less costly and more adaptive way of motivating and controlling staff than reliance on structural/bureaucratic mechanisms).

It is acknowledged that such value-based organizing involves difficulties. Writing of mutual support organizations, Hudson says:

> *'Unless values are fully acknowledged, as happens successfully in many hospices, anger, despair and resentment can spill over into the management of the organization. Members can become angry with staff and sometimes with each other as well. Debates and decisions become highly politicised and increasingly separated from the facts.*
>
> *The point is that values are central in mutual support organizations, both explicitly and implicitly. Management's task is to make things happen within the framework of the organization's values. Management may sometimes have to challenge those values (for example, to persuade members of the need to modernise their approach to services), but they will achieve significant change only if they carry the members with them'* (Hudson, 1995: 279).

A similarly blunt warning is given by Barnard and Walker:

> *There are dangers in developing a statement of values. Members of some organizations may share only the values needed to do the job and disagree on other values. An exercise that brought all values to the surface might then cause unnecessary disagreement. The statement must also be lived out in practice. Few things can do more damage to the faith of staff in management than to see managers not living by the values they have proclaimed (Barnard and Walker, 1994: 60).*

The dilemma is poignantly encapsulated by two leading writers on equal opportunities in voluntary organizations:

> *For many organizations, the attempt to implement an equal opportunities policy has involved major conflicts and difficulties, and has swallowed up large amounts of resources without producing demonstrable benefits ... Despite recent history and experience, most people still feel that at a fundamental level, equal opportunities is one of the crucial principles of the voluntary sector. The voluntary sector is built on the foundation stones of fairness, justice, accessibility and accountability (Cheung-Judge and Henley, 1994: 4).*

Nevertheless, such authors do not doubt that these difficulties can be overcome. Cheung-Judge and Henley go on to say that the real problems were 'caused largely by the way [equal opportunity] has been handled'. In general, the prescriptions offered have the following characteristics:

- they are consistently positive and optimistic – the difficulties are presented as pitfalls to be avoided, tensions to be contained and acknowledged, and balances to be struck;
- they confidently advocate using a range of management methods – some rationalistic, many participative – to integrate the competing claims of diverse stakeholder groups, and to ensure staff are motivated in support of agreed goals, standards and priorities; and
- they stress the vital contribution of managers, especially in providing leadership in relation to values issues (in one recent book on voluntary sector management (Osborne, 1996) the first substantive chapter is on managerial ethics).

These three characteristics are vividly and persuasively presented in Saxton (1997) in which exhortations for charities to become moral leaders in society are mixed with 'how to do it' advice (suggested exercises for an 'awayday'; possible performance indicators) and uplifting tales of leadership in major charities. These characteristics are also familiar – they run through much recent popular management writing, including much that has been aimed at the managers of public services (Pattison, 1997).

FOUNDATIONS OF SAND?

Some of the criticisms of popular managerialism (see for example, Pattison and Paton, 1996) can also be levelled at this voluntary sector variant, but mercifully it still has some way to go before it reaches the same pitch of fervour and over-simplification. It is, however, open to other criticisms instead.

In the first place, it exaggerates the difference between voluntary and other organizations in respect of value commitments. In a recent study comparing governance processes in local authority-controlled schools and voluntary agencies for the homeless, Otto (1997) examined the proposition that the 'loose and ambiguous structures' characteristic of many voluntary agencies 'give people the opportunity to enact deeply held values in the workplace, thereby providing them with a vital source of intrinsic motivation'. She reported:

> *The more regulated and bureaucratic environment of the schools did not seem to diminish passionate beliefs and moral commitments. There was a common currency of personal conviction in both cultures (Otto, 1997: 30).*

More generally, a large body of evidence exists about the importance of professional and public service values in a wide range of public bodies.

Secondly, the sorts of individual and organizational commitments to which the term 'value' is applied are not 'givens'. They do not not have essential and permanent meanings, prior to and independent of context. Values usually belong to someone or some group, and the values that are acclaimed as 'core' or 'underlying' tend to be those of the people exercising power. Moreover, these commitments are constantly discovered, absorbed, reconstructed, elaborated, selectively emphasized, and above all *used* – with an eye to internal and external legitimacy. The high drama recorded in Michels's (1949) classic study of political parties – involving emergent oligarchy, colossal goal displacement and the gradual institutionalization of socialist organizations – is re-enacted on a lesser stage in the life cycles of many voluntary organizations.

Thirdly, the presumption that it should always be possible to integrate the differing values of divergent stakeholder groups is, in the face of the historical record, heroically optimistic. Indeed, as Batsleer and Randall (1992) argue, quite different strategies are currently available to voluntary agencies and they are incompatible; the choices will involve contestation and are highly political. Similarly, it would be naive to imagine that the challenge currently being mounted by, for example, the disability movement, could, if only it were subject to appropriate management techniques, be, before very long, meaningfully reconciled with the values underpinning professional service provision in the public and voluntary services. Such techniques may indeed be helpful in generating temporary agreements and precarious compromises. But in these and other cases, voluntary agencies are playing host to wider struggles. Agreeing a statement of organizational purpose, priorities or standards is the occasion for another skirmish, not the signing of an armistice.

Fourthly, the presumption that an organization's values and commitments can be consistently and reliably implemented by 'mechanisms' is extremely questionable, flying in the face both of everyday experience and a large body of theory. As I have argued elsewhere (Paton, 1996: 37–38):

> ... the problem is that organisations, like people, espouse many values and pursue multiple goals, which may be more or less ambiguous, and between which all sorts of tensions and inconsistencies inevitably arise. Thus, if any single commitment is resolutely pursued, without considering the web of other related commitments in which it is embedded, the results will always be contentious and, indeed, morally questionable. In general, decision-making becomes ever more difficult the stricter and more diverse the criteria that must be satisfied. Hence the familiar strategies of the functional separation of activities, the quasi-resolution of conflict, local rationality, and the sequential attention to goals (Cyert and March, 1963). Viewed this way, some inconsistency between values and action is inevitable – indeed it may even be desirable in maintaining the aspirations of an organisation. We know that organisational commitments (like personal standards of, say, honesty) can be important in influencing organisational behaviour even if they do not and cannot determine it in the short-term or in every case – this is the wisdom in everyday, conventional 'hypocrisy' (March, 1988).

The fifth problem is that these ideas exaggerate the autonomy of voluntary agencies in respect of their values. Organizations choose to project images and values in order to earn legitimacy, build relations with supporters, and attract resources; and in consequence they must, to a greater or lesser degree, adapt their messages to maintain their audiences or win new ones – as substantial bodies of professional training and practice in the fields of marketing and public relations testify. Hence voluntary agencies cannot help but be influenced by the rise and fall of different concerns in the wider society. Indeed, it is ironic that the voluntary sector has been deftly importing managerial values (professionalism, efficiency and effectiveness, quality and standards) even as it has proclaimed its distinctiveness and autonomy.

Finally, value-based conduct is not necessarily as admirable as the writing on voluntary sector management seems to assume. It can also be oppressive. Eric Miller (1990) notes the frequent tension between the frontline staff in voluntary agencies (the 'blue jeans') and those, perhaps with commercial backgrounds and experience, who 'sell need' as fundraisers (the 'grey suits'). He suggests that the psychological mechanisms of splitting and projection are often involved, leading to sharp polarizations between good and bad.

> *Often the conflict gets displaced onto individuals, particularly those in roles that have to bridge the two cultures: the head of finance or operations or personnel becomes a casualty role with a high turnover. The organization behaves as if, by extruding the individuals, the problems will go away. Or excessive stress manifests itself in other ways, such as binge-drinking, psychosomatic illness, or break-down (Miller, 1990: 66).*

The dark side of value commitments is illustrated by the following instance. A full time student became involved with a substantial but completely volunteer-run organization taking material help to a war zone. Those closely involved were exposed to hardship, danger and terrible human suffering on the long journeys and became very close-knit as well as committed. As with others, this became an increasingly important part of her life, and she gave up her course to work full time in the organization's office. However, she gradually became disaffected and took a course on voluntary sector management partly in the hope of finding a way out. On the course she spoke with deep bitterness (but also considerable confusion) about the domination of the organization by its founder and a small clique, the way he used it to meet his own personal needs, and the exploitation of over-committed volunteers. For example, she claimed that the marriage of the volunteer who ran the office, and upon whom the organization most depended, had broken up and and her home was about to be repossessed, as a direct consequence of her non-stop involvement. The leadership, she said, knew of this but was indifferent. Listening to her trying to make sense of her experience in discussion with others on the course, it became apparent that she was in a comparable situation to a person breaking away from a cult with which he or she has merged identities.

More generally, when the values of communities or organizations become a basis for separateness, exclusivity and righteousness they can easily become internally oppressive as well as externally xenophobic.

CONCLUSION – TWO VIEWS OF VALUES

The positive account of the place of values in voluntary organizations that is contained in recent writing on voluntary sector management can be contrasted with the more sceptical or even jaundiced views that emerge from the broader field of organizational studies. This is done in Table 7.1 over.

Two points need to be emphasized about this contrast. The first is that, arguably, the two theoretical positions are not alternatives; it is a case of 'both/and', not 'either/or'. Second, the critique of the managerial view that has been offered is the critique of an intellectual position rather than a social project. Indeed, as a citizen, and as a sometime manager in an organization with strong value commitments, I am broadly sympathetic to the managerial position. I believe the writing in question does help make sense

Table 7.1 *Two Views of the Role of Values in Voluntary Organizations*

	Model I: Managerial	Model II: Socially Embedded
Conception of Voluntary Organizations	A special, largely autonomous type of agency	Another arena for value enactment
Relevant Theories of Organization	Agency theory; organic views (eg the learning organization)	Resource dependence; institutional theory; social constructionism; chaos–theoretic models.
Nature of Values	Stable, specific, universalistic, positive – a source of virtue	Fluid, contested, contingent, problematic – potentially oppressive, or a mask for interests
Sources of Values	Founding purpose, as interpreted by trustees or members	Funders, donors, professional and other staff, social networks and movements, institutional environment
Relation to Wider Publics	Influencing: promoting the brand	Adapting: discovering the brand
Organizational Problematique	Managerial: mission – identity and autonomy; coherence – promoting a shared culture; consistency – practising what we preach	Power and conflict: 'iron law of oligarchy'; goal displacement and co-optation; splitting and projection

of many people's experience in positions of responsibility in voluntary organizations; it offers hope and a suite of generally practical ideas.

So what is the problem? Is it not harsh, unfair and misconceived to criticize professionally-oriented or popular management writing for not being an academic analysis? Indeed, 'What else have you got to offer?' would be an obvious and fair question for some of the authors cited to pose in response.

There are essentially two answers – for managers and for researchers respectively. For the former, the implication of the argument is simply a caution: yes, values are important, but they have their dangers, too. We need to recognize the limits of managing through values, and remember that the ecology of values being enacted in any lively organization will always, and rightly, be subtler and richer than those magnificent specimens captured and mounted in the display cases of mission and value statements. Of course, in times of confusing changes and contradictory pressures, the managerial urge is for greater clarity and certainty – organizations and those who work in them need some fixed points (even if they prove illusory). But if values are not kept alive by critical dialogue and discussion they gradually become rigid and static. They foreclose thought and debate, and constrict development. But it is equally true that debate around values may be uncomfortable, making the manager's job more difficult and carrying its own dangers (Paton, 1996). Whatever their benefits and importance, values are troublesome.

For researchers, the answer is that this discussion raises a number of questions. What difference is voluntary sector managerialism, with its emphasis on values, actually making? What are its effects on the managers and the managed? There is precious little phenomenology of management – we know very little, either in voluntary or any other organizations, about how and how far the new managerialism shapes the perceptions and actions of managers (as opposed to being used by them to justify and exhort). But there are glimpses, suggesting this would be a fruitful line of enquiry; one wonders whether management ideas help those experiencing the contradictions and dilemmas of intensely divergent stakeholder expectations to construct stable identities, survive the stresses, and maintain services. Or do they further encourage unrealistic expectations of self or others? How often is the talk of values sometimes a touch self-righteous and a mask for careerism? How often are the 'recipes' actually implemented, and how well do they work?

We also lack 'worm's-eye views' of the new managerialism, with its emphasis on values. How does it look to those on the receiving end? In what circumstances does it earn respect and in what circumstances does it stimulate cynicism, driving people's real beliefs and commitments underground? Is it damaging the bond of trust with supporters? Indeed, would a different, perhaps more measured and ironic 'voice', sometimes be preferred in the confusing, rhetoric-laden circumstances surrounding the work of many voluntary agencies?

These are empirical questions, more or less, and arguably they deserve attention.

BIBLIOGRAPHY

Barnard, H and Walker, P (1994) *Strategies for Success*, NCVO, London

Batsleer, J and Randall, S (1992) 'Creating common cause' in Batsleer, J, Cornforth, C and Paton, R (eds) *Issues in Voluntary and Non-Profit Management*, Addison-Wesley, Wokingham

Bruce, I (1994) *Meeting Need: Successful Charity Marketing*, ICSA, Hemel Hempstead

Cheung-Judge, M-Y and Henley, A (1994) *Equality in Action*, NCVO, London

Cyert, R and March, J G (1963) *A Behavioural Theory of the Firm*, Prentice Hall, New Jersey

CFVS (1996) *Meeting the Challenge of Change: Voluntary Action into the 21st Century*, report of the Commission on the Future of the Voluntary Sector, NCVO, London

Gann, N (1996) *Managing Change in Voluntary Organizations*, The Open University Press, Buckingham

Gerard, D (1983) *Charities in Britain: Conservatism or Change?* Bedford Square Press, London

Hind, A (1995) *The Governance and Management of Charities*, The Voluntary Sector Press, Hertfordshire

Hudson, M (1995) *Managing Without Profit*, Penguin Books, Harmondsworth, Middlesex

James, E (ed) (1989) *The Non-Profit Sector in International Perspective: Studies in Comparative Culture and Policy*, Oxford University Press, New York

March, J G (1988) *Decisions and Organizations*, Blackwell, Oxford

Michels, R (1949) *Political Parties*, Free Press, New York

Miller, E (1990) *Missionaries or Mercenaries? Dilemmas and Conflicts in Voluntary Organizations*, reprinted in B789 Resource File, The Open University, Milton Keynes

Osborne, S (1996) *Managing in the Voluntary Sector*, International Thomson Business Press, London

Otto, S (1997) 'Clarity and commitment – friends or foes?', *Non-Profit Studies*, Vol 1, No 2

Paton, R (1992) 'The social economy: value-based organizations in the wider society', in Batsleer, J, Cornforth, C and Paton, R (eds) *Issues in Voluntary and Non-Profit Management*, Addison-Wesley, Wokingham

Paton, R (1996) 'How are values handled in voluntary agencies?', in Billis, D and Harris, M (eds) *Voluntary Agencies: Challenges of Organisation and Management*, Macmillan Press, Basingstoke

Pattison, S (1997) *The Faith of the Managers*, Cassell, London

Pattison, S and Paton, R (1996) 'The religious dimensions of management belief', *Iconoclastic Papers*, Vol 1, No 1: <http://www.solent.ac.uk/busmgmt/iconoclastic.html>

Rose-Ackerman, S (1997) 'Altruism, ideological entrepreneurs and the non-profit firm', *Voluntas*, Vol 8, No 2, pp120–134

Saxton, J (1997) *What Are Charities For?* Third Sector Publications/Arts Publishing International, London

Wolfenden (1978) *The Future of Voluntary Organizations*, Report of the Wolfenden Committee, Croom Helm, London

6, P and Leat, D (1997) 'Inventing the British voluntary sector by committee', *Non-Profit Studies*, Vol 1, No 2

8

Citizen Organizations as Policy Entrepreneurs

Adil Najam

THE RISE AND RISE OF THE CITIZEN SECTOR

Writing in *Foreign Affairs*, Lester Salamon (1994: 109) proclaims that 'a striking upsurge is underway around the globe in organized voluntary activity and the creation of private, nonprofit or nongovernmental organizations … Indeed, we are in the midst of a global associational revolution that may prove to be as significant to the latter twentieth century as the rise of the nation-state was to the later nineteenth.' Strong words indeed; but a view increasingly being shared by others. Julie Fisher (1993: xi–xii), for example, points towards 'a nongovernmental revolution… already sweeping the Third World' and considers citizen organizations to be 'essential contributors' in being able to cope with 'the "steep and rocky path" that we must locate, construct, and somehow pull ourselves along if we are to survive without destroying the lives of future generations'. Princen et al (1995: 54) propose that 'by supplementing, replacing, bypassing, and sometimes even substituting for traditional politics, [citizen associations] are increasingly picking up where governmental action stops – or has yet to begin'.

Citizen organizations – whether you prefer to label them as nongovernmental organizations, as nonprofit entities, or by any of their many other names – are not a new phenomenon. What is new, however, is:

- the realization that there is a rapid and sustained growth in their numbers across the globe (for example Fisher, 1993; Uvin, 1996);
- the more nuanced recognition that the rise of such organizations is a global phenomenon, not simply because they are growing all across the globe but because they are leaving significant imprints on global processes ranging from economic development to democracy to ecology (for example Gordenker and Weiss, 1996; Mathews, 1997); and

- the resulting growth of scholarly interest – to which this volume is itself a testament – in studying them at the international, and even global, level in a comparative as well as a theory building sense (for example Hulme and Edwards, 1997; Salamon and Anheier, 1997).

The same trends which point towards the increasing influence these organizations are having at all levels of operation in all corners of the world are leading some to wonder if the act can live up to the advertisement and whether reality may not have been overextended by rhetoric. Even as the global rise in stock of the citizen sector is celebrated by all, the perceptive scholar is left to unravel the implications of this newfound fascination:

> *The Media love NGOs. The world's public – at least those who have any compassion for the struggling poor – love NGOs. And increasingly official aid agencies and many Third World governments are courting them. Is this glowing image realistic? Can NGOs deliver all that is expected from them? (Clark, 1991: 52)*

Thomas Dichter (1988: 36) ponders upon the dilemma that citizen organizations everywhere face: 'they are being asked to take on more and more even while not, in truth, being certain of what will work over the long haul … this means new opportunities and a great challenge ahead. But the risks are also great, especially given [their] tendency to shortchange reflection in favor of action.' It is worth nothing that such concerns are being raised by the sector's long-time friends and supporters. This heightened sense of introspection is a sea change worth noting, especially when juxtaposed with the unadulterated admiration of erstwhile distracters who have suddenly become new converts to the magic of civic association.

The task of unraveling these concerns while keeping track of the meteoric rise in the size and scope of the sector is not an easy one. This is so in no small part because the terrain of the global citizen sector is characterized by an amazing degree of diversity in size, scope, structure, goals, ideological leanings, operational approach, financial base, etc (see Clark, 1991; Fisher, 1993; James, 1987). More relevantly, our conceptual and analytic understanding of this terrain is even more scant than the terrain is expansive (Cernea, 1988; Drabek, 1987). Despite a few notable exceptions, the broader literature on the subject continues to be restrictive for at least three important reasons.[1] First, the scholarship has been overwhelmingly descriptive with little effort to synthesize the wealth of descriptive evidence into analytic frameworks, empirical typologies or holistic conceptual maps of the entire sector as a sector. Second, the focus of the literature is largely sectarian in that studies have tended to concentrate on restricted bands of the larger, and much broader, spectrum of activities that these organizations indulge in. Third, much of the literature is parochial in that most studies focus exclusively on narrow segments of the sector that they are familiar with (or aware of) with little effort to establish connections with other segments. The result of these chronic deficiencies is a sporadic and temperamental appreciation of the behaviour of this sector, as a sector.

These ailments are brought sharply into focus by the existence of what David Lewis (this volume) calls the two 'parallel universes' of research into the set of organizations that collectively make up the global citizen sector;[2] one devoted to understanding the so-called non-governmental organizations in the developing countries of the South and the other to the study of the so-called nonprofit organizations in the industrialized countries of the North. For a very long time an unhealthy, and in many ways unnatural, chasm has existed between the two universes. There has been little to no contact between the scholars of the two domains and each has remained ambivalent (at best) to apprehensive (at worst) about the extent that it could learn from the other. Very little exists in the way of attempts to bridge this chasm and, for the most part, studies that focus on NGOs in developing countries tend to ignore the learning on nonprofits in industrialized countries as consistently, unabashedly and routinely as studies that focus on the latter ignore the former.

As this book testifies, this is finally – and not a moment too soon – beginning to change. Appropriately, much of the emerging literature in this stream focuses on aspects that are unique to citizen organizations in each respective universe and how the two differ from each other. While not denying the utility of mapping these differences, this chapter takes a somewhat different route towards the same ultimate goal of getting these two worlds to talk to and learn from each other. It seeks to build on that which is common between the two universes.

In doing so, the lens of policy influence provides us with a useful starting point. Although policy is no less context driven than issues related to governance, legitimacy and effectiveness (the other themes discussed in this volume), it does have one distinct advantage over the others. There exist large and robust general literatures on public policy in the developing and industrialized countries respectively; and while those literatures also do not tend to talk to each other as much as they should, they do talk more than do the literatures on non-governmental and nonprofit organizations. As a result, we already know that policy processes in the two contexts do have some important commonalties and, at the broadest level, the process can be diagrammed along the same lines whether it is in the South or the North (see Najam, 1995). At the same time, and again at the same broad level, the separate literatures on non-governmental and nonprofit organizations tend to throw up very similar categories of ways in which citizen organizations try to influence the policy process in their respective contexts.

By placing these two elements together, this chapter proposes a simple yet effective template for mapping the ways in which citizen organizations, whether they be in the North or South, influence policy. It is argued that having a common template, even if it is at the broadest level of generality, is a first step towards enabling a dialogue. More importantly, the dialogue can be enriched by enabling a better view of the overall richness of the tapestry that is the global citizen sector. The hope is that by being able to view the full tapestry we will be better positioned to appreciate the embedded grains and textures of the various strands that are either common or differentiated between citizen organizations in North and South.

To make the analysis more manageable, this chapter will survey citizen organizations working in the broadly defined area of 'sustainable development'. This allows us to capture two segments in which the sector tends to be heavily engaged – environment and development – while casting a wide enough net to capture the richness of organizations in both North and South. A conscious effort is made to use examples from both North and South, from various sub-regions within each, and from organizations that range in size from multinational to national to local. The purpose is not to camouflage the many important differences between these organizations, but to highlight how, despite the differences, they tend to operate in broadly similar ways in trying to influence the public policy process at its various stages.

In summary, this chapter seeks to better understand how citizen organizations, in their various roles, interact with the policy process. To resist the temptation of being either too descriptive, too sectarian or too parochial it sets itself the task of constructing an analytical template of the full range of policy services that citizen organizations provide in a selected substantive area (in this case, sustainable development) using examples from both North and South. In doing so, it argues that at the broad level the same template can be used for organizations in North as well as South and that starting from points of broad similarities can bring us closer to developing behavioural explanations that span the entire global citizen sector rather that only its various substantive or geographic sub-sectors.

A DEFINITIONAL NOTE

A discussion about what we mean by the terms citizen sector, sustainable development or policy could easily land us into a definitional quagmire. This paper will avoid prolonged definitional debates about any of the above because despite their pervasive use none has a precise definition attached to it. Although seeking greater conceptual clarity regarding any of the three is a challenge with great intellectual appeal, it is an endeavour of limited productive relevance to our immediate purpose. However, for the very same reasons it is necessary to lay out what this chapter understands each of the three concepts to mean.

Trying to define the citizen sector – or the set of institutions which is variously referred to as civil society or the nonprofit, the non-governmental, the voluntary, the independent, the charitable, the people's, the philanthropic, the associational, or the third sector – has been a confounding exercise for many.[3] Those who have taken such expeditions of faith have been quick to recognize the arduousness of their trek (Brown and Korten, 1991; Douglas, 1987; Esman and Uphoff, 1984; Hansmann, 1987; Najam,

1996a; Salamon and Anheier, 1997; Weisbrod, 1988). For example, at the very onset of their typological endeavour, Esman and Uphoff (1984: 58) warn their readers that '[a]lmost anything that one can say about [the citizen sector] is true – or false – in at least some instance, somewhere'. On a similar note Cernea (1988: 9) observes that 'the residual nature of the term itself offers such a broad umbrella for a kaleidoscopic collection of organizations, that attempts at simple definitions are quickly rendered meaningless'. Clark (1991: 40) all but gives up the attempt by starting from the premise that such organizations 'do not comprise a tight community but a broad spectrum – too broad, perhaps, to leave the term with much meaning'.

In fact, as I have argued elsewhere (Najam, 1996a) the absence of a robust conceptual definition for the sector as a whole and the residual nature of the terms non-governmental or nonprofit organizations has intellectually impoverished our understanding of the sector. Building on earlier works by Nerfin (1986), Brown and Korten (1991) and others, I have argued that citizens' organizations do in fact constitute a distinct institutional sector, with distinct motivations and structural preferences. I suggest that the institutional landscape, especially for any policy relevant discussion, is best understood as constituting three distinct sets of institutions: those of the prince, the merchant and the citizen. The first of these – the state sector – is primarily concerned with the preservation of social order; does so through its legitimate authority and coercive sanction from society; represents the interests of the majority (or dominant groups); and operates in the realm of the political system. The second – the market sector – is concerned with the production of goods and services; does so through mechanisms of negotiated economic exchange and profit maximization; represents individual self-interest; and operates in the realm of the market. The third – the voluntary associational, or citizen, sector – is most concerned with the articulation and actualization of particular social visions; does so through the shared normative values of its patrons, members and clients; represents the interests of those who consider their interests marginalized; and operates in the realm of civil society.[4]

If the citizen sector is a difficult concept to define, sustainable development is even more so. In using the term, this chapter makes no claim of possessing a precise definition for the term. It is used here in its popular, if vague, sense of implying the quest for a balance between ecological and economic imperatives. The most popularly quoted definition of the term comes from the World Commission on Environment and Development (WCED, 1987: 8) which defined it as development 'that meets the needs of the present without compromising the ability of future generations to meet their own needs'. Although lacking in analytic detail for meaningful policy use, this definition is as good as any. Politically, and semantically, the term is a convenient marriage between the desire for sustaining ecological integrity and furthering economic and human development. One of the most comprehensive reviews of the literature on defining sustainable development is provided by Lélé (1991: 607) who points out that 'to some extent, the value of the phrase does lie in its broad vagueness'. The term is used here in a similar spirit of being a constructive ambiguity. In an operational sense, organizations working on issues that lie on the nexus of environment and development concerns will be described as working in the field of sustainable development.

The popular understanding of the term 'policy' also tends to be expansive and all-consuming. This chapter's conception of policy emanates from three related streams in the policy literature. First, in *Agendas, Alternatives, and Public Policies*, John Kingdon (1984) describes the generation of policy alternatives as being 'best seen as a selection process, analogous to biological natural selection. In ... the policy primeval soup, many ideas float around, bumping into one another, encountering new ideas, and forming combinations and recombinations.' Importantly, he adds that 'in the process of consideration in the policy community, ideas themselves are important'. Second, in *Policy Paradox and Political Reason*, Deborah Stone (1988: 14) asserts that 'public policy is about communities trying to achieve something as communities. This is true even though there is almost always conflict within a community over what its goals should be and who its members are ...' Finally, in *Evidence, Argument and Persuasion in the Policy Process*, Giandomenico Majone (1989) introduces the notion that the policy process is not simply one of presenting objective evidence but of dialectical argumentation and persuasion.

At a minimum, then, policy is seen as a social device to accelerate, decelerate, circumvent or create particular changes. The narrow view of policy as a set of legally binding edicts handed down by some competent authority is rejected. Instead, the policy enterprise is conceptualized as a dynamic dialectic dialogue (Majone, 1989) between the sometimes competing and sometimes converging notions of the public interest held by the various actors and interests in the larger community (Stone, 1988) – it is in the interaction between these various notions in the policy stream that policy is shaped, reshaped and reshaped again in a constantly evolving process (Kingdon, 1984). Within such a conception of the process, citizen organizations – which, by definition, are agents of change and whose goal is to articulate and actualize a particular social vision – are best identified as being policy entrepreneurs (Najam, 1996a). The normative values they represent and the social visions they seek to actualize are their contribution to what has been called the 'primeval policy soup' or 'policy stream'.

CITIZEN ORGANIZATIONS IN THE POLICY STREAM

Citizen organizations have an abiding interest in the content of public policy. As McCormick (1993: 142) puts it, 'the fundamental objective of an NGO is to influence public policy from outside the formal structure of elected government'. One of the more robust definitions of the sector, provided by Hall (1987: 3), describes them firmly as policy entrepreneurs in the very same sense as that used here:

> *... a nonprofit organization [is] a body of individuals who associate for any of three purposes: (1) to perform public tasks that have been delegated to them by the state; (2) to perform public tasks for which there is a demand that neither the state nor for-profit organizations are willing to fulfill; or (3) to influence the direction of policy in the state, the for-profit sector or other nonprofit organizations.*

Indeed, we can define citizen organizations as 'para-policy organizations' on the basis of their principal normative characteristic being (a) the bringing together – in associations – of actors with shared normative values, (b) for the purpose of actualizing particular social visions (Najam, 1996a). The latter are the goals and the former are the interests that the organizations bring to the policy stream. It is in interacting with other actors in the stream that they seek to express these interests and forward these goals so as to influence the ever emerging shape of policy.[5] The work of Smith and Lipsky (1993: vii–viii) on the rise of public service contracting in the US supports this view of citizen groups as policy entrepreneurs: 'We believe that the experiences and behaviors of the people who work in nonprofit organizations and other parts of the service system, taken together *add up* to – in a sense, become – the nation's social policy' (original emphasis). Organizations operating in the South are similarly preoccupied with issues of public policy. In fact, so much of what they do – for example, building roads and wells or providing education and health care – is so much like what governments are supposed to do that one might sometimes confuse them with governmental agencies were it not for their having proudly labelled themselves as being non-governmental.

The other actor in the policy stream that we focus on is the government or, in our earlier conceptual metaphor, the prince. Although interaction in the policy stream with other policy players – including other citizen organizations, donor agencies and philanthropists, commercial sector organizations, political parties, etc – will also have an impact on their ultimate influence on policy, it is the shape of policy as enunciated by government institutions that the policy enterprise is most directly concerned with. It therefore makes sense to select this as a focus of our enquiry.[6]

It is not without irony that the government sector should be as central as it is to the activities of the very group of organizations that so often define themselves as non-governmental.[7] That they are, in themselves, not governmental is seen to be a badge of honour by most citizen organizations; this, however, does not imply that they are not interested in the government. Far from it, much of citizen action and aspiration – in developing as well as industrialized countries – can be boiled down to doing itself, or wanting the government to do, things that it (that is the government) either a) refuses to do, b) does not do enough of, c) is incapable of doing or d) is unable to do.[8]

Some mutual apprehension will always be a part of all citizen–prince relationships because, as Clark (1991: 74) points out, citizen groups 'are often distrustful and critical of governments and ... these sentiments are often reciprocated'. Within the sustainable development area, for example, the 1992 United Nations Conference on Environment and Development (UNCED) is often considered a major breakthrough in close collaboration between governments and the citizen sector on a set of global issues. Yet, as Finger (1994: 186) reports, 'a fundamental tension existed throughout the UNCED process, a tension between [a citizen] role as defined by states and one defined by [citizen organizations] themselves' (also see Enge and Malkenes, 1993; McMahon, 1993). Having said that, the growing trend is towards more, rather than less, cooperation between the domains of the prince and the citizen (Fisher, 1998; Najam, 1996c; Uvin, 1996). To stick with the UNCED case, for example, its principal document (*Agenda 21*) extols governments to explicitly invite citizen organizations to take part in the formulation and implementation of sustainable development policies.

Noting this global trend, Lester Salamon (1994: 120) strips away at what he calls the 'myth of voluntarism' to point out that contrary to popular opinion, even amongst scholars, 'the relationship between government and the nonprofit sector has been characterized more by cooperation than conflict'. Moreover, he suggests that such cooperation is on the rise and is likely to remain so into the next century. According to Smith and Lipsky (1993), for example, the considerable growth in the use of nonprofit groups as public service contractors is one of the more striking trends in this sector in the US today. The evidence from the developing countries suggests that this trend is not unique to industrialized welfare states (see Fisher, 1998; Hulme and Edwards, 1997; Najam, 1996b and 1996c; Opoku-Mensah, 1997).[9] For example, Diaz-Albertini (1993: 332) reports from Peru:

> *The relations between the government and the NGDO [non-govern-mental development organizations] ... are becoming frequent and intricate, making the differentiation between the actors more difficult. In Peru, NGDOs are collaborating in diverse projects under many different kinds of arrangements: as consultants, as managing or co-managing government programs and services, as large-scale projects in conjunction with multilateral lending institutions, and so on.*

Paul Opoku-Mensah (1997: 19), in studying the relationship between citizen organizations and the government in Ghana, finds that 'contrary to the rhetoric of conflict, relations between the [citizen] sector and the state in Ghana have generally been collaborative'. He goes on to extrapolate this discussion to Africa in general and argues that accommodation between citizen organizations and governments is on the rise throughout the continent.

Korten (1991: 30) reports a similar trend in Asia:

> *NGOs in many Asian countries have demonstrated substantial adeptness in building alliances with those in government who are both influential and sympathetic to their cause. Alliance building is*

often a conscious political strategy aimed at securing political protection for the NGO and its activities. With time the alliance may become the basis of a coalition advocating constructive policy changes to which the NGO and the concerned officials have mutual commitment.

Annis (1987: 132), focusing on citizen organizations in Latin America, forwards a possible explanation:

Just as the poor are deeply interested in the resources of their governments, so too, their governments are deeply interested in them – even if for all the wrong reasons ... First, extending services implies political obligation ... Second, local organizations are often viewed by the state as appropriate instruments for carrying out high profile, state-sponsored service campaigns ... Third, states are able to see potential benefits of 'cost sharing' and 'cost recovery'... Fourth, even the most unenlightened and bureaucratic state agencies recognize that services are likely to be delivered more efficiently if there is input from those who are supposed to receive the service ... In other words, at the same time that grassroots organizations are trying to wrest services and concessions from the state, the state is generally trying to break itself into finer units of political and bureaucratic control. What happens in practice is a kind of interpenetration – a blending in which the so-called 'governmental' and 'non-governmental' meld together.

This growing trend towards increased citizen–prince contacts should, however, not necessarily be seen as a threat either to state sovereignty or to citizen autonomy.[10] As Drabek (1987: xiii) points out, 'one of the fundamental reasons that NGOs have received so much attention of late is that they are perceived to be able to do something that national governments cannot or will not do. Yet NGOs have no intention or desire to supplant or compete with the state in their development efforts; on the contrary, in both the North and South most NGOs continue to interact heavily with governments.' Instead, this trend should be viewed as an expected corollary of increasing citizen presence in the policy domain. Indeed, it could be viewed as de facto recognition of citizen organizations having come of age and being taken seriously by other – especially governmental – actors in the policy stream. As the level and sophistication of citizen–government relations increases, it is important to invest scholarly attention and enquiry into understanding the nature of and variance in such relations, and the possible sources of variance.[11]

This growing interaction between citizen organizations and governments suggests that the citizen shadow over the policy enterprise is likely to enlarge rather than shrink. As the following discussion will illustrate, much of the citizen influence on policy comes not from conventional advocacy but from more subtle forms of interaction within the primeval soup that is the policy stream. To limit our investigation of the policy influence of citizen organizations to the conventionally narrow confines of policy advocacy is to limit our understanding of this shadow.

CONSTRUCTING A POLICY MAP

There is a wealth of descriptive literature from all over the world which suggests that citizen organizations are both interested in and have influence upon the policy process. Much of this happens through conventional advocacy but even more happens in other, more indirect, ways. The rest of this chapter will survey that part of this vast literature which deals with the broad area of sustainable development to develop an improved understanding of how citizen organizations operate within the policy stream. Since the scale, scope and diversity of the examples can be overwhelming, we will begin by constructing an organizing template to assist us in better appreciating the different roles that citizen organizations play as entrepreneurs in the various stages of the policy enterprise.

The proposed framework is a two-dimensional matrix of policy competencies with the various stages of the policy process defining one axis of the matrix and the different roles that citizen organizations play in the policy enterprise defining the other. Given the meandering nature of the policy stream and the diversity of roles that the citizen sector plays within this stream, one could potentially draw out long laundry lists along either dimension. However, for this exercise to be conceptually and analytically useful it is important that the number of categories along both axes be few enough to be manageable, defined enough to be meaningful and broad enough to (between them) cover the conceivable spectrum of possibilities.

Although the policy process is complex and unsympathetic to simple conceptualizations – and although the term 'stages' is itself misleading in that policy moves less along well-defined linear stages and more in seemingly haphazard patterns better defined by metaphors such as 'garbage cans' (Cohen et al, 1972) and 'primeval soups' (Kingdon, 1984) – most scholars of policy sciences would agree that at its broadest level the process can be reasonably depicted as one of agenda setting, policy development and policy implementation.[12]

- **Agenda setting** is about setting priorities. At this stage, the various actors in the policy stream seek to highlight the importance of the issues and interests that they most closely identify with. The essential task is to decide the issues on which policy should focus. By the very nature of the policy enterprise, there are always more interests to be satisfied than there are resources or time. Therefore, prioritization becomes a key task.
- **Policy development** is about choosing from alternatives and options. It is here that policy takes a formal, sometimes legally binding, shape. In national and local politics this could range from legislative action

to judicial edict to agency regulation to norms of community practice. In international politics it could range from a binding convention or treaty (hard law) to a normative declaration (soft law). The key issue in this phase is the battle about which, of the invariably many, options or alternatives is selected to seek the desired effect. While the debate in agenda setting is related more to which issues should be tackled as priority, the question here is what approach should be adopted in tackling it.

- **Policy implementation** is about action. It is in this phase that steps are taken to convert intent into action. Often, but not always, broad policy statements are converted into more specifically defined projects in this phase. The key issue here is to ensure that the tasks set out in the policy are carried out. However, the process of implementation is never as clean as this and very often policy is itself, de facto, reformulated during implementation (Najam, 1995).

A survey of the literature throws up a long list of roles that citizen organizations play in the policy stream at the local, national and international levels. Rejecting the laundry list approach preferred by some, this paper identifies four broad areas as the key loci of citizen involvement in the policy stream. One way of conceptualizing these four roles is as follows: as monitors, citizen organizations ensure that government (and the commercial sector) is doing what it is supposed to be doing; as advocates they prod government agencies to do what they consider to be the right thing; as innovators they suggest how things might be done differently; and as service providers they themselves act directly to do what – in their opinion – needs to be done.[13]

- As monitors, citizen organizations perform the function of keeping policy 'honest'. In this capacity, they not only act as whistleblowers for policies that are not being implemented properly but they also keep track of events that are likely to, or should, impact upon the shape of new policies.
- As advocates, citizen organizations lobby directly for the policy options they prefer, or against the ones they oppose. They build strategic coalitions and public support which might tilt the balance in favour of their preferred policy option. This includes a multitude of related functions including information dissemination, public education and resource mobilization.
- As innovators, citizen organizations develop and demonstrate ways of doing things differently and highlight the policy value being missed by options that are not adopted or considered. This includes the innovative contributions they can make to policy by virtue of their practical, technical and managerial expertise. This is one of the more catalytic roles they play in the policy stream and it is not uncommon for the citizen innovation of today to become the government wisdom of tomorrow.

Table 8.1 *Citizen Organizations as Policy Entrepreneurs –*
The Policy Space they Occupy

	Monitors	Advocates	Innovators	Service Providers
Agenda Setting				
Policy Development				
Policy Implementation				

• As service providers, citizen organizations directly act to fulfil a service need, especially to the marginalized and under-served. This would also include services provided directly to communities in substantive sectors that are considered to be part of governmental competency or mandate such as the provision of clean water, reliable roads or even telecommunication infrastructure.[14]

Citizen organizations perform all four of these roles at the three stages of the policy process described above. To get a full picture of their involvement in the policy enterprise we can construct a 3x4 matrix with the policy roles they play on one axis and policy phases on the other. Table 8.1 defines a map of the policy space within which citizen organizations influence public policy. As will be highlighted later, it is important that the matrix should not be seen as a set of rigid boxes. It should be seen instead as a map of the larger policy space that the global citizen sector inhabits; a space which is characterized not by stringent internal and external compartmentalization but by a set of very porous and somewhat dynamic boundaries.

The following sections will discuss examples from all over the world of how citizen organizations working for sustainable development have influenced policy in each of these roles and at each of these stages. This discussion will lead to a composite matrix which will lay out, with examples, the broad map of citizen involvement as policy entrepreneurs in the quest for sustainable development (Table 8.2). Although the examples used in this chapter are predominantly positive – partly because the literature on the subject has tended to highlight the sector's positive contributions far more extensively than its negative impacts – this chapter does not imply any value judgement regarding such contributions being necessarily positive. Similarly, that the chosen examples are generally ones where citizen organizations have played such policy roles effectively should also not be taken to imply that they always do so as effectively. Indeed, as a number of perceptive scholars have pointed out, not all goals of citizen organizations may be socially desirable; not all organizations are alike; not all organizations possess the much publicized strengths of the sector; and, in fact, not all publicized strengths are necessarily always strengths (see Annis, 1987; Clark, 1991; Dichter, 1988; Tendler, 1982).

Citizen Organizations as Monitors

Some of the biggest, and certainly the most visible, policy successes of environmental organizations – and more generally of citizen organizations in other substantive areas, especially in the human rights area – have come in their role as monitors, especially as whistleblowers and watchdogs over policy implementation (Dawkins, 1991; Lindborg, 1992; Stairs and Taylor, 1992). They have been effective monitors at both the national and international levels; at the latter this has become one of their principal hallmarks (Chayes and Chayes, 1993). So much so that Spiro (1995: 45–46) considers them to be 'prime movers' in this area, and they are now seen as 'a sort of new world police force', and that 'international regimes protecting human rights and the environment would arguably amount to nothing without initial and continuing NGO pressure'.

The institutional strengths that citizen organizations bring to their role as policy monitors include their claim of independence from the governmental and commercial sectors, their substantive expertise in a number of environmental issues and their ability to gather information not easily available to individual citizens which they then disseminate to their constituents and the media. Importantly, as Princen et al (1995: 51) point out, they 'do not have to be nice to anyone. They can be, and often are, in the business of monitoring, exposing, criticizing, and condemning. They need not compromise on either ecological or ethical principles, or at least they need do so much less than states for which the essence of maintaining good relations is, indeed, compromise.'

Moreover, there is an implicit moral claim that these organizations make in their role as policy monitors on behalf of citizens. This is made explicit by Korten (1990: 187) who reminds his readers: 'Abuse feeds on silence. Often the fear of exposure is in itself enough to check the potential abuser.' He adds that 'the judiciary is a passive instrument' and 'the press can communicate only the information it has'; it is, therefore, up to citizen organizations to become the 'eyes and ears' that call attention to abuses of policy.

Although the monitoring role is most intensive at the policy implementation stage, it is not inconsequential at the other two stages. In the agenda setting phase, the monitoring role of the citizen sector is most often related to collecting and publicizing information that can help the shape of the emerging policy agenda. Although related to the advocacy role, this needs to be recognized as a separate activity which is conceptually a precursor to advocacy and deals more with the identification of problems than of solutions. Many environmental groups have literally defined the agenda for policy through their monitoring activities. An immediate example is the role played by IUCN – The World Conservation Union in extensively researching and documenting the effects of trade in endangered species which was significantly instrumental in making this an issue worthy of an international treaty (Porter and Brown, 1991: 61–62). Another powerful example is the series of *Citizen's Reports on the State of India's Environment* (CSE, 1982) coordinated by the New Delhi-based Center for Science and

Environment (CSE). Written in collaboration with, and with contributions from, local and national organizations dealing with environment and development issues, these reports served as well documented monitoring efforts that can be credited for having a substantial impact on India's policy agenda definition in the general area of sustainable development.

The monitoring carried out by various citizen organizations as part of their publications strategy has also had significant influence on the shape of national and international policy agendas. For example, periodicals such as *World Watch* (Worldwatch Institute, US) and *Third World Resurgence* (Third World Network, Penang, Malaysia) and the bi-annual publication of *World Resources* (World Resources Institute, US) have had such an impact. Similarly powerful as a monitoring effort is *Vital Signs*, an annual publication of the Worldwatch Institute, which traces trends (mostly quantitatively) in environmental quality. Figures, charts and arguments from such publications have an uncanny way of showing up in policy debates regarding the agenda direction and are frequently used not only by other citizen organizations but also by government decision makers.

The monitoring role played by citizen organizations at the policy development stage has also benefited from advances in information technologies and the attendant ease in information gathering and dissemination. One prominent example from the international policy arena is that of the *Earth Negotiations Bulletin* (ENB) of the Canada-based International Institute for Sustainable Development (IISD). This initiative has electronically produced and distributed regular reports – often on a daily basis – on most of the prominent sustainable development-related policy negotiations since UNCED. This serves the very valuable purpose of monitoring the evolving shape of extremely complex, time-consuming, distant and protracted policy developments on a regular and immediate basis. This has had the significant impact of enabling other citizen organizations and activists – and even government officials – to keep abreast of events without exorbitant costs in time, energy and money.

There also seems to be a growing trend at the national level towards citizen organizations closely monitoring policy development to keep the process honest. In the US, for example, most major environmental groups maintain an office in Washington which tracks policy development discussions on issues of particular interest to the membership. While the principal function of these offices is advocacy, a separate monitoring function should not be neglected and is most evident in the various policy updates that such groups periodically send to their supporters. In a Southern context, the development of the Pakistan National Conservation Strategy (PNCS) was publicly monitored through a special newsletter published by IUCN-Pakistan with inputs from other citizen organizations. At the completion of the policy development phase the newsletter turned into the magazine *The Way Ahead* whose primary mandate is to monitor the implementation of the strategy, but which also serves the important function of monitoring the development phase of other related policies. Most recently, this included the new national law pertaining to NGO registration.

The most visible and consistent impact that the citizen sector has in its role as a policy monitor is at the level of policy implementation. Examples abound at all levels – local, national and international. Examples from international policy include the success of Greenpeace and the Environmental Defense Fund (EDF) in documenting and publicizing violations of the Antarctic Treaty System (Laws, 1991); Greenpeace has had similar success in bringing world attention to violations of the International Convention on Regulation of Whaling (Stairs and Taylor, 1992). Monitoring as part of policy implementation – as opposed to monitoring of policy implementation – is also a task that citizen groups have been adept at. For example, Princen et al (1995: 53) remind us that in wildlife trade, Trade Records Analysis of Flora and Fauna in Commerce, the Environmental Investigation Agency, IUCN and other NGOs assume a major share of what would otherwise be a primarily intergovernmental function, namely monitoring.

Examples at the local level are similarly numerous. Bolivia's Beni land reserve, for instance, was declared a UNESCO Man and Biosphere Reserve in 1986 but over the next two years loggers continued to operate in the reserve in violation of the concession granted to them; a local organization of the Moxos Indians has been monitoring this violation and has been able to direct national as well as international attention to this infringement (Dawkins, 1991: 83). In Malaysia, the Consumers' Association of Penang was able to win a suit against a Japanese company that was mining rare earths and polluting the waterways on the basis of having monitored the firm's activities and documenting how it violated national policy (Livernash, 1992: 226). In Pakistan, local citizen groups, such as Shehri (literal translation 'urban citizen') have begun playing a similar monitoring role and are pioneering the use of legal action as a strategy for environmental activism by highlighting instances where policy is not being implemented as it should (Yusuf, 1992).

Citizen Organizations as Advocates

If monitoring serves as the eyes and ears of citizen interests otherwise unrepresented in the policy stream, advocacy (or lobbying) serves as the mouthpiece. A conceptual distinction between the two roles is highlighted by Korten (1990: 186):

> ... *unlike the monitoring and protest role ... the first priority of the [citizen organization] in the catalyst role is* pro-action *to create positive change more than* re-action *to police negative behavior. Thus the focus is on* advocacy – *acting* for – *rather than* protest – *acting* against *(original emphasis).*

All citizen organizations are, by definition, advocates. Yet, for some of them formal advocacy is not only an overarching theme but the bulk of their formal activity. It is advocacy as a specific activity rather than as the overarching defining theme that we are concerned with here. Advocacy in this more specific sense is by far the most recognized of the policy roles played by citizen organizations. Efficacy in this role is enhanced, especially in established electoral democracies, by the ability to mobilize public opinion which can translate to direct and indirect pressure on government decision makers:

> *Backed by the credibility they bring to an issue, [citizen organizations] can effectively use the media, public demonstrations, consumer boycotts and other grassroots channels to mobilize public opinion. This capability is critically important for two reasons: the ability of the media, consumers and voters to pressure – and thereby influence – actions of government officials engaged in the [policy development] process, and the impact of public opinion and resulting changes in behavior on the problem itself (Lindborg, 1992).*

However, as Diaz-Albertini (1993: 323) points out, such strategies are not always available or applicable in 'weakly institutionalized political systems' where the advocacy role played by the citizen sector hinges more on 'attempting to strengthen or restructure state agencies so that they become capable of processing political claims ... by institutionalizing channels for representation – bargaining, negotiating, and building capability for assuming long-term agreements and development programs'. The ability to mobilize resources and training opportunities can be a source of strength in this task – it can give advocacy efforts similar legitimacy with state agencies as the ability to mobilize mass public support might do elsewhere.

McCormick (1993: 140) seems to believe that 'lobbying and other forms of interest-group activity are essentially Western concepts, and although there are effective and vocal national NGOs in many non-Western countries, they are not always relevant or appropriate in terms of understanding how policy is influenced and made in those countries'. This is an ill-informed view. While the nature of advocacy and lobbying may be different in Southern countries, all evidence suggests that citizen groups in these countries are no less active, or successful, in their advocacy. In focusing on the experience in Africa, for example, Bratton (1990: 87) found that organizations in non-Western settings are able to lobby effectively, albeit differently. He also identified some key structural attributes for effective advocacy: 'policy advocacy is most likely to be effective in organizations that have several key characteristics: an homogeneous membership, a federated structure, a focused programme, informal ties with political leaders, and a domestic funding base'.

Citizen organizations have had dramatic success as advocates for sustainable development policy at the agenda setting stage.[15] Princen et al (1995: 52) testify that citizen organizations 'are increasingly prominent forces in framing environmental issues. They help establish a common language and, sometimes, common world views. Indeed, the history of international environmental politics shows that new ideas have not come from governments or even designated international organizations, but from environmental lobbies and activist groups' (also see Najam, 1993; Porter and Brown, 1991). Most of the big international groups such as the Sierra Club, Friends of the Earth, Greenpeace, etc are particularly adept at advocacy at all, and especially at the agenda setting stages. More recently, a number of developing country groups such as the Malaysia-based Third World Network (TWN) and the Philippine-based Green Forum have also become active in lobbying at the agenda setting stage of international environmental policy making.

A specific example of the impact that citizen organizations can have as advocates at the agenda setting stage is of the International Waterfowl Research Bureau (IWRB). Advocacy efforts by this group and a series of meetings convened by it in the 1960s resulted in the signing of the 1971 Ramsar Convention on Wetlands of International Importance (Lyster, 1985). The Women's Environment and Development Organization (WEDO) has been similarly instrumental in influencing the agenda of many recent international policy negotiations (Chen, 1996). In relation to more domestic policy, various advocacy campaigns launched by the Sustainable Development Policy Institute (SDPI) in Pakistan have successfully afforded increased prominence to environmental issues – for example the use of plastic grocery bags, domestic water conservation and so on – on the policy agenda. The advocacy work of the Union of Concerned Scientists (UCS) in the mid-western states of the US on renewable energy options has, similarly, given a new prominence to the issue in domestic US energy policy debates. Population groups in a number of countries, such as the Indonesian Planned Parenthood Association (PBKI) which began operating in 1957, have been particularly successful in advocacy at the agenda setting stage and in many cases have succeeded in bringing population issues from the policy wilderness to prominence (Fisher, 1993: 128).

Probably the most widely cited example of the impact that citizen organizations can have in the policy development phase relates to their participation in the UNCED negotiations (Enge and Malkenes, 1993; Lindborg, 1992).[16] Examples abound, however, of less visible but equally profound impacts elsewhere. One such example is the role played by citizen organizations in the US in influencing the final shape of the North American Free Trade Agreement (NAFTA). Without advocacy and lobbying by such groups in Canada, the US and Mexico the shape of the ultimate agreement would have been significantly different from what it now is – instrumental in this role was the tri-national coalition of citizen groups which came about as a result of efforts initiated by the Mexican advocacy organization Grupo de los Cien (Ferber et al, 1995; Nunez, 1994). These examples suggest a trend towards more sophisticated advocacy by citizen organizations:

Environmental NGOs [have begun to] use the law for strategic political purposes as an instrument of advocacy and influence,

> *rather than as a means of achieving a substantive legal end ... [This]*
> *does not suggest that the use of law by environmental NGOs is new,*
> *but that it is increasing, that it is increasingly sophisticated, and*
> *that it is increasingly international (Sands, 1992: 31).*

Despite such successes at the international level, the domestic setting remains the locus of most advocacy by citizen groups in both North and South. For example, a mix of activism and advocacy by the California Coalition for Clean Air and the Sierra Club forced the US Environmental Protection Agency to 'reluctantly' issue guidelines in 1990 calling for days in which southern California drivers would not be permitted to use their cars if state and regional plans by the year 2000 are unsuccessful in reducing carbon monoxide emissions; a month later the California Air Resources Board adopted the strictest 'smog laws' in the nation calling for mass production of low-polluting cars and other measures (Dawkins, 1991: 82). As another example, the Committee of Earthquake Victims (CUD) formed as a coalition of various barrio organizations, local voluntary organizations and university groups and coordinated by the Urban Popular Movement (MUP) in Mexico City in the aftermath of the 1985 earthquake articulated, advocated for, and was able to get the government to accept a defined policy package, which they had designed, setting out the ground rules for reconstruction (Annis, 1988).

Policy advocacy at the local level is often ignored because it is so dispersed. One should, however, not assume that it does not exist. For example, it was policy advocacy by literally thousands of local groups all around the US that led local governments to adopt policies relating to recycling, landfills, wetlands, etc. Parallel examples in developing countries, although often undocumented, are nonetheless available; one instance being in the Pakistani village of Gunyar where a youth group (ABNJ) was able to convince village elders to experiment with 'social fencing' as an alternative to the prevalent approach of open grazing (Ali, 1993). This example is an interesting one because it demonstrates the policy influence that grassroots organizations can have even in situations where operational policy comes not through governmental dictates but via community practice.

Examples of advocacy by citizen organizations at the policy implementation stage – which very often means the project level – are also abundant. Since citizen organizations, especially in the South, are most involved at the level of project implementation it is not surprising that this has also been the setting for much advocacy by them. Very often, advocacy at this level takes the shape of protesting against particular policy implementation or project choices; implicit in this rejection, however, are notions of what alternatives are preferred. Similarly, advocacy on particular episodes of implementation or on specific projects often has a feedback relationship to broader policy advocacy. In advocating against a particular project an organization is de facto advocating for broader policy choices; however, since it is easier to mobilize opposition (or support) for tangible projects than for the more distant notions of policy, citizen organizations (especially smaller ones) often concentrate their advocacy efforts on project implementation.[17]

One of the most publicized recent episodes of citizen advocacy at the policy implementation level is the controversy over the construction of the Narmada Dam in Gujarat, India. The lead group in this continuing saga is the Indian activist coalition, the Narmada Bachao Andholan (NBA), but a large number of other groups in India and internationally – especially the International Rivers Network (IRN) – have also been active in the effort. Although the Narmada saga is a continuing one, citizen advocacy has, until now, resulted in the World Bank taking back its decision to fund the project and the Indian Water Resources Ministry having conceded to a number of project design changes advocated by the NBA (Triedman, 1993).[18]

Another less publicized example is from Pakistan where a coalition of Pakistani citizen organizations – including the Sustainable Development Policy Institute, Shirkat Gah Women's Resource Center and Sungi Development Foundation – and Greenpeace International averted the import of polluting mercury-based chloro-alkali production technology from Denmark to Pakistan. The plant had been legislatively closed down in Denmark, but a local Pakistani company managed to gain permission to relocate it in Pakistan. National citizen advocacy triggered the very first environmental hearing in the Pakistan Senate. Following the hearing, negotiations between these groups and the local firm importing the plant resulted in a decision by the firm to voluntarily upgrade the plant to a cleaner level (Samee, 1995).

Other instances of advocacy by citizen organizations at the policy implementation level include the Green Belt Movement in Kenya, which has successfully advocated for national tree plantation programmes which have reportedly resulted in the plantation of some 10 million trees with the involvement of 50,000 Kenyan women; in doing so the Green Belt movement has itself taken on the role of defining the national tree planting policy (Livernash, 1992: 225). Similarly, a women's community group in Uttar Pradesh, India, successfully lobbied against a soapstone mining concession that would have blocked their access to fuelwood by destroying the forest that they depended upon – in doing so they were able to reverse the government's mining concession (Starke, 1990: 69–70).

Citizen Organizations as Innovators

Many scholars of the subject consider innovation in the policy stream to be a distinctive contribution of the citizen sector. Brown and Korten (1991: 48) argue that citizen organizations have important advantages over government as catalysts of social and institutional innovation because they 'can test innovative programs that governments would not undertake until the programs are proven politically feasible'. Korten (1991: 35) adds that organizations in this sector are in a position to take such risks where government might not because their institutional motivation is essentially different and intrinsically biased in favour of innovation:

> *The bottom-line question for the technocrat is whether NGOs are more cost-effective than government in the delivery of basic services. By contrast, some social activists may argue that the question is irrelevant and reflects a lack of understanding of the real business of NGOs, which is to serve as catalysts of social change.*

Clark (1991: 59) echoes this view, pointing out that citizen organizations 'are less subject to the straightjacket of development orthodoxy than official aid agencies and governments. Their staff normally have greater flexibility to experiment, adapt and attempt new approaches. This is partly because the numbers involved in decision making are smaller, because local officials will probably not be as minutely involved, because scrutiny from outside is slight, the consequences of failure are much less, and because the ethos of "volunteerism" encourages the individual to develop his or her ideas.' However, he poignantly adds that 'the same factors could be cited as a problem – namely "amateurism". It fosters idiosyncrasy, lack of continuity and poor learning abilities.'

Citizen organizations working in the broad area of sustainable development, especially in the South, have a more than impressive record in this area. Arguably, much of the credibility that environmental groups currently enjoy is because of their achievement in championing innovative policy approaches at the local, national and international levels.

At the agenda setting phase citizen organizations as innovators play what Clark (1991: 59) calls a 'seeding role' by 'demonstrating the efficacy of a new idea, publicizing it, perhaps persuading those with access to greater power and budgets to take notice, and then encouraging the widespread adoption by others of the idea'. It is no mean testimony to the agenda setting role that citizen organizations have been able to play that a term like 'participatory planning' – which was once mocked by government decision makers – is now lingua franca for governmental development planners. Or, for that matter, 'sustainable development' – a term coined by IUCN and WWF in the 1980 *World Conservation Strategy* on the basis of earlier work done at the London-based International Institute for Environment and Development (IIED) and elsewhere – has become the mantra of governments around the globe. The concept of 'ecological accounting' now being developed with pioneering inputs from citizen organizations such as the World Resources Institute (WRI), is another concept that is fast gaining currency on policy agendas.

Very often what gives a citizen organization the ability and the credibility to place innovative ideas on policy agendas is that they have already demonstrated the efficacy of these innovations through small scale implementation. An example of an idea that began as a citizen sector project and now enjoys currency all over the world is the provision of credit to the very poor by the Grameen Bank in Bangladesh. The idea that giving credit to the very poor is indeed a very bankable proposition would not, until recently, have been considered a serious suggestion. However, today it is considered a model for micro-credit schemes throughout the world, even including the US, and enjoys a place of prominence on policy agendas of international development agencies and national governments in many countries (Clark, 1991: 59). Another example of citizen innovations influencing policy agendas is the role that Ralph Nader and his groups have played in the field of consumer rights or which the Rocky Mountain Institute (RMI) has similarly played in influencing the US energy agenda.

We have defined innovation at the agenda setting stage as instances where citizen organizations are able to place novel or previously unaccepted notions on the policy agenda. Innovation at the policy development stage is defined here as instances where novel approaches championed by citizen groups are accepted as the policies of choice. One example of such policy innovation is that of the so-called 'debt-for-nature swaps' in which developing country debts are 'bought' off at discounted rates and, in return, the debtor country agrees to take mutually agreed environmental measures. This innovative idea has been championed by a number of environmental groups in the North as well as the South, including Conservation International, the Nature Conservancy, Rainforest International, the Brazilian Institute for Economic and Social Analysis (IBASE) and the Ecuadorian Fundación Natura. These citizen groups have been active partners in a number of such deals which have now been completed in many countries including Bolivia, Ecuador, Costa Rica, the Philippines, Zambia and Madagascar (Porter and Brown, 1991).

Citizen organizations have also spurred policy innovations nationally. For example, the Aga Khan Rural Support Programme (AKRSP) in northern Pakistan has been so successful in facilitating village level community development that the model is now being used as the government's preferred approach to rural development (de Silva, 1994: 13). Similarly, in Peru, PROTERRA's land tilting activities in the Lurin valley influenced the shape of agrarian reform laws; and in India, the Amul Dairy cooperative provided the model for the government's National Dairy Development Program (Livernash, 1992: 226).

That citizen organizations as innovators have been able to contribute as much as they have to the agenda setting and policy development stages is, in fact, a testimony to the level of innovation that they invest at the project, or the policy implementation, stage. It is here, more than anywhere else, that they are able to both nurture and apply what Tom Dichter calls 'strategic knowledge'.[19] A particularly relevant example in this area is that of the Pakistan Institute of Environmental–Development Action Research (PIEDAR) whose action research in rural Punjab is geared specifically towards demonstrating the benefits of community-based irrigation management over bureaucratized irrigation management as a potentially more efficient implementation alternative.

Citizen organizations innovate as much by choice as out of necessity. Not all groups innovate, nor are all innovations worthy of emulation. Yet, some very spectacular examples of innovations can be listed which have made significant contributions towards operationalizing the otherwise nebulous concept of sustainable development. The Sukhomajri Watershed Restoration project, in the foothills of the Himalayas in India, for example, demonstrates how an innovative community approach to water management can succeed where more elaborate technical approaches would not. Similarly, the Cassava Integrated Pest Management initiative of the Nigeria-based International Institute for Tropical Agriculture (IITA) demonstrates how innovative biological solutions can be worthwhile alternatives to environmentally costly chemical pesticides. In yet another example, the spread of the Jiko Charcoal Stove in Kenya by the Kenyan Energy and Environment Organization (KENGO) demonstrated how a simple but innovative technology that is better both for the environment and human health can be popularized on a mass scale (Reid et al, 1988).

Technical innovation – especially innovations that seek to meet the needs of the grassroots while learning from the latest advances but not forgetting traditional practices – is an area where citizen organizations working on sustainable development are particularly active. Fisher (1993: 126) lists some examples: the Appropriate Technology Development Association in Lucknow, India; the Technology Consulting Center in Ghana; the CAMERTIC (Center for Agricultural Mechanization and Rural Technology) in Tanzania; Dian Desa in Indonesia and CEMAT in Guatemala. The list could go on indefinitely and could also include many citizen groups in industrialized countries such as the Boston Solar Energy Society and Appropriate Technology International.

Citizen Organizations as Service Providers

Service delivery is what more citizen organizations do more of than anything else. Whether it is providing food to the hungry, shelter to the homeless, employment opportunities to the unemployed or dispensing the benefits of education and health, the common impression of a citizen organization is one of providing services to the impoverished and needy. Although traditional relief services still remain a very large part of what citizen organizations do, recent research suggests that if one is to consider their activity at a global scale, then a large bulk of what they do would be better classified as dealing with human and economic development – and increasingly with sustainable development (Clark, 1991; Drabek, 1987; Fisher, 1993). Moreover, as Smith and Lipsky (1993: 3) remind us, the movement from charity to public service contracting translates into an enhanced political role for the sector:

> *Voluntary associations [have long enabled] citizens to express their collective interests and solve community problems. Today, in addition, they play a new political role in representing the welfare state to its citizens, providing a buffer between state policy and service delivery.*

A simultaneous trend is towards the glamourization of more political citizen activities such as policy advocacy which, some fear, will come at the cost of the service delivery role. However, Charlton and May (1995: 241) remind us that a 'service delivery role should not be marginalized as an adjunct to activities –from advocacy through citizenship education to lobbying – arbitrarily defined as "more" political; nor should it be dismissed as a distraction from these more important "political" missions'. This chapter's definition of service delivery builds on Charlton and May's notion that service delivery, even in its narrowest meaning and even in the most isolated project sense, is an essentially political – and, in fact, policy – mission. Moreover, we expand on this definition to include the delivery of policy services not only to the communities that citizen organizations serve, but to governments who are increasingly using citizen organizations both as official or unofficial advisers inducted to represent various community interests, and also as contracted policy consultants.

Citizen involvement at the agenda setting phase of the policy enterprise (in the form of actually providing the service of defining a policy agenda) comes overwhelmingly in their role as monitors, advocates and innovators. There are, however, occasional instances where citizen organizations are called in formally as service providers (often as public service contractors) in this capacity. A flurry of such examples came during the preparatory process for UNCED.[20] However, these should not be considered the norm.

One such example is that of the Business Council for Sustainable Development (BCSD), the creation of which was essentially facilitated by the UNCED secretariat and which was then formally invited by the secretariat to write a report outlining the business community's vision of sustainable development. This report, although not an official document, was nonetheless an exceptionally influential one. Another, more interesting example was of an initiative led by the IIED and other international environmental groups in collaboration with the United Nations Environment Programme (UNEP). This consortium provided assistance to selected developing countries in preparing their national reports for UNCED. In fact, a large number of countries in industrialized as well as developing countries directly involved citizen organizations in the preparation of these reports which, in many cases, have since influenced their policy agendas.

Another, somewhat unusual, example of involvement as a service provider at the agenda setting stage was when the government of Pakistan invited IUCN-Pakistan to hold a series of search conferences with various government agencies and citizen organizations to discuss whether a national conservation strategy should be developed for Pakistan. This turned out to be amongst the most significant agenda setting events for much of Pakistan's subsequent environmental policy initiatives; it exposed a set of individuals and institutions to environmental concerns which have since played important roles in shaping the country's environmental policy.

Citizen organizations as direct service providers have been far more active at the policy development stage. Although the presence of the citizen sector in an observer capacity at most international environmental treaty (that is policy) negotiations is considered to be an advocacy role within our framework, some international groups have, in fact, played a direct service delivery role. The most prominent amongst such organizations is IUCN. Not only does IUCN actually host the secretariats of particular international environmental treaties at its headquarters in Gland, Switzerland, but it has also been instrumental in shaping the language of a number of such treaties. These include the Convention Concerning the Protection of the World Cultural and Natural Heritage, signed in 1972, which was based on a draft produced by IUCN in 1971; and the Convention on International Trade in Endangered Species (CITES), signed in 1973, which was based on an IUCN initiative that went through three drafts over nearly a decade (McCormick, 1993: 134; Porter and Brown, 1991: 62).

Regional and country offices of IUCN have also played a significant role at the national level as policy development service providers. Since having co-initiated the concept of national conservation strategies (NCSs) in the 1982 *World Conservation Strategy* IUCN has taken it upon itself to propagate these cross-sectoral policy reviews; since then, over 60 countries, most of them in the South, have produced such strategies, many with the active collaboration of IUCN. In most of these cases other, more local, citizen organizations have also been involved in the policy development process. More recently, other international groups, such as IIED, have also become involved in similar initiatives, prominently including the preparation of national environmental action plans (Carew-Reid et al, 1994).

At the national level, citizen organizations are often invited to governmental commissions and similar initiatives which are directly or indirectly involved in policy development. This has been a common practice in Northern countries for quite some time and is now a growing trend in the South. This trend has been especially prevalent in environmental policy development because a) citizen organizations, in their advocacy capacity, often have a major role in bringing environmental issues to the policy table, and b) they bring a level of technical and practical knowledge of environmental issues as well as a sense of community interests that government agencies may not possess. Such interaction during policy development is one of the stated goals of the SDPI in Pakistan which has played an influential role in a number of government policy development exercises on both national and international issues. Similarly, like many other such groups all over the world, Canada's National Roundtable on the Environment and the Economy (NRTEE) has representation from a number of citizen organizations including the Island Nature Trust, the Ecology Action Center and Canadian Ecology Advocates (see Roseland, 1992).

Examples of the citizen sector playing a service provider role at the policy implementation stage are the most numerous. As suggested earlier, governments and donor agencies are rapidly realizing the strategic value of using citizen organizations for policy implementation tasks.

According to Charlton and May (1995: 246–247) this may be because the sector's reputation for 'probity (qua honesty)' is the most significant of the NGO sector's 'qualitative advantages' over state functionaries, and government agencies are realizing that 'if rehabilitation of the policy implementation process is to occur under contemporary conditions, it will almost certainly require the direct assistance and support of the non-governmental sector to achieve what the governmental sector can no longer be expected to aspire to unaided'. This is not without strategic advantages for the citizen sector:[21]

> The insertion of [citizen organizations] into the policy and programme cycles of governments and their donors principally as project implementers places the sector in a strategic position, pursuing roles as policy mediators and service providers that may appear mainly economic in form but are as clearly perceived by their beneficiaries as political in their content (Charlton and May, 1995: 240).

We are most concerned here, however, with citizen initiatives which serve to fill a major void in what might otherwise be considered an area of state responsibility. These, then, are the areas where citizen organizations are filling in for the state either because they are able to provide services which the state is unable to, or are able to provide them more efficiently and effectively than state agencies. Examples that immediately come to mind include the Bangladesh Rural Advancement Committee (BRAC) which works in 2225 villages and, as only one of its many diverse development projects, has provided oral rehydration training for 11 million households; and the Organization of Rural Associations for Progress (ORAP) in Zimbabwe whose employment generation projects reach over 60,000 people (Fisher, 1993: 95). The AKRSP runs a similarly broad development programme in northern Pakistan. All three are large enough in size and comprehensive enough in scope to rival some government agencies and, in fact, are looked upon both by their beneficiaries and by governmental agencies in the areas they serve as pseudo-government agencies, or what Salamon (1987) might call 'third party government'. Similar programmes also abound in Northern countries, with one obvious example being planned parenthood clinics all over the US which have been at the forefront of providing contraceptive education and services. Given the volatile politics that surrounds issues of contraception, and by extension abortion, such clinics are able to provide a service that the US government is unwilling to provide.

Another way in which citizen activity is harnessed in the policy implementation phase is through what Durning (1989: 78) calls 'broad community-government mobilizations'. He points out that extraordinary gains have followed in the (admittedly rare) cases where local–national alliances have been forged:

> During World War II millions of American, Asian, European, and
> Soviet civilians recycled materials, conserved energy, and planted
> victory gardens to boost food production. Later, South Korea used
> village-level organizations to plant enormous expanses of trees,
> implement national population policies, and boost agricultural
> production. Zimbabwe has trained more than 500 community-
> selected family planners to improve maternal and child health and
> control population growth. And after the 1979 Nicaraguan revolu-
> tion a massive government literacy campaign sent 80,000
> volunteers into the countryside ... in one year they raised literacy
> from 50 to 87 per cent.

Populating the Policy Map

The principal conclusion that emerges from the evidence and examples
presented above is that in the various roles that citizen organizations play
as policy entrepreneurs, they have been active in all stages of the policy
stream. Populating the policy space we had defined in Table 8.1 with some
of the examples discussed above gives us Table 8.2. Significantly – but not
surprisingly – it demonstrates the sheer breadth of citizen occupancy of
the policy map. It is presented here to highlight the conclusion that in the
area of sustainable development the global community of citizen organizations has been very active at all policy stages and in all policy roles.
Moreover, this trend encompasses organizations of various sizes and structural features, working in various geographic locations and operating
under a variety of different contextual constraints.

The purpose of the matrix Table 8.2 is not to suggest that all citizen
organizations are necessarily – or equally – adept and effective in the
various roles discussed. It is only to point out that these are roles that
citizen organizations are demonstrably capable of playing and are likely to
continue playing as their involvement in the policy process increases. One
must also reiterate that the matrix should not be seen as being composed
of rigid pigeonholes. Nor should it be seen as a classification schema. For
example, any contribution made at the policy development stage will
necessarily be informed by, and have an impact upon, policy implementation and agenda setting. Similarly, particular organizations which invest
effort, resources and expertise in a particular policy issue are often likely to
follow it through the various policy stages or in various roles.[22]

In short, the policy map defined by the matrix should not be seen as a
rigid edifice of 12 neatly defined boxes, but rather as a flexibly structured
constellation of categories with permeable boundaries. Constructed as
such, we should allow for cross-influences along both axes.

Table 8.2 *Examples of Citizen Organizations Inhabiting all Nooks of the Policy Space*

	Monitors	Advocates	Innovators	Service Providers
Agenda Setting	Worldwatch Institute Center for Science and the Environment Third World Network World Wide Fund for Nature (WWF)	Green Forum Union of Concerned Scientists International Waterfowl Research Bureau (IWRB)	Grameen Bank World Resources Institute (WRI) Rocky Mountain Institute (RMI)	International Institute for Environment and Development (IIED) Business Council for Sustainable Development (BCSD)
Policy Development	International Institute for Sustainable Development (IISD) US Citizens Network for Sustainable Development	Women Environment and Development Organization (WEDO) Groupo de los Cien Urban Popular Movement (MUP) Sierra Club	Fundación Natura Nature Conservancy Brazilian Institute for Economic and Social Analysis (IBASE) PROTERRA	International Union for the Conservation of Nature (IUCN) Sustainable Development Policy Institute (SDPI)
Policy Implementation	Friends of the Earth Consumers Association of Penang (CAP) Shehri	Greenpeace International Narmada Bachao Andholan (NBA) Greenbelt Movement	Pakistan Institute for Environment– Development Action Research (PIEDAR) Sukhomajri Watershed Restoration Dian Desa	Bangladesh Rural Advancement Committee (BRAC) Organization of Rural Associations for Progress (ORAP)

PUTTING THE POLICY MAP TO USE

Two important points emerge from the preceding discussion. First, the policy influence of citizen organizations – in both North and South – extends beyond narrowly defined notions of conventional advocacy and we need to look at the full range of roles in which these organizations can, and do, influence the substance and process of public policy. Second, the broad roles that citizen organizations play at the various stages of the policy process are, in fact, similar enough in North and South for a general framework to be constructed that can be applicable to studies from either domain and, therefore, also to comparative research within or between them.

The policy map matrix, as defined above, has the virtue of being independent of the geographic or economic location (for example North or South, Asian, European or North American), the substantive sector (for example environment, health, disaster relief) or the political system (democratic or dictatorial, unitary or federal and so on) in which an organization operates. Although it is necessarily broad in scope, the applicability of the framework to data on citizen organizations from either North or South can provide a basis for the type of systematic comparative research that is required for meaningfully bridging the chasm that exists between the sectors in these two worlds.[23] Such research can make use of the policy map matrix either as a tool for organizing data or as a device for analysing it.

A Tool for Organizing Data

A practical utility of the policy map matrix is in providing scholars and practitioners with a handy device for organizing data on the policy influence of citizen organizations. Applied to any given policy episode, country, region or organization, the matrix can help organize our understanding of who (that is, which organizations or sub-components thereof) is influencing public policy, how (that is, in which role) and when (that is, at what stage). This is how the preceding section used the matrix. There are, however, a number of other ways in which the matrix could be used as a tool for organizing data on citizen organizations.

For instance, instead of populating the policy space with examples from around the globe as we have done in Table 8.2, we could focus on a single policy episode and see which organizations have been active in which role and at which stage of the process. One example that has already been mentioned above is of the PNCS process.[24] This was a major cross-sectoral policy review which aimed to align national development priorities with the need for sustainable development planning. The agenda setting stage began in the early 1980s, gathered momentum towards the middle of the decade and by 1988 actual policy development had begun in earnest. In 1992 the government of Pakistan adopted the PNCS as the de facto environmental policy of the country. Its implementation is now in its second phase. Table 8.3 highlights the influence that selected citizen organizations had on this policy process in Pakistan.

Citizen organizations have been actively involved in all stages of the PNCS process, and in Pakistan and abroad it is often quoted as a model of collaboration between government agencies and the citizen sector. In fact, the growth of environmental organizations in Pakistan has been directly influenced by the PNCS process. IUCN-Pakistan was the key impetus behind the entire process and was actually responsible for bringing it onto the policy agenda. It did so first through arranging visits by international

Table 8.3 *Examples of Citizen Organizations which Influence the PNCS Process in Pakistan*

	Monitors	Advocates	Innovators	Service Providers
Agenda Setting	—	WWF-Pakistan	Aga Khan Rural Support Programme (AKRSP)	IUCN-Pakistan
Policy Development	SHEHRI– Citizens for a Better Environment	Shirkat Gah Women's Resource Center	PNCS Unit	IUCN-Pakistan
Policy Implementation	Journalist's Resource Center (JRC)	Sustainable Development Policy Institute (SDPI)	Pakistan Institute for Environment– Development Action Research (PIEDAR)	Sungi Development Foundation

experts and finally by hosting a conference in 1986 where government agencies were brought together with international and national experts and some citizen organizations to study the need for, and the possible shape of, such a strategy for Pakistan. IUCN was later appointed as the lead organization in the preparation of the actual policy document. As such, IUCN-Pakistan played the critical service provision role at both the agenda setting and policy development stage. It continues to play this role at the implementation stage but is now joined by a vast array of other citizen organizations, such as Sungi Development Foundation.

Partly due to the dearth of citizen organizations working in the environmental area at the time, there was no particular organization which played a major monitoring role at the agenda setting stage. However, during policy development a number of organizations, such as Shehri (Citizens for a Better Environment) and Shirkat Gah Women's Resource Center began playing this role by being involved in the discussions both for the purposes of keeping the process honest and for advocating their particular interests. An even larger number of citizen groups are now indirectly playing a monitoring role at the implementation stage while the Journalist's Resource Center is playing it directly through its magazine *The Way Ahead*.

Apart from IUCN-Pakistan itself, the key advocacy role at the agenda setting stage was played by WWF-Pakistan. During the policy development stage this role was played by a number of organizations including, as already mentioned, Shehri and Shirkat Gah Women's Resource Center. Now, during the implementation stage, the key advocate for implementation is the SDPI which was established as a result of the PNCS process with such advocacy being one of its principal mandates.

Organizations which influenced the agenda setting stage as policy innovators included IUCN-International which had pioneered the idea of national conservation strategies and the AKRSP whose projects in northern Pakistan highlighted both the need and potential direction for such a strategy. At the policy development stage, the innovation principally came from the PNCS Unit which had been set up to foster a collaborative effort between key government agencies and IUCN-Pakistan's strategy team. Importantly, the PNCS Unit tapped into a vast reservoir of innovative ideas through a series of experts meetings and public hearings in which a number of citizen organizations actively participated. At the implementation stage, a number of citizen organizations are playing the role of innovator. A key example is the PIEDAR which was also created as a direct result of the PNCS process and one of whose principal projects is seeking innovative policy responses to the issue of water use efficiency in the agricultural sector.

Amongst the many other alternative uses for the matrix would be to populate the policy space it defines with examples of how a single citizen group has tried to impact public policy at its various stages in different roles. A citizen organization may undertake such a study as part of its own strategic planning to better grasp the efficacy of its policy efforts. For example, such an enquiry may suggest that the organization in question is much more effective and efficient in a particular role, at a particular stage, on a particular type of issue. It would be advisable, then, for it to shift the focus of its policy efforts in that direction to get the biggest bang for its buck. Yet another use may be to populate the matrix at a country, regional, or substantive issue level to highlight examples of different citizen organizations influencing public policy. Such a study would allow scholars to get a better profile of the policy influence of the citizen sector in that geographic or substantive area.

A Tool for Analysing Data

The much more important task that necessarily follows the organization of data within any framework is to make analytic sense of the cases being reviewed. The policy map defined in Table 8.1 can also assist in organizing this analysis. More than that, it can be a useful device for generating and studying questions about citizen organizations in the policy stream. For example, a few of the questions that emerge from the preceding discussion include: are particular forms of relationships between citizen organizations and governments likely to be more dominant at particular points on the policy map? Are there particular areas of citizen competencies within the larger policy stream? What type of citizen organizations are more or less likely to be successful at which particular area on the policy map? A much larger list of such questions could potentially be generated from the framework.

Answering any of the above would require much more systematic research and detailed analysis of particular cases than has been available for this study. However, even with the broad information that was used here, some tentative ideas begin to emerge which can be considered hypotheses for more detailed future research. Consider, for example, the question of whether there are particular roles or stages in the policy process where citizen organizations are more (or less) likely to have a significant impact on public policy? As a way of hypothesizing about the possible answer one might reflect upon the array of examples discussed earlier and attempt an informed – albeit necessarily subjective and qualitative – assessment about organizations working in the general area of sustainable development.

Based on the examples discussed, Table 8.4 presents the tentative results of such hypothesizing about which roles have provided the citizen sector with the opportunity to make either strong, moderate or weak impacts at the various policy stages.[25] This should be seen as a descriptive rather than a normative assessment. That the citizen impact in a particular role at a particular policy stage has tended to be weak should not be interpreted as a call to strengthen that role but to ponder upon the institutional reasons behind this situation. For example, given how jealously governments in all polities guard their prerogatives as the societal fonts of policy articulation, it should not be surprising that the impact of citizen organizations during the policy development stage tends to be strong only in their roles as advocates.

By similar token, it should not be a surprise that citizen organizations working towards sustainable development goals tend to have the strongest impact in their role as advocates or at the policy implementation stage. As advocates –which for them is a fundamental defining function – they best invoke their organizational motivation of actualizing particular visions shared by their workers and constituencies. By the implementation stage policy has often lost its fuzziness and become concrete – often taking the shape of specific projects – and it is therefore easier for citizen groups to mobilize their constituents for the purpose of actually getting things done.

In the absence of detailed case-based studies, the value of something like Table 8.4 is obviously limited. However, such an exercise can be a useful first step towards developing a well-defined and systematic research regime on the policy impact of citizen organizations. For example,

Table 8.4 *Towards Hypotheses: The Potential Policy Impact of Citizen Organizations Working on Issues Related to Sustainable Development*

	Monitors	Advocates	Innovators	Service Providers
Agenda Setting	Moderate	Strong	Moderate	Weak
Policy Development	Weak	Strong	Weak	Moderate
Policy Implementation	Strong	Strong	Strong	Strong

in light of Table 8.4 one might devise a research programme to look systematically at a set of organizations (or a set of policy episodes) either within a country or between countries to see whether any general patterns of efficacy exist. In controlling for similarities or differences between the type of organizations being studied one could shed light on the question of what type of organizations are more suited for what type of policy activities, in what role and at what stage of the policy enterprise. Similarly, one might run parallel studies in Northern and Southern contexts to see what may or may not be common. The possibilities are many, but in each instance detailed case-based research would be required. However, in starting from a general framework, that research could then be plugged back into the framework to see what, if any, generalizations can be defended and what lessons might be drawn from experiences in different contexts. Such research would have much to contribute to our understanding of the global citizen sector.

LESSONS LEARNED

Focusing on the substantive area of sustainable development, this paper has attempted to construct a general framework for understanding how citizen organizations influence the process and substance of public policy. It has done so using examples of citizen organizations from both North and South. A conscious effort has been made to use examples of organizations of varying structural features, working at all levels (grassroots to international) in a variety of political, economic and social settings. Any conclusions that emerge from this discussion must be accompanied by the disclaimer that in trying to understand the big picture of policy influence by the citizen sector we have, by necessity, used a very broad brush. That many finer details may have been lost in adopting such an approach does not imply that such details are not considered to be important, but only that they have been beyond the scope of this exercise. Having said that, some general lessons begin to emerge about the activities of the citizen sector within the policy stream.

*   There is a case to be made for actually defining citizen organizations in both North and South as policy entrepreneurs or para-policy organizations. We can do so on the basis of their normative characteristic being a) the bringing together – in associations – of actors with shared normative values, b) for the purpose of actualizing particular social visions. Much of the action and aspiration of the citizen sector (even where it calls itself the non-governmental sector) can be boiled down to either doing itself, or wanting governments to do, things that governments either a) refuse to do, b) do not do enough of, c) are incapable of doing or d) are prevented from doing.
*   Whether they define themselves explicitly as advocacy organizations or not, most citizen organizations are in the business of influencing

policy. We need to broaden our understanding of such influence by looking beyond narrow and restrictive notions of policy advocacy as the only, or even principal, role that citizen organizations play in the policy stream. Citizen organizations also influence public policy through their activity as policy monitors; as innovators of new approaches; and as service providers.

- Expanding our conception of how citizen organizations influence the policy enterprise shows that, in fact, they influence policy at all its stages: agenda setting, policy development and policy implementation. Moreover, the broad roles that such organizations play – monitors, advocates, innovators and service providers – in the policy stream are, in fact, the same in Northern and Southern contexts. Placing the three policy stages on one axis and the roles in which citizen organizations influence policy on the other defines a map of the policy space within which citizen organizations operate in trying to influence policy. This policy map can be used as a tool for organizing as well as analysing data. It can also help in generating and studying key questions about the impact of citizen organizations on the policy enterprise. Most importantly, such a framework can be useful for comparative research within and between countries which can facilitate better North–South learning and possibly lead to broader theory-building studies on the policy influence of the citizen sector.

ENDNOTES

1   There have been some brave, even seminal, attempts at expanding our conceptual understanding of this genre of organizations (for example Brown and Korten, 1991; Clark, 1991; Esman and Uphoff, 1984; Fisher, 1998; Kramer, 1981; Weisbrod, 1988; Wolch, 1990). However, most of these have focused either solely on NGOs in the South or on nonprofit organizations in the North.

2   This chapter uses the term 'citizen sector' to refer to what is variously called civil society or the nonprofit, the voluntary, the independent, the charitable, the people's, the philanthropic, the associational or the third sector. A more detailed treatment of this choice of terminology is provided in the section on definitions.

3   Salamon (1992) points out that each of these various terms highlights one aspect of the sector while overlooking others. Each, therefore, shows only part of the picture. In fact, if the purest interpretation of these terms were to be applied, non-governmental would include the market sector just as nonprofit would encompass the government.

4   This conception is designed to be expansive. It makes no distinction between organizations by size, geographic locale, financial base or substantive interest, and would include industrialized as well as developing country groups. Moreover, no moral claim is implied in the usage and the Ku Klux Klan would be accepted as no less of a citizen organization by definition than, say, the American Civil Liberties Union (ACLU). Bigotry, after all, can be as much of a citizen trait as altruism.

5   The concept of citizen organizations as 'para-policy organizations' is not dissimilar to notions of nonprofits as 'semi-public institutions' or 'third party government' as used by Salamon (1994) in advancing his theory of 'voluntary failure'.

6   With some exceptions (eg Esman and Uphoff, 1984; Fisher, 1998; Kramer, 1981; Smith and Lipsky, 1993; Tandon, 1987) citizen organization–government relations have received less scholarly attention than relations between these organizations and philanthropist or international assistance agencies, or between citizen organizations of various types such as grassroots and grassroots support organizations.

7   This, however, should not be a surprise. The 'non' in non-governmental is as much a statement about what these organizations are not like in form, structure, vision and values as it is a statement about what institutional sector they are most like in the issues and activities that concern them the most.

8   Such reasoning can be linked back to theories about 'government failure' being the rationale for non-governmental or nonprofit organizations (see Douglas, 1987; Weisbrod, 1988; Wolch, 1990).

9   Using extensive examples from Asia, Africa and Latin America, Julie Fisher (1998) provides an insightful discussion on the growing depth and breadth of the global trend towards more citizen–prince relations.

10 Camilleri and Falk (1992: 3) have argued that the concept of state sovereignty is being challenged by 'the emergence of new social movements with both local and transnational consciousness'. For more discussions on the threat to citizen autonomy from increasing interaction with government agencies see Tandon (1989) and Fisher (1998).

11 In Najam (1996c) a '3Cs' model of understanding citizen–prince relations is proposed. This interests-based model is based not on the nature of the host regime (eg democratic, autocratic, bureaucratic, dictatorial etc) but on the degree of convergence or divergence of the goals and interests of particular citizen organizations and particular governmental agencies on particular issues. The 3Cs model argues that three types of relationships are likely: confrontation, complementarity or collaboration. In the first, governmental and citizen organizations are likely to have opposing objectives and act to thwart each other's efforts; in the second, they are likely to act separately but towards converging objectives; in the third, they would tend to work jointly towards joint objectives. It suggests that a robust approach towards studying citizen sector–government relations is through the complex lens of inter-institutional interests, rather than simpler notions of comparative advantage, or the even simpler perceptions of antipathy for all governmental motivations. It is suggested that even where government is the dominant and dominating institutional player, the ultimate relationship is a strategic institutional decision made by both the government and the citizen organizations in question.

12 The descriptions of the three policy 'stages' or 'phases' are necessarily simplistic. They do *not*, however, imply a linear, top-down view of the policy enterprise. Moreover, none of the three phases are static or finite. Each is an ongoing or overlapping process. Much like music that has to be rewritten in the act of playing it, agendas, policies and implementation are ever evolving and ever responding to changing balances of institutional interests, alliances and negotiation. For a literature review on the complex nature of the policy process, and especially the policy implementation process, see Najam (1995).

175

13 At one level, the four roles defined here are in a natural progression. As monitors, citizen groups keep an eye on what may be wrong, as advocates they actively seek steps towards what they believe to be the right direction, as innovators they suggest what these steps might be and as implementers they carry out such steps. Having said that, it is acknowledged that this progression, while seemingly (and simplistically) natural, is not necessarily realistic and is hardly ever this neat.

14 In *Getting to the 21st Century: Voluntary Action and the Global Agenda*, David Korten (1990: 185–197) suggests four critical codes for voluntary action: 1) catalyzing the transformation of institutions, policies and values; 2) monitoring and protesting against abuses of power; 3) facilitating reconciliation; and 4) providing essential community services. The first of these corresponds roughly with what we are calling innovation and advocacy, the second with monitoring and the fourth with service provision. The third – facilitating reconciliation – is, in fact, less of a policy function; and the parts that are so may be covered under innovation.

15 Unlike other issues where citizen interest was triggered by existing political concern (eg human rights) one can generally say that interest in the environment was propelled onto the political agenda significantly because of activism and advocacy by citizen organizations. Arguably, although citizen advocacy in the human rights area has certainly made it a bigger political issue than it otherwise might have been, it was the issue's already latent political importance that fertilized the growth of citizen organizations in that area. The distinction to be made is that between expanding an existing space in the policy agenda on the one hand, and the identification of a crack, the elbowing in, and then the pushing at its sides to create a new space on the other. Citizen organizations seem to have played the latter role in the case of environment and development.

16 The advocacy effort of the Center for International Environment Law (CIEL) with island states vulnerable to climate change and sea-level rise was so successful that it resulted in the creation of the Association of Small Island States (AOSIS) and CIEL became an official adviser to these governments (McMahon, 1993).

17 The distinction between monitoring and advocacy at this phase can often become blurred and needs to be reiterated. Monitoring is a reporting task – to track what is happening and how it is different from what was supposed to happen. Advocacy is different in that it entails a judgement call on what ought to happen.

18 Citizen organizations played an important advocacy role at all stages of the Narmada Dam process. What is highlighted here is the role they played at the implementation stage, ie after the Indian government had already decided to build the dam. Even at this late stage advocacy by citizen organizations was able to have an impact on the details of how the project was ultimately carried out.

19 Dichter's notion of 'strategic knowledge' comes to me via Julie Fisher (personal communication).

20 This flurry may be partly attributed to the sense of euphoria that the Earth Summit generated about the prospect of global cooperation for sustainable development, and about the role that the citizen sector may play in such cooperation. Moreover, the scale and visibility of the conference caught a lot of governments, especially in the South, by surprise, and forced them to do their

environmental policy thinking on fast forward; any help they could get from citizen organizations in this regard was, therefore, very welcome.

21 As Clark (1991: 45) points out, there are also disadvantages and dangers attached to such collaboration: 'Public Service contractors will often tailor their projects and indeed their organizations to suit the official aid agencies who fund them. They are happy for the project initiative to come from governments and for their role to be that of a subcontractor implementing a component of another's project. And they are equally content to act on strong hints they receive from official donors that the latter would "welcome" funding applications for a particular type of project' (see also Smith and Lipsky, 1993).

22 Consider, as an example, the role of service provider that IUCN-Pakistan played in the development of the PNCS. As discussed later, IUCN played this role at the agenda setting stage as well as at the policy development stage, and is now playing it equally at the policy implementation stage (de Silva, 1994). In another example, also from Pakistan, the SDPI was involved in all stages of policy implementation regarding the transfer of a mercury-based chloro-alkali plant from Denmark; as a monitor it tracked the import of this dirty technology, as an advocate it protested against this import, as an innovator it worked with technical experts to devise innovations to the technology that would reduce its environmental impact, and as a service provider it worked with industry and government to implement and institutionalize these innovations (Samee, 1995).

23 This is not to suggest that this is a unique framework for such comparative research. It is only to stress that applying some common framework to cases in North and South will be necessary if we want to nurture learning between the two worlds.

24 All the discussion on the PNCS is based on the author's direct involvement in that process. For a detailed analysis of the process see Runnalls (1995).

25 A related question which Table 8.4 does not address concerns the type of organization (eg large international organization, grassroots organization, coalition of citizen groups etc) that may be more, or less, influential in a particular role or stage.

26 Although different in both focus and form, this chapter has grown out of an earlier article, *Nongovernmental Organizations as Policy Entrepreneurs: In Pursuit of Sustainable Development* (Najam, 1996; PONPO Working Paper No 231, Program on Non-Profit Organizations, Yale University, New Haven.

BIBLIOGRAPHY

Ali, S (1993) 'Gunyar: leading by example', *NCS Bulletin*, Vol 5, No 2, pp25–27
Annis, S (1987) 'Can small-scale development be a large-scale policy? The case of Latin America', *World Development*, 15 (Supplement), pp129–134
Annis, S (1988) 'What is not the same about the urban poor: the case of Mexico City', in Lewis, J P et al (eds) *Strengthening the Poor: What Have We Learnt*, Overseas Development Council, Washington, DC
Bratton, M (1990) 'Non-governmental organizations in Africa: can they influence public policy?', *Development and Change*, Vol 21, No 1, pp87–118
Brown, L D and Korten, D C (1991) 'Working more effectively with nongovernmental organizations', in Paul, S and Israel, A (eds) *Nongovernmental Organizations and the World Bank*, The World Bank, Washington, DC

Camilleri, J A and Falk, J (1992) *The End of Sovereignty? The Politics of a Shrinking and Fragmenting World*, Edward Elgar, Aldershot, UK

Carew-Reid, J, Prescott-Allen, R, Bass, S and Dalal-Clayton, B (1994) *Strategies for National Sustainable Development: A Handbook for their Planning and Implementation*, Earthscan, London

Cernea, M M (1988) *Nongovernmental Organizations and Local Development*, World Bank Discussion Paper No 40, The World Bank, Washington, DC

Charlton, R and May, R (1995) 'NGOs, politics, projects and probity: a policy implementation perspective', *Third World Quarterly*, Vol 16, No 2, pp237–255

Chayes, A and Handler Chayes, A (1993) 'On compliance', *International Organization*, Vol 47, No 2, pp175–205

Chen, M A (1996) 'Engendering world conferences: the international women's movement and the UN', in Weiss, T G and Gordenker, L (eds) *NGOs, the UN and Global Governance*, Lynne Rienner, Colorado

Clark, John (1991) *Democratizing Development: The Role of Volunteer Organizations*, Earthscan, London

Cohen, M D, March, J G and Olsen, J P (1972) 'A garbage can model of organizational choice', *Administrative Science Quarterly*, Vol 17, No 1, pp1–25

CSE (1982) *The People's Report on the State of India's Environment (1981–82)*, Center for Science and the Environment, New Delhi

Dawkins, K (1991) *Sharing Rights and Responsibilities for the Environment: Assessing Potential Roles for Non-governmental Organizations in International Decisionmaking*, Masters Thesis, Department of Urban Studies and Planning, MIT

de Silva, D (1994) 'Government versus the NGOs', *The Way Ahead – Pakistan's Environment and Development Quarterly*, Vol 1, No 2, pp12–13

Diaz-Albertini, J (1993) 'Nonprofit advocacy in weakly institutionalized political systems: the case of NGDOs in Lima, Peru', *Nonprofit and Voluntary Sector Quarterly*, Vol 22, No 4, pp317–337

Dichter, T W (1988) 'The changing world of northern NGOs – problems, paradoxes and possibilities', *Development – Journal of SID*, No 4, pp36–40

Douglas, J (1987) 'Economic theories of nonprofit organization', in Powell, W W (ed) *The Nonprofit Sector: A Research Handbook*, Yale University Press, New Haven

Drabek, A G (ed) (1987) 'Development alternatives: the challenge for NGOs', Supplement issue of *World Development*, Vol 15

Durning, A B (1989) 'People power and development', *Foreign Policy*, Fall, No 76, pp66–82

Enge, E and Malkenes, R I (1993) 'Non-governmental organizations at UNCED: another successful failure?', in Bergesen, H O and Parmann, G (Fridtjof Nansen Institute, Norway) (eds) *Green Globe Yearbook of International Co-operation on Environment and Development 1993*, Oxford University Press, New York

Esman, M J and Uphoff, N T (1984) *Local Organizations: Intermediaries in Rural Development*, Cornell University, Ithaca

Ferber, B, Ferretti, J and Fischer, L M (1995) 'Building an environmental protection framework for North America: the role of the non-governmental community', in Bergesen, H O and Parmann, G (Fridtjof Nansen Institute, Norway) (eds) *Green Globe Yearbook of International Co-operation on Environment and Development 1995*, Oxford University Press, New York

Finger, M (1994) 'Environmental NGOs in the UNCED process', in Princen, T and Finger, M (eds) *Environmental NGOs in World Politics: Linking the Local and the Global*, Routledge, London

Fisher, J (1993) *The Road from Rio: Sustainable Development and the Nongovernmental Movement in the Third World*, Praeger, Connecticut

Fisher, J (1998) *Nongovernments: NGOs and the Political Development of the Third World*, Kumarian Press, Connecticut

Gordenker, L and Weiss, T G (1996) 'Pluralizing global governance: analytical approaches and dimensions', in Weiss, T G and Gordenker, L (eds) *NGOs, the UN and Global Governance*, Lynne Rienner, Colorado

Hall, P D (1987) 'A historical overview of the private nonprofit sector', in Powell, W W (ed) *The Nonprofit Sector: A Research Handbook*, Yale University Press, New Haven

Hansmann, H (1987) 'Economic theories of nonprofit organization', in Powell, W W (ed) *The Nonprofit Sector: A Research Handbook*, Yale University Press, New Haven

Hulme, D and Edwards, M (eds) (1997) *NGOs, States and Donors: Too Close for Comfort?* St Martin's Press, New York

James, E (1987) 'The nonprofit sector in comparative perspective', in Powell, W W (ed) *The Nonprofit Sector: A Research Handbook*, Yale University Press, New Haven

Kingdon, J (1984) *Agendas, Alternatives, and Public Policies*, Harper Collins, New York

Korten, D C (1990) *Getting to the 21st Century: Voluntary Action and the Global Agenda*, Kumarian Press, Connecticut

Korten, D C (1991) 'The role of nongovernmental organizations in development: changing patterns and perspectives', in Paul, S and Israel, A (eds) *Nongovernmental Organizations and the World Bank*, The World Bank, Washington, DC

Kramer, R M (1981) *Voluntary Agencies in the Welfare State*, University of California Press, Berkeley

Laws, D (1991) 'The Antarctic minerals regime negotiations', in Susskind, Lawrence E, Siskind, E and Breslin, J W (eds) *Nine Case Studies in International Environmental Negotiation*, MIT–Harvard Public Disputes Program, Cambridge

Lélé, Sharachandra M (1991) 'Sustainable development: a critical review', *World Development*, Vol 19, No 6, pp607–21

Lindborg, N (1992) 'Nongovernmental organizations: their past, present, and future role in international environmental negotiations', in Susskind, L E, Dolin, E J and Breslin, J W (eds) *International Environmental Treaty Making*, Program on Negotiation at Harvard Law School, Cambridge

Livernash, R (1992) 'Policies and institutions: nongovernmental organizations: a growing force in the developing world', *World Resources 1992–93*, a report by the World Resources Institute in collaboration with UNEP and UNDP, Oxford University Press, New York

Lyster, S (1985) *International Wildlife Law*, Grotius Publications, Cambridge

Majone, G (1989) *Evidence, Argument and Persuasion in the Policy Process*, Yale University Press, New Haven

Mathews, J (1997) 'Power shift', *Foreign Policy*, Vol 76, No 1, pp50–66

McCormick, J (1993) 'International nongovernmental organizations: prospects for a global environmental movement', in Kamieniecki, S (ed) *Environmental Politics in the International Arena: Movements, Parties, Organizations, and Policy*, State University of New York Press, Stony Brook

McMahon, V M (1993) 'Environmental nongovernmental organizations at intergovernmental negotiations', in Susskind, L E, Moomaw, W R and Najam, A (eds) *Papers on International Environmental Negotiations*, volume 3, Program on Negotiation at Harvard Law School, Cambridge

Najam, A (1993) 'International environmental negotiation: a strategy for the South', in Susskind, L E, Moomaw, W R and Najam, A (eds) *Papers on International Environmental Negotiation*, volume 3, Program on Negotiation at Harvard Law School, Cambridge

Najam, A (1995) 'Learning from the literature on implementation: a synthesis perspective', IIASA Working Paper WP–95–61, International Institute of Applied Systems Analysis, Laxenburg, Austria

Najam, A (1996a) 'Understanding the third sector: revisiting the prince, the merchant and the citizen', *Nonprofit Management and Leadership*, Vol 7, No 2, pp203–219

Najam, A (1996b) 'NGO accountability: a conceptual framework', *Development Policy Review*, Vol 14, No 4, pp339–353

Najam, A (1996c) 'The 3Cs of NGO–government relations: confrontation, complementarity and collaboration', paper presented at the 2nd International Conference of the International Society for Third Sector Research (ISTR), July 18–21, 1996, Mexico City

Nerfin, M (1986) 'Neither prince nor merchant: citizen – an introduction to the third system', in Ahooja-Patel, K, Drabek, A G and Nerfin, M (eds) *World Economy in Transition*, Pergamon Press, Oxford

Nunez, A M (1994) *NAFTA and its Environmental Parallel Agreement*, Masters thesis, Department of Urban Studies and Planning, MIT

Opuku-Mensah, P (1997) 'Allies or adversaries? NGOs and the Africa state: the case of Ghana', paper presented at the 26th Annual Conference of the Association for Research on Nonprofit Organizations and Voluntary Action (ARNOVA), Indianapolis, December 4–6

Porter, G and Welsh Brown, J (1991) *Global Environmental Politics*, Westview Press, Boulder

Princen, T, Finger, M and Manno, J (1995) 'Nongovernmental organizations in world environmental politics', *International Environmental Affairs*, Vol 7, No 1, pp42–58

Reid, W V, Barnes, J N and Blackwelder, B (1988) *Bankrolling Successes: A Portfolio of Sustainable Development Projects*, Environmental Policy Institute and National Wildlife Federation, Washington, DC

Roseland, M (1992) *Toward Sustainable Cities: A Resource Book for Municipal and Local Governments*, National Roundtable on the Environment and the Economy, Ottawa

Runnalls, D (1995) *The Story of Pakistan's NCS: An Analysis of its Evolution*, IUCN-Pakistan, Karachi

Salamon, L M (1987) 'Partners in public service: the scope and theory of government–nonprofit relations', in Powell, W W (ed) *The Nonprofit Sector: A Research Handbook*, Yale University Press, New Haven

Salamon, L M (1992) *America's Nonprofit Sector: A Primer*, The Foundation Center, New York

Salamon, L M (1994) 'The rise of the nonprofit sector', *Foreign Affairs*, Vol 73, No 4, pp109–122

Salamon, L M and Anheier, H K (eds) (1997) *Defining the Nonprofit Sector: A Cross-National Analysis*, Manchester University Press, Manchester

Samee, M (1995) 'A first for environmental advocacy', *The Way Ahead –Pakistan's Environment and Development Quarterly*, Vol 2, No 1, pp23–26

Sands, P (1992) 'The role of environmental NGOs in international environmental law', *Development – Journal of SID*, No 2, pp28–31

Smith, S R and Lipsky, M (1993) *Nonprofits for Hire: The Welfare State in the Age of Contracting*, Harvard University Press, Cambridge

Spiro, P J (1995) 'New global communities: nongovernmental organizations in international decision-making institutions', *The Washington Quarterly*, Vol 18, No 1, pp45–56

Stairs, K and Taylor, P (1992) 'Non-governmental organizations and the legal protection of the oceans: a case study', in Hurrell, A and Kingsbury, B (eds) *The International Politics of the Environment*, Oxford University Press, New York

Starke, L (1990) *Signs of Hope: Working Towards Our Common Future*, Oxford University Press, New York

Stone, D A (1988) *Policy Paradox and Political Reason*, Scott, Foresman, and Co, Illinois

Tandon, R (1987) 'The relationship between NGOs and government', paper presented to the Conference on the Promotion of Autonomous Development, New Delhi, PRIA, mimeo

Tandon, R (1989) 'The state and voluntary agencies in Asia', in Holloway, R (ed) *Doing Development: Government, NGOs and the Rural Poor in Asia*, Earthscan, London

Tendler, J (1982) *Turning Private Voluntary Organizations Into Development Agencies: Questions for Evaluation*, USAID Program on Evaluation Discussion Paper No 12, USAID, Washington, DC

Triedman, J (1993) 'Narmada dam suicide averted: Indian government accepts demands for dam review', *Third World Resurgence*, September, No 37, pp39–40

Uvin, P (1996) 'Scaling up the grassroots and scaling down the summit: the relations between third world NGOs and the UN', in Weiss, T G and Gordenker, L (eds) *NGOs, the UN and Global Governance*, Lynne Rienner, Colorado

WCED (1987) *Our Common Future: Report of the World Commission on Environment and Development*, Oxford University Press, New York

Weisbrod, B A (1988) *The Nonprofit Economy*, Harvard University Press, Cambridge

Wolch, J R (1990) *The Shadow State: Government and Voluntary Sector in Transition*, The Foundation Center, New York

Yusuf, Z (1992) 'Legal notice: the environment as a human rights issue', *NCS Bulletin*, Vol 4, No 2, pp10–11

9

Influencing Policy: A UK Voluntary Sector Perspective

Marilyn Taylor

INTRODUCTION

In evidence to the recent Commission on the Future of the Voluntary Sector in the UK, many organizations in that country commented on the sector's ability to 'articulate the interests of, and give a voice to, disadvantaged people or empower people to take more control over their lives' through participation in the democratic process or direct action (Hutchison, 1996: 4). But as Salamon (1993) suggests, it cannot be automatically assumed that the voluntary sector is the protector of democracy – he reminds us that in France, voluntary organizations were illegal until 1901, precisely because they were seen to represent a threat to the democracy that the Revolution had ushered in over a century earlier.

Much existing research on the Northern voluntary or nonprofit sector focuses on service-providing organizations. As Kendall and Knapp (1996) point out, the international classification of nonprofit organizations (ICNPO) highlights the sector's service provision rather than its political and empowerment functions. The very term 'nonprofit' which dominates Northern research on the sector relates to its economic rather than its political contribution – as does the European alternative of *'l'economie sociale'*. Even the separate political science literature on pressure groups is mainly concerned with sectional (producer) associations and their economic interests – business, trade unions, professional associations – rather than cause groups (Grant, 1995).

This chapter will explore the ways in which the voluntary sector in one Northern pluralist democracy – the UK – has contributed to policy. It will examine how this role has developed over time and identify the challenges that it faces in the policy environment of the 1990s. It will close by suggesting a framework for understanding the different roles and challenges voluntary organizations face under different political regimes.

THE POLICY ROLE

Voluntary organizations in the UK have contributed to policy in the following ways:

- creating an active and informed citizenry;
- building 'social capital' (Putnam, 1993) – networks, confidence, skills and knowledge;
- contributing to policy formulation:
  - research and information;
  - providing channels for consultation; and
  - advising on legislation; and
- acting as a vehicle for policy pressure:
  - pioneering and demonstrating alternatives;
  - public and professional education;
  - direct campaigning (through lobbying, advocacy and protest).

These various contributions give voluntary organizations the potential to ensure the representation of a diversity of interests in a pluralist society. But how far do they fulfil this role?

A recent survey by the UK National Council for Voluntary Organisations found that 77 per cent of national voluntary organizations they surveyed reported that they engaged in lobbying (NCVO, 1990); and a third employed policy officers with lobbying responsibilities. Local surveys in the UK and in the US, however, give much lower figures.

Table 9.1 *Campaigning Activities of Nonprofit Organizations*

	Campaigning is Primary Purpose	Engaged in Campaigning	Involved in Consultations with Local Government
Salamon, 1993: various locations, US	3 per cent	18 per cent	n/a
Shore et al, 1994: Liverpool, UK	2 per cent	15 per cent	n/a
Taylor et al, 1995: various, UK	7 per cent	n/a	n/a
Taylor* (unpublished): East Sussex, UK	n/a	25 per cent	33 per cent

Source: author's own research
* this information comes from yet unpublished research by the author on the impact of local government reorganization in East Sussex
n/a indicates not available

Government has long accepted the role of the voluntary sector in advocacy in the UK and other Northern countries. In some areas – the environment, mental health, disability, for example – it relies on the specialist information that the sector provides and has involved specialist voluntary organizations in the drafting of legislation. And yet, a certain ambivalence towards campaigning is betrayed by the legal position of charities in this country. The UK is one of relatively few Northern countries where charities do not have full rights of free speech – others are the US, Ireland, Canada and Australia (6 and Randon, 1995). The UK Charity Commission has issued successive guidelines over the years which countenance representational activities so long as they remain 'ancillary to a charity's primary purposes, which must be clearly charitable and nonpolitical' (Charity Commissioners for England and Wales, 1981). Guidelines issued in 1981 and reprinted in 1986 (Charity Commissioners for England and Wales, 1981; 1986) counsel charities against:

- seeking to influence or remedy those causes of poverty which lie in the social, economic and political structures of countries and communities; and
- seeking to eliminate social, economic, political or other injustice.

The Policy Role Throughout History

The campaigning role of the sector has a long and sometimes distinguished history in the UK. At the same time as the French Revolution was proclaiming the superiority of the state in dealing with matters of inequality and social injustice, the British voluntary sector and its equivalents elsewhere were showing their mettle as advocates for the poor and oppressed, most famously through the anti-slavery campaigns. Although by no means all its campaigns reflected this enlightened view, over the 19th century the sector also campaigned on issues as diverse as the preservation of open spaces, clean air, the prevention of cruelty to animals and later children, better housing and prison reform.

The sector's campaigning has been central to the establishment of basic political and human rights (for example through its campaigns on the franchise, birth control, divorce law, homosexuality and civil liberties). Throughout its history, the sector has also been a way for 'groups excluded from political and economic power to gain a stake in society, develop networks, discuss and formulate strategies and gain an organisational base' (Taylor and Kendall, 1996: 60). From the dissenters' schools of the 17th and 18th centuries to the corresponding societies of the late 18th century, the emerging middle class, argues Marsh (1983), was cemented through associations and campaigns to wrest control from the existing oligarchies. Provincial local government, with its opposition to the London-based central government, was founded on these traditions.

The evident failure of laissez faire policies fuelled campaigns to force the state to take increasing responsibility for welfare, as legislator, funder or provider. These were rewarded by the legislation of the mid-1940s which created a welfare state based on universal rights guaranteed by the state rather than charity. It might have been assumed that the arrival of the welfare state would take away the need for campaigning. However, the very range of governmental responsibilities, coupled with improved education, developments in the mass media and growing evidence that the welfare state had not eradicated poverty, provided the sector with new targets. After a period of apparent complacency over the immediate post-war period (Knight, 1993), the sector developed a role as a watchdog of the state and over the rights that state welfare had introduced.

From the late 1950s on, a series of high profile campaigning organizations were set up: liberal, reformist and radical. Marsh (1983) reports that of the listed pressure groups in 1976, half had been formed since 1960 (the equivalent figure for all voluntary organizations, including service organizations, is a third). Predominantly small scale and middle class, these tapped into the changing values of the time. One author notes that, with the decline of religion, the members of these campaigns can be seen as the 'new dissenters' (Schwarz, 1989). The poverty lobby alone saw the foundation of 17 new campaigning organizations in the ten years between 1965 and 1975.

These were followed by a renewed interest in campaigning from the more traditional organizations who had been seeking a new role. By the 1970s, these were becoming 'sources of information, centres of excellence and *means of responsible pressure*' (Younghusband, 1978: 270, my emphasis). 'Out of the political darkness', Davies adds, 'voluntary organisations joined the political mêlée; a decade earlier this would have led to mass resignations amongst their membership' (Davies, 1985). At the same time, those whom the welfare state had failed were finding their own voice. Self-help groups, disabled people and black and ethnic minority groups challenged the power of professionals and the failure of universalist services to meet their needs. Their criticism was directed as much at the traditional charitable sector as at government itself.

Table 9.2 summarizes the factors in the changing role of the sector over history and the key players at each stage. With the franchise limited in a period of laissez faire pluralism, philanthropists and churches – the relatively powerful – were advancing the claims of those 'less fortunate' in a spirit of benevolent paternalism. With growing evidence of voluntary and market failure, the growing middle class was central to the pressure to introduce state responsibility for welfare – indeed Perkin (1993) suggests that the welfare state was more a creation of the professional classes who were to be the major beneficiaries both as consumers and producers of welfare. Both traditions continued after the introduction of the welfare state, but with growing evidence of government failure and in a period of relative affluence, the sector moved to monitor the implementation of welfare policies. Particularly significant in this new role was the challenge posed to both benevolent paternalism and state welfare by the 'less fortunate' themselves – disabled people, black and ethnic minority communities and other excluded groups – who were now demanding a voice of their own and the full rights of citizenship.

Table 9.2 *The UK Voluntary Sector Through History*

	Pre 20th Century	Late 19th Century On	1960s On
Environment Voluntary Sector Role	Laissez faire Advancing the claims of the less fortunate	Market failure Advancing the need for state intervention	Government failure Monitoring and transforming the state
Key Actors	Philanthropists and churches	Middle classes	Excluded citizens Middle classes
Driving Force	Charity, not rights	Introduction of rights	Implementation of rights

Source: author's own research

THE CHANGING ENVIRONMENT

So far this chapter has described a move towards state responsibility and universal rights, with the voluntary sector acting as a watchdog on the implementation of welfare policy. But over recent years, the features of the political environment have shifted again in the UK as they have elsewhere. Four particular features concern us here. The first is the move towards the market. The second is the decline of popular trust in the democratic system. The third is a new emphasis on partnership in a pluralist policy environment. The fourth is the restructuring of government in Europe with the growing importance of the European Union.

The move to the market, with the introduction of a mixed economy of welfare, the introduction of business values (the 'new managerialism') into government and the rise of a consumerist philosophy, has a number of implications for the UK voluntary sector: first, it involves the transfer of services previously provided by the statutory sector to voluntary and commercial organizations through the use of contracts. Secondly it has introduced a contract culture dominated, some feel, by financial bottom lines and managerialism rather than political and service values. Thirdly, it has placed an emphasis on the individual consumer rather than the citizen. The emphasis on the rights of the consumer has the potential to increase the importance of the sector's individual advocacy work and to support the growth of service user organizations, but places a question mark over the democratic system as a framework for lobbying, campaigning and citizenship.

At the same time, the UK, with other Northern countries, has seen a marked decline of popular confidence in the democratic system. Membership of political parties is falling (although the advent of New Labour with its formidable marketing machine stemmed the tide for a while) and voting patterns are becoming increasingly volatile. Membership of single issue campaign groups has increased dramatically to the point where 'taken as a whole (voluntary) organisations now have much larger memberships than the political parties and can often claim an authority that politicians lack' (Mulgan and Landry, 1995: 60). In 1987, for example, Whiteley and Winyard claimed that the poverty lobby had a membership of some 3 million people – far bigger than any trade union or political party. In a post-modern world, this represents a shift away from a representative to a more participatory democracy, based on differentiation and choice rather than universality and collectivism (Gyford, 1986) – a trend compatible with the ideology of the market.

Thirdly, a new emphasis from the UK state on user involvement in local welfare services and on partnership with 'the community' in economic and social regeneration has opened up new opportunities for the voluntary sector to become involved in formulating policies and planning implementation. As a result there has been a growth in the range and sophistication of pressure group activity at local level (Grant, 1995).

Taken together, these three trends are blurring the boundaries between state and voluntary organizations. In the UK, the language of government is being replaced by a language of 'governance', with local statutory authorities being urged to take on an 'enabling' role. Rather than standing on the outside throwing stones, the voluntary sector is being enticed inside.

Table 9.3 *The UK Voluntary Sector in the 1990s*

	Pre 20th Century	Late 19th Century On	1960s On	1990s
Environment	Laissez faire	Market failure	Government failure	Partnership
Voluntary Sector Role	Advancing the claims of the less fortunate	Advancing the need for state intervention	Monitoring and transforming the state	Contributing as a partner
Key Actors	Philanthropists and churches	Middle classes	Excluded citizens Middle classes	Partners Consumers
Driving Force	Charity, not rights	Introduction of rights	Implementation of rights	Responsibilities; consumer rights

Source: author's own research

The fourth major trend that concerns us here is the globalization of the economy, which has placed a new emphasis on cross-national campaigning in the North and put new players on the policy stage. The increasing significance of the European Union to business is evidenced by the way in which industry has geared up its lobbying machine in Brussels. But, though Europeanization is geared mainly to commercial and business interests, European measures can have a considerable and often unanticipated impact on operations within the sector – in the field of tax, for example, or transport issues. Beyond this, the European Union has offered

UK voluntary organizations opportunities to make progress on human rights and environment issues which have not always been available at national level. Changes are also taking place at subnational level, although these vary from country to country. An element of regionalization has been introduced in the UK which is expected to accelerate with the election of a New Labour government. However, the erosion of local government powers in the 1980s and early 1990s in the UK runs against the European trend – other European countries (for example France and Italy) have introduced major initiatives to decentralize government functions and powers (Taylor and Bassi, forthcoming).

THE CHALLENGES FOR THE VOLUNTARY SECTOR

UK voluntary organizations have long had to balance their political activities against the requirements of charity legislation. But the changes described above pose a number of challenges to their campaigning role. Does their increased profile in both service delivery and policy making compromise their ability to maintain an independent voice? Three major challenges can be identified:

1) the compatibility of campaigning with an increasingly central role in the delivery of welfare;
2) the dilemmas of co-option in gaining insider status at the policy making table; and
3) the danger of a kind of Darwinism in policy, where access to the policy process is limited to the larger, more middle class organizations – a trend which would reduce rather than increase democratic pluralism.

Is Public Benefit Campaigning Compatible with the Contract Culture?

As the voluntary sector assumes a more central role in the delivery of welfare, the scope for influencing the implementation of policy clearly increases. But there have been fears within the sector that the scope for criticizing government policy will diminish: because of censorship, because of vested interests or simply because it is impractical to try and maintain a separate advocacy role alongside the demands of service delivery.

Some writers maintain that advocacy and government funding are incompatible, because government cannot be expected to fund its critics. But most research in the UK finds this assumption unsubstantiated. Government funding to the voluntary sector in the UK doubled in real terms over the 1980s, but Kramer found that government funding did not affect the advocacy role of the social care organizations he studied (Kramer et al, 1993). Indeed, it may have reinforced it: 'Sometimes', argue 6 and Forder (1996: 226), 'campaigning against a government that also provides funding can be the watermark of an agency's independence'. Whiteley and Winyard's 1987 study reported that three-quarters of the organizations in the poverty lobby received some funding from government. And I have argued elsewhere that the voluntary sector benefited from battles between a radical right central government in the 1980s and left wing local governments, who invested in organizations that gave voice to excluded groups (Taylor and Bassi, forthcoming; see also Wolch, 1990).

Nonetheless, Whiteley and Winyard (1987) do cite examples of organizations in the poverty lobby exercising self-censorship. There are also a number of examples where government funders have threatened to withdraw funding or control employment policy in the past:

- In 1980, MIND was told by central government that unless it withdrew allegations of brutality in secure psychiatric hospitals, it would lose part of its government grant (Whiteley and Winyard, 1987: 30).
- In 1983, the central government grant to a national advice organization was suspended, apparently because of the prominence of a local part time advice worker in the national Campaign for Nuclear Disarmament. Later in the decade a review by its central government funder raised questions about the political judgement exercised in certain of its campaigns.
- Centres and agencies which received funding through central government's special employment funding in the 1980s found their funding at risk if they displayed political posters, and funds were taken away from community arts and unemployment centres for this reason (Brenton, 1985: 94).
- In the mid-1980s, central government unsuccessfully sought powers of veto on the appointment of staff to local development agencies supported under one of its programmes, following publicity over the political track record of one employee.

Generally, however, government funding per se is not seen to be a problem. It is the changed nature of the funding relationship which is giving cause for concern. The growth of purchase of service contracting has, some feel, given government purchasers more control over their voluntary sector 'agents'. Comparing the UK voluntary sector with its equivalents in Europe and the US, Brenton (1985) argues that it was the low profile of the voluntary sector in the UK during the years of the welfare state that prevented its incorporation and allowed it to retain a relatively independent voice. With the transfer of mainstream services to the voluntary sector, this may change. A closer relationship with government might lead to censorship by the purchaser or self-censorship by providers as they seek to keep on the right side of the purchaser.

Research so far finds these fears unsubstantiated (Nicholls, 1995; Richardson, 1995; Unwin and Westland, 1996). Unwin and Westland report that the three authorities they studied were all 'very conscious of the important role of voluntary organisations, not simply as providers of services, but also as articulators of need, as representatives and advocates and as proxies for communication and consultation with the community' (1996: 10–11). They also found evidence of continuing government investment in the advocacy work of the sector.

Despite this, voluntary organizations remain concerned about the potential impact of contracting on their advocacy and campaigning roles (Deakin, 1996). There is some evidence to support their concern. In contrast to the other studies mentioned, Lewis (1993) finds evidence of tensions between advocacy and service provision, not because of censorship – the organization she studied had made a conscious decision to maintain its advocacy function – but because the administration of a contract in one of her case studies simply left no time for advocacy. Russell et al (1995) report that some organizations in their studies were finding it difficult to combine advocacy with service provision, a finding echoed by Lindow and Morris in relation to user-led organizations (1995).

Why this discrepancy in research findings? Are those voluntary organizations who fear the loss of the advocacy role simply crying wolf? One explanation of the discrepancy is that a number of studies report considerable variation between local authorities with respect to their implementation of contracting (Bemrose and MacKeith, 1995; Deakin, 1996; Taylor and Lansley, 1992). Another clue may come from Nicholls (1995), who reports that, in her study of four local branches of a national mental health charity, one branch said that it campaigned mostly on national issues, so no local tension was created. It may be that, in some cases, the fact that national organizations can keep clear blue water between their national campaigning role and their local service provision means that advocacy is not suffering.

It is too early to state with any confidence what the long term trend will be. Experience elsewhere gives some cause for concern, however. Overseas aid agencies have reported that, as they have increasingly taken on the role of administering government overseas aid, their campaigning edge has been blunted, and that they have 'been put on the defensive by critical remarks about their work by government ministers' (Robinson, 1991: 175, cited in Grant, 1995). In the US, Salamon (1993) cites Lowi's conclusion in the 1970s that nonprofit organizations 'naturally possess political power, but only occasionally are they politicized. The rest of the time they administer' (Lowi, 1979: 28, cited in Salamon, 1993).

Another explanation for the gap between fears and evidence so far may be that voluntary organizations do not recognize how their advocacy role is being eroded. As they are drawn into mainstream service provision, they may – in the words of one voluntary sector director – be subject to 'cultural take-over by stealth'. Kumar (1997) reports on the increasing similarity in culture between senior managers in the voluntary and statutory sectors, with considerable overlap of personnel.

A further possibility is that the nature of advocacy might change – at least for those organizations which move into the welfare market. Taylor et al report in their 1995 study that, in a market where distinctions between the voluntary and commercial sectors were becoming increasingly blurred, one of the key remaining distinctions between the voluntary and the private organizations in their social care sample was the campaigning role of voluntary organizations. Commercial organizations did not campaign for the cause of their clients. Nor did those agencies in the housing and residential care field defining themselves as 'not-for-profit' agencies, one of which said that it did not consider itself a voluntary organization because 'we do not campaign'. Commercial organizations, however, did lobby as a sectional interest group to defend their market share as may 'not-for-profits'. As voluntary organizations become more commercialized, the boundary between self-interest and client interest in their campaigns is likely to become blurred (Smith and Lipsky, 1993) and they too might move in this direction; from pursuing a cause to promoting and defending their stake in the welfare economy. They are also likely to become the target of campaigns rather than initiators. In the South, Hulme and Edwards (1997) acknowledge similar problems, foreseeing a gradual 'hardening of the arteries' as organizations become more bureaucratic and less prone to take risks or bear the costs of listening to those they seek to assist.

Partners in Policy: Opportunity, Appeasement or Incorporation?

In the 1990s, government is seeking actively to engage disadvantaged groups and service users in the policy making process. The aim is partly to release new resources, partly an expression of new consumerist views of welfare (especially in social care) but partly the outcome of experience from a succession of failed urban regeneration policies which suggested that unless the excluded were involved in policies to address their exclusion, they would continue to represent a threat to the rest of society.

As the universal language of partnership gives the voluntary sector a more central role in policy making, planning and development, 'their main opportunity to promote their mission may ... be through participation in the local planning process, rather than by carrying out activities at the periphery' (Bemrose and MacKeith, 1995: 38).

Has this opportunity to operate from the inside given voluntary and community organizations more opportunity to influence policy and provision? The drive from above has certainly changed the rhetoric at local level and increased contact between authorities and their voluntary sectors. In some areas, considerable strides have been made. Partnership has given voluntary and community organizations opportunities to deliver particular projects or elements of a strategy and to get involved in the detail of implementation. In some cases, they have been able to get social issues onto predominantly economic agendas. But, generally speaking, the evidence from partnership is that the voluntary sector is more likely to be involved in delivery than in policy development (Alcock and Craig, 1995;

Hastings et al, 1996; MacFarlane, 1993). And while Hambleton et al (1995) argue that even imperfect partnerships can be valuable in releasing resources for voluntary and community organizations and other partners, this falls some way short of the rhetoric of partnership and the expectations of communities. As in the case of service contracting, experience varies across authorities, but Hastings et al (1996) conclude from their study of ten partnerships that, while progress has been made, the impact of involvement is modest in return for the investment made. The consultation that is on offer is, as Hulme and Edwards report also from the South (1997), 'supply-side rather than demand-led'.

If we think of the policy process as a game, then the problems experienced by voluntary and community organizations can be classified under four headings: they don't have the resources to play on equal terms; they don't determine the rules of play; they're probably in the wrong game; and the cards are stacked in favour of more powerful players. This leaves them with one of the classic dilemmas of interest groups: is it worth playing the game or should they choose to remain on the outside?

Roberts et al (1995) comment on the resource 'lopsidedness' in many partnerships – few voluntary and community organizations have financial resources, information or officer back-up that other partners take for granted. Few have the assets to give them real leverage. The power imbalance is reinforced by the fact that the agenda, the language, the rules of engagement and the assumptions behind those rules are usually defined by the government partner, in an illustration of Lukes's second and third faces of power (1974):[1]

> *Cultures are in place which at every step obstruct the sharing of power. For much of the time, power holders are not even aware of the ways in which they hold onto power – they do not recognise the impenetrability of their language and procedures or the extent to which these need to be changed (Stewart and Taylor, 1995: 71).*

Unfamiliarity and power tactics among the initiated mean that many user and community representatives are inhibited about making a contribution (Kumar, 1997). Partners are expected to 'deliver' their constituencies rather than go back and consult with them (Skelcher et al, 1996), and a drive to consensus and containment discourages those from outside the system from rocking the boat (Hambleton et al, 1995; Hastings et al, 1996).

Voluntary and community partners either find themselves excluded by this culture or they learn the ropes and, in doing so, run the risk of incorporation into the agendas and mindsets of other partners. 'As Skelcher et al report, activists also became isolated from their communities by constant demands on their time from network for a' (1996: 22). Research on user-led and self-help organizations certainly suggests that the increased demands of consultation are in danger of diverting these organizations from their own agendas (Lindow and Morris, 1995; Wann, 1995; Wilson, 1995).

The creation of official partnership forums can also co-opt people into decisions that they are not happy with. In the words of a mental health development worker in the UK voluntary sector:

> *It may be difficult to query or campaign against a decision or do anything like that if you've sat there and agreed with it, either pro-actively agreed with it or reactively agreed by the fact that you missed a meeting, you've actually passed some sort of document through (Bewley and Glendinning, 1994: 23).*

In fact, a number of voluntary and community organizations find that they are in the wrong game. The real decisions still tend to be made through informal channels, with formal bodies simply a rubber stamping mechanism. Some writers distinguish between outsiders, peripheral insiders (or thresholders) and specialist or core insiders (Grant, 1995; Maloney et al, 1994). Getting a ringside seat as a peripheral insider is easy; getting into the core is much more difficult. Reid and Iqbal (1996: 31) distinguish between two network 'cultures'. The more informal, 'competitive' networks are flexible and confer a lot of autonomy on members. They are entrepreneurial and opportunistic but they are also more exclusive, relying on organizations using their skills in managing inter-organizational relationships to secure their own entry. The more formal 'collaborative' networks are less exclusive, more concerned about legitimation, but are also less entrepreneurial and appear to achieve a great deal less than the effort expended by participants.

The Survival of the Fittest?

Knight predicted in 1993 that the voluntary sector would become polarized between not-for-profit service providers and more social change oriented community-based organizations. This echoes Hulme and Edwards' concerns in developing countries about a growing rift between well-resourced service providers and poorly funded social mobilization agencies, for example, in South and Central America (Hulme and Edwards, 1997). Increasingly, lobbying demands technical expertise, and the ability to deliver the research that the policy makers want. Research also suggests that it is the larger organizations that are most likely to be on policy networks (see, for example, Russell et al, 1995; Smith and Lipsky, 1993). They are more likely to have the time and resources, to move in similar circles as the decision makers (Kumar, 1997), to be familiar with the rules and to have assets to bring to the table. There is a further tendency in some government circles to equate the voluntary and community sectors and assume that voluntary organizations can speak for local communities, although central government guidance has sought to counter this in the regeneration field. Grant (1995) also comments on the middle class dominance of the cause group community – 64 per cent of members of the environmental campaign group Friends of the Earth have been or are in higher education, for example. In this situation, disadvantaged communities tend to remain excluded from the policy process.

However, this may be unduly pessimistic. The success of the disability movement shows what can be achieved by groups outside conventional lobbying circles. A number of writers from the disability movement comment on how disabled people's confidence and expectations have been transformed by this success. In evaluating the achievements of the disability lobby, Oliver (1996) considers that it has given disabled people a voice, brought necessary civil rights legislation closer and achieved legislation to give disabled people control over the money they receive for personal assistance. The movement has now created an institutional base. It has also gained considerable public support and begun to change disabling images in the media. Maybe its greatest achievement has been the mobilization of disabled people, not only as service users but also as citizens.

But the explosion of consultation opportunities over recent years has a downside: and that is the number of demands it makes on ill-resourced organizations. Having found their way into the game, the next challenge for smaller user and community-based organizations is to find ways of engaging in the policy process without becoming detached from their roots. Opportunities for involvement have also been patchy. Lindow and Morris (1995) report that the development of user involvement in services for older people has lagged behind developments elsewhere. Beresford and Croft (1996: 82) describe how poor people have been excluded from a poverty debate dominated by middle class organizations: 'non-poor experts collecting "scientific evidence" to bring pressure to bear on government ... a small group of experts who know the laws, who are recognised as authorities on the subject and who have detailed schemes for negotiation'.

Amongst the larger, more established organizations there is some evidence that radical protest is increasingly discarded as unsophisticated and counterproductive – environmental groups in the UK recently refused to go on a protest against fox hunting because they distrusted the methods used. Being on the outside throwing stones is no longer the place to be. Is this 'incorporation' or a more realistic assessment of how policy is actually changed? Will an insider strategy be more effective or will the sector lose its critical edge? Voluntary organizations, as writers about the South have argued, have to ask themselves whether their seat at the table has been won because 'they now have the social grace not to persist with awkward questions and the organizational capacity to divert the poor and disadvantaged from more radical ideas about how to overcome poverty' (Hulme and Edwards, 1997: 3).

Nonetheless, the division that Knight (1993) draws between the large, co-opted not-for-profits and the politically uncontaminated grassroots is by no means as clear as he would have us believe. The large household names are still associated with major campaigns on poverty which have scored real legislative successes. Some of the major international aid organizations with head offices in the UK are using their weight to campaign on poverty 'at home'. And their voice is needed. In the register of winners and losers in the policy game, it is business that is way out in front. In his paper on the role of the voluntary sector in democracy, Salamon (1993) gives the statistics of that dominance in the US: 70 per cent of all organizations having a Washington presence represent business compared with 5 per cent of voluntary organizations representing disadvantaged groups (Schlozman and Tierney, 1986) and 4 per cent of citizen's groups. The picture is similar in the European Union. Grant (1995) reports that the number of people employed by pressure groups in Brussels doubled between the late 1980s and 1994 (to almost one per European Union employee). But of the 518 groups analysed by Kohler-Koch (1994), 416 may be placed in the business category. Commission officials and Members of the European Parliament may positively seek voluntary sector input to balance the forceful promotion of the interests of commerce and industry. But the scale of the imbalance is demonstrated by Grant's comparison of the European Environment Bureau, one of the better resourced offices, which in 1992 had three or four full time staff, with CEFIC (a pharmaceutical interest group), with its 80 staff and 4000 company representatives.

The Legitimacy of Campaigning

The increase in lobbying activity over recent years has been phenomenal. As the example in the previous section shows, even City interests have found it necessary to formalize their lobbying activities and employ specialist lobbyists. But legislative constraints on campaigning still place obstacles in the way of the sector's campaigning, even in one of the world's most advanced liberal democracies, and suggest an ambivalence towards the democratic role of the voluntary sector which has many parallels elsewhere. Despite the fact that successive reviews of charity law and government funding to the sector find little evidence of charities overstepping the mark, right wing critics in particular continue to find fault with their involvement in pressure group activity. A charity law based on precedent can be a powerful weapon in the hands of those seeking to control freedom of speech, as investigations into charities like Oxfam have shown.

Mulgan and Landry (1995) summarize some of the arguments that have been advanced in favour of this political prohibition. They note the criticism from the right that the power of pressure groups overloads the state and constrains the policy maker. 6 and Randon cite a deep-seated belief on the part of a conservative establishment that the concept of charitable purpose is one of service provision and not one that permits of any political campaigning. They argue, however, that a 'mature democracy should be able to sustain a much looser ecology of argument and to respect the natural links between service provision and political activity' (cited in Mulgan and Landry, 1995: 66). A politically engaged voluntary sector contributes to the free competition of ideas and by encouraging the maximum pluralism in political organization, campaigning and argument, drives up quality in policy information.

The Charity Commission has repeatedly issued guidelines which clarify the position of charities. Nonetheless, Mulgan and Landry do not consider that this goes far enough. They propose that charitable status be attached to activity rather than to the organization and that the remaining restrictions on free speech be removed from charities, to enable them to play a full part in political life.

Meanwhile, some organizations have resolved the problem by separating off their political arms into non-charitable companies. An alternative is to join with other organizations in a legally separate campaigning alliance: this has been a significant trend in the UK, both for reasons of strength in numbers and for keeping campaigning separate from other activities. It allows voluntary organizations to maintain both insider and outsider status. Voluntary organizations have also made common cause with commercial organizations: the poverty lobby joined with small businesses in lobbying for amendments to the 1986 Social Security Act and more recently with landlords to persuade the New Labour government not to implement housing benefit cuts proposed by their predecessors.

CONCLUSIONS

The impact of globalization of the economy, structural adjustment and the advance of market principles on the people on the margins of society mean that the campaigning role of the voluntary sector is as necessary as ever. But these trends also pose new challenges. This chapter has dealt primarily with the UK, but the pressures faced by the UK voluntary organizations in the current policy environment – of incorporation, diversion and polarization – are shared not only in other Northern countries but across the globe, as the references to the work of Hulme and Edwards in this chapter illustrate. However, in commenting on the policy role of the sector, we do well to remember its democratic shortcomings. Some writers, like Hirst (1994) in the UK and Barber in the US (1984) have constructed a vision of a future democracy based on voluntary associations and unmediated interest groups. Communitarianism has developed a considerable appeal among those disenchanted with both the state and the market. But, as Biggs and Neame (1995) argue, considerable dangers lie in the belief that NGOs alone can ensure the 'delivery of democracy and civil society' either in the North or South. Voluntary organizations can make up for government failure, not just in economic, but in political terms. If the state does not represent the interests of certain groups in society then voluntary organizations will emerge to both serve and advocate for those groups. But, in politics as in the economic market, government failure is matched by voluntary failure (Salamon, 1987). Voluntary organizations can be particularist, patchy and exclusive and if society's needs are to be met, a partnership is required between the state and the voluntary sector.

What kind of partnership should this be? Dunleavy (1987) differentiates between three different roles that the state can play. The cipher state is passive, leaving the ultimate power to the groups in civil society, as Hirst and some adherents of the communitarian agenda seem to suggest. In this scenario, the voluntary sector and other interest groups become the policy makers, competing with each other for supremacy. In such a state, it can be argued that the mischief of factions will reign and the fittest will survive, with the excluded dependent on the enlightened paternalist to promote their cause, as they were in earlier centuries (see Table 9.2). The partisan state is concerned with its own interest in a public choice agenda and will favour those interest groups that serve its own agenda. During the years of the welfare state, this was a professional agenda; in the 1980s, some would argue, the state served the interests of capital (Dearlove and Saunders, 1984). The danger for the voluntary sector in this scenario is that it will be co-opted into that dominant agenda. It is in this role, too, that the state is least likely to countenance an independent advocacy role. Dunleavy's third role is that of the guardian state. In this role, the state is concerned with rebalancing society's interests, which normally entails readjusting public policy in favour of socially non-dominant interests. It is in this role that the state will be most open to bottom-up influence and indeed likely to provide the resources that are the prerequisite for such influence (see also Taylor and Lansley, 1992).

Where any country lies in this framework will depend on the period under study, the policy area and the level of government. In the past, the UK has – as Table 9.2 showed – experienced a cipher state and a partisan state. The reality in the UK over recent years seems to lie somewhere between the partisan and the guardian state. Recent moves towards partnership promise greater access particularly insofar as they offer a place in the policy making game for non-dominant interests. Government funders are also insisting that voluntary sector providers have mechanisms in place to involve their own users in policy making. But the analysis in this chapter suggests that, even in a guardian state, the cards are not evenly distributed and the game may be rigged. In this context, the voluntary sector has to find a balance between insider access through the quality of its information, advice and research and the less cosy outsider position which can ensure that those excluded from society have their own voice and are heard.

Such a strategy requires three things from the sector. The first is that organizations articulate and keep to their mission, weighing up the costs as well as the benefits of partnership. This counsel is frequently given, but perhaps less easy to follow through the maze of new opportunities – the line between judicious strategy and co-option is very fine and missions can remain at the level of aspiration rather than reality. A second require-ment therefore is that both government and the major players in the voluntary sector foster the diversity within the sector, to ensure that there is a spread of organizations along the continuum from outsider to insider and that there is a balance between containment and creative tension. It is rarely possible for individual voluntary organizations to operate at all the levels required for effective campaigning. The large can easily lose touch with their roots; the small do not have the resources to be present in important arenas. Effective alliances need to be built along the continuum from insider to outsider, so that overall strategies can be loosely articulated along that spectrum, exploiting the different assets of different parts of the sector. It will not always be easy, but without that articulation, the split foreseen by Knight (1993) and Hulme and Edwards (1997) could become reality and the voice of any part of the sector will be weakened.

Finally, related to this is the need to ensure that excluded groups are empowered to influence policy and to hold the rest of the sector as well as government to account. Evidence from the disability movement suggests that it is from this bottom-up, demand-led base that the rules of the game can sometimes be changed. This requires that the more powerful voluntary organizations as well as government make an investment in building the social capital that gives excluded and less powerful groups the confidence, the skills and the organizational capacity to make their voice count and makes, in Putnam's 1993 analysis, for effective governance.

ENDNOTE

1 Stephen Lukes (1974) distinguishes between three faces of power: where A has power over B; where A sets the agenda in which power relationships are played out; and where B internalizes A's version of how power works and accepts it as a 'given'.

BIBLIOGRAPHY

Alcock, P and Craig, G (1995) 'Anti-poverty strategies in Britain: partnership between local authorities and the voluntary sector', paper presented to *Researching the UK Voluntary Sector*, NCVO, London, September 7–8

Barber, B (1984) *Strong Democracy: Participatory Politics for a New Age*, University of California Press, Berkeley

Bemrose, C and MacKeith, J (1995) *Partnerships for Progress: Good Practice in the Relationship between Local Government and Voluntary Organisations*, The Policy Press, Bristol

Beresford, P and Croft, S (1996) 'It's our problem too! Challenging the exclusion of poor people from poverty discourse', *Critical Social Policy*, Vol 15, Nos 2/3, pp75–95

Bewley, C and Glendinning, C (1994) *Involving Disabled People in Community Care Planning*, Joseph Rowntree Foundation, York

Biggs, S and Neame, A (1995) 'Negotiating room for manoeuvre: reflection concerning NGO autonomy and accountability within the new policy agenda' in Edwards, M and Hulme, D (eds) *Nongovernmental Organisations – Performance and Accountability: Beyond the Magic Bullet*, Earthscan, London

Brenton, M (1985) *The Voluntary Sector in British Social Services*, Longman, Harlow

Charity Commissioners for England and Wales (1981; 1986) 'Political activities by charities', CC9, Charity Commissioners for England and Wales, London

Davies, M (1985) *Politics of Pressure*, BBC Publications

Deakin, N (1996) 'The devil's in the detail', *Social Policy and Administration*, No 30, p1

Dearlove, J and Saunders, P (1984) *Introduction to British Politics: Analysing a Capitalist Democracy*, Polity Press, Cambridge

Dunleavy, P (1987) *Theories of the State: The Politics of Liberal Democracy*, Macmillan, Basingstoke

Grant, W (1995) *Pressure Groups, Politics and Democracy in Britain*, Harvester Wheatsheaf, London

Gyford, J (1986) 'Diversity, sectionalism and local democracy', Committee of Inquiry into the Conduct of Local Authority Business, *The Conduct of Local Authority Business: Research Volume IV: Aspects of Local Democracy*, Cmnd 9801, HMSO

Hambleton, R, Essex, S, Mills, L and Razzaque, K (1995) *The Collaborative Council: A Study of Inter-Agency Working in Practice*, LGC Communications, London

Hastings, A, McArthur, A and McGregor, A (1996) *Less Than Equal: Community Organisations and Estate Regeneration Partnerships*, The Policy Press, Bristol

Hirst, P (1994) *Associative Democracy*, Polity Press, Cambridge

Hulme, D and Edwards, M (eds) (1997) *NGOs, States and Donors: Too Close For Comfort*, Macmillan in association with Save the Children, London

Hutchison, R (1996) 'General summary', in *Meeting the Challenge of Change: Voluntary Action into the 21st Century*, Commission on the Future of the Voluntary Sector, London

Kendall, J and Knapp, M (1996) *The Voluntary Sector in the UK*, Manchester University Press, Manchester

Knight, B (1993) *Voluntary Action*, The Home Office, London

Kohler-Koch, B (1994) 'Changing patterns of interest intermediation in the European Union', *Government and Opposition*, Vol 29, No 2, pp166–180

Kramer, R, Lorentzen, H, Melief, W and Pasquinelli, S (1993) *Privatisation in Four European Countries: Comparative Studies in Government–Third Sector Relationships*, M E Sharpe, New York

Kumar, S (1997) *Accountability Relationships Between Voluntary Sector 'Providers', Local Government 'Purchasers' and Service Users in the Contracting State*, York Publishing Services, York

Lewis, J (1993) 'Developing the mixed economy of care: emerging issues for voluntary organisations', *Journal of Social Policy*, Vol 22, No 2, pp173–192

Lindow, V and Morris, P (1995) *Service User Involvement: Synthesis of Findings and Experience in the Field of Community Care*, Joseph Rowntree Foundation, York

Lukes, S (1974) *Power: A Radical View*, Macmillan, London

MacFarlane, R (1993) *Community Involvement in City Challenge*, NCVO Publications, London

Maloney, W J, Jordan, G and McLaughlin, A (1994) 'Interest groups and public policy: the insider/outsider model revisited', *Journal of Public Policy*, Vol 14, No 1, pp17–38

Marsh, D (1983) *Pressure Politics: Interest Groups in Britain*, Junction Books, London

Mulgan, G and Landry, C (1995) *The Other Invisible Hand*, Demos, London

Nicholls, V (1995) 'Contracting and the voluntary sector: a critique of the impact of markets on MIND organisations', *Critical Social Policy*, No 51, pp101–114

NCVO (1990) *Cause and Effect: A Survey of Campaigning in the Voluntary Sector*, National Council for Voluntary Organisations, London

Oliver, M (1996) 'User involvement in the voluntary sector – a view from the disability movement', in *Voluntary Action into the 21st Century: Meeting the Challenge of Change*, Commission on the Future of the Voluntary Sector, London

Perkin, H (1993) *The Rise of Professional Society*, Routledge, London

Putnam, R (1993) *Making Democracy Work: Civic Traditions in Modern Italy*, Princeton University Press, Princeton

Reid, B and Iqbal, B (1996) 'Redefining housing practice: interorganisational relationships and local housing networks', in Malpass, P (ed) *The New Governance of Housing*, Longman, London

Richardson, J (1995) *Purchase of Service Contracting*, National Council for Voluntary Organisations, London

Roberts, V, Russell, H, Harding, A and Parkinson, M (1995) *Public/Private/Voluntary Partnerships in Local Government*, Local Government Management Board, Luton

Robinson, M (1991) 'An uncertain partnership: the Overseas Development Agency and the voluntary sector in the 1980s', in Bose, A and Burnell, P (eds) *Britain's Overseas Aid Since 1979*, Manchester University Press, Manchester

Russell, J, Scott, D and Wilding, P (1995) *Mixed Fortunes: The Funding of the Voluntary Sector*, Manchester University, Manchester

Salamon, L M (1987) 'Partners in public service: the scope and theory of government–nonprofit relations', in Powell, W W (ed), *The Nonprofit Sector: A Research Handbook*, Yale University Press, Connecticut

Salamon, L M (1993) 'The nonprofit sector and democracy: prerequisite, impediment or irrelevance', presentation to the Aspen Institute Nonprofit Sector Research Fund Symposium, *Democracy and the Non-profit Sector*, December 14

Schlozman, K L and Tierney, J T (1986) *Organized Interests and American Democracy*, Harper and Row, New York

Schwarz, W (1989) *The New Dissenters: The Nonconformist Conscience in The Age of Thatcher*, Bedford Square Press, London

Shore, P; Knapp, M, Kendall, J and Carter, S (1994) 'The local voluntary sector in Liverpool', in Saxon-Harrold, S and Kendall, J (eds) *Researching the Voluntary Sector*, Volume II, Charities Aid Foundation, Tunbridge Wells, pp113–128

Skelcher, C, McCabe, A, Lowndes, V and Nanton, P (1996) *Community Networks in Urban Regeneration*, The Policy Press, Bristol

Smith, S R and Lipsky, M (1993) *Nonprofits for Hire: The Welfare State in The Age of Contracting*, Harvard University Press, Cambridge

Stewart, M and Taylor, M (1995) *Empowerment and Estate Regeneration: A Critical Review*, The Policy Press, Bristol

Taylor, M and Bassi, A (forthcoming) 'Unpacking the state: local government, national government and the third sector', to be published in *Voluntas*

Taylor, M and Lansley, J (1992) 'Ideology and welfare in the UK: the implications for the voluntary sector', *Voluntas*, Vol 3, No 2, pp153–174

Taylor, M and Kendall, J (1996) 'History of the voluntary sector', in Kendall, J and Knapp, M (eds) *The Voluntary Sector in the UK*, Manchester University Press, Manchester

Taylor, M, Langan, J and Hoggett, P (1995) *Encouraging Diversity: Voluntary and Private Organisations in Community Care*, Arena, Aldershot

Unwin, J and Westland, P (1996) *Trends, Myths and Realities: Funding Policies and the Local Voluntary Sector*, Association of Charitable Foundations/Charities Aid Foundation, London

Wann, M (1995) *Building Social Capital: Self Help in the Twenty-First Century Welfare State*, Institute for Public Policy Research, London

Whiteley, P and Winyard, S (1987) *Pressure for the Poor: The Poverty Lobby and Policy Making*, Methuen, London

Wilson, J (1995) *Two Worlds: Self-Help Groups and Professionals*, British Association of Social Workers, Birmingham

Wolch, J (1990) *The Shadow State: Government and Voluntary Sector in Transition*, The Foundation Center, New York

Younghusband, E (1978) *Social Work in Britain: 1950–75, Volume 1*, Allen and Unwin, London

6, P and Forder, J (1996) 'Can campaigning be evaluated?' *Nonprofit and Voluntary Sector Quarterly*, Vol 25, No 2, pp225–247

6, P and Randon, A (1995) *Liberty, Charity and Politics: Non-Profit Law and Freedom of Speech*, Dartmouth, Aldershot

10
Evaluation and the Voluntary (Nonprofit) Sector: Emerging Issues

Jeremy Kendall and Martin Knapp

INTRODUCTION

The introduction to any paper on evaluation and the voluntary (or nonprofit) sector would be obliged to note the apparently growing importance of this topic and the developing (and yet enormously varied) contexts within which this importance is recognized and expressed. An opening question to address, therefore, is why evaluation matters (or seems to matter). We also feel obliged to note that the topic of voluntary sector evaluation has variously been described as a 'minefield', a 'nightmare' and 'intractable'. The heterogeneity of activities to be found within the sector, the multiplicity of stakeholders, the diversity of their motives and the absence of a simple 'bottom line' are among the root causes of these difficulties. Appropriately warned, but foolishly undaunted, we provide a review in this chapter of the state of play.

An accumulating body of empirical data suggests why evaluation matters as far as the voluntary sector is concerned. One reason is surely the changing resource context within which many voluntary organizations currently operate. There is no shortage of evidence from the UK and other Northern countries of the extent to which voluntary organizations are now working with, and are often substantially funded by, 'evaluation-prone' state agencies (Kendall and Knapp, 1996; 6 and Kendall, 1997; Salamon and Anheier, 1996). But state funders are not the only stakeholders with an interest in evaluation; even if only implicitly, all opinions, attitudes and expectations expressed about efficiency or performance clearly suggest that other stakeholders have a view. Examples from the UK would include grant-making trusts' interests in evaluating the endeavours they support (Ashford and Clarke, 1996; Leat, 1992), Charity Commission demands for 'evaluation stakeholders', some volunteers' wishes to understand better the nature of the organizations they serve and their performance, the effects of user advocacy on users' views about what they receive and growing concerns among the general public about mismanagement of charitable funds (cf Saxon-Harrold, 1993).

The broader context for any discussion of evaluation also helps to explain why it matters. We can note the greater interest in the topic from the 1960s onwards, the initial hegemony of putatively rational and managerial approaches that followed, and the enthusiastic embrace of evaluation by many governments as an element of so-called New Public Management during the 1980s. Consumer charters, the 1998 Best Value initiative in local government and the nebulous stakeholder rhetoric of the 1990s represent more recent developments. However, just as such approaches were explicitly permeating state decision making, so scepticism and doubts about their usefulness were coming strongly to the fore in the social science community (Parsons, 1995). This is just one facet of the changing context within which to view attempts at evaluating voluntary organizations.

THEORETICAL STARTING POINTS

In order to try to identify different approaches to evaluation and their utilization, and also to identify what it is about the voluntary sector and voluntary organizations which may make its evaluation especially problematic or challenging, we review some of the received theoretical understandings as to its conceptualization, rationale and functions. While much of this literature will be familiar to most Northern nonprofit scholars, and indeed many from the South who are part of the self-defined international nonprofit research community, it may be less so to those from outside this field and from other backgrounds. We cannot offer an exhaustive review. Rather we selectively present a number of perspectives which appear to us to have obvious and immediate relevance to questions of evaluation.[1] For convenience, these are discussed sequentially, but this didactic device should not encourage the view that these are distinct theoretical perspectives. To a degree, the theories overlap and often complement one another. As it turns out, we *do* observe a major fault line between theories which have a rationalist character and those which do not, reflecting the familiar divide within broader social science. Notwithstanding this important distinction, we shall observe a lot of common ground.

There are two primary reasons for reviewing this apparently large quota of theories, and drawing out implications for evaluation. First, with the present state of knowledge on, and understanding of, the rationale for and functions of the voluntary sector, it is not possible to choose between them as grand theories. A second reason for keeping the field open derives from our scepticism concerning the possibility of arriving at a single overarching theory which can adequately capture the voluntary sector's contribution across all fields, locales and times. It seems likely that those theories which can be operationalized will have more utility and explanatory insight in some contexts than in others. But because of the exceptionally broad remit of this chapter – we have been asked to examine the question of evaluation and the voluntary sector as understood from a Northern point of view, with no (other) narrowing of scope or qualifiers – we feel obliged to attend to a rather wide range of views.

Before proceeding with our telegraphic account of the theories, we should make clear what we understand by voluntary organizations. We assume these to be entities with a formal structure, not profit distributing, constitutionally independent of government and benefiting from a meaningful degree of voluntarism (Kendall and Knapp, 1995; Salamon and Anheier, 1997). This last property – which embraces organizations as volunteer-involving, and/or beneficiaries of private giving – has traditionally been emphasized in classical sociological approaches to the sector (Herman, 1990; Van Til, 1988), and – as we shall see below – is also a key theme cutting across the modern formulations reviewed here.

Rationalist Theories

The first theory to highlight is Weisbrod's (1975; 1988) economic conceptualization of voluntary organizations as providers of public/externality-generating goods and services. In orthodox economics, the private market is usually seen as an efficient mechanism for ensuring provision in line with citizens' tastes and expressed preferences. However, this optimality breaks down in the case of jointly consumed, non-excludable and non-rival goods – in part because of the so-called free-rider problem wherein the benefits of consumption can be reaped without paying. This instance of market failure provides an efficiency rationale for government provision (with consumer preferences expressed through the democratic process). Yet Weisbrod points out that the state itself (treated as a neutral aggregator of electors' demands) is likely to be able and willing to meet only some of the demands that arise in this fashion, and the combination of both market and government failures leaves a residual demand or a set of unmet needs. Voluntary organizations are then represented as responses to these failures (although how they can correct for the free-rider problem is only loosely sketched through unspecific references to informal social pressures and sanctions).

A second, supply side approach extends the analysis by focusing on the question of nonprofit entrepreneurship (James, 1987). Inter alia, this alerts us to the distinctive contribution of voluntary organizations as mobilizers of voluntarism: the commitment and character of the individual or institutional entrepreneurs who found and run them – often motivated by religious and ideological goals – is taken to allow them access to volunteer inputs of human and financial resources (ie volunteering and private giving). This leaves them well positioned to provide many human services at lower cost than other providers (James, 1989; but see Badelt, 1997).

Third, we have Hansmann's (1980) contract failure perspective. Like Weisbrod and James, this also takes the free market as the benchmark for thinking about the voluntary sector, but focuses on a different set of difficulties in its operation; those arising from asymmetries in the distribution of information. The theory places particular emphasis on what is often taken as a defining characteristic of voluntary organizations – the non-distribution constraint under which they operate. From this perspective, legal and constitutional constraints on organizations' abilities to distribute net earnings act as powerful signals to consumers about the motives, intentions and behaviours of those who control them. Hansmann argues that, in situations of consumer vulnerability, where the characteristics of output are difficult or impossible to measure or monitor (particularly when funder and direct consumer are separated), nonprofit organizations are likely to be regarded as more trustworthy than for-profit organizations because the goals of the latter mean that they have a more obvious incentive to cut corners on quality, or otherwise take advantage of the situation (including of supporters). Moreover, consumers may be reassured by these organizations' volunteer-utilizing character, taking their involvement to be an indicator that that those involved are not just in it for the money.

Implicit in Hansmann's formulation is the assumption that the existence of nonprofits which are motivated to act in accordance with consumer expectations is efficient from a societal point of view because this implies that the costs of monitoring or exploitation which would be incurred in a purely for-profit world are avoided. Thus, in a further theoretical approach, the model of nonprofits as an efficient institutional response to asymmetric information has been recast more broadly as a model of nonprofits as an efficient institutional response to transaction costs. The latter can be extended to embrace a wider range of transaction costs – not just the costs that arise between consumer and producer, but in mobilizing supply side resources in the first instance. These include the interpretation of the free-rider problem as a question of transaction costs between consumers (Krashinsky, 1986); and the modelling of nonprofits as coalitions of simultaneously demand and supply side stakeholders, who lack incentives to cut corners on quality because to do so would be to inflict self-harm (Ben-Ner and Van Hoomissen, 1993).

While these arguments were developed deliberately as explanations of the voluntary sector and quickly became well established in the dedicated nonprofit literature, the use of a fifth concept – social capital – is relatively new. It was originally brought to the attention of a wide audience by sociologist James Coleman (1990), building upon earlier work by other writers, as a more general theoretical device for understanding the relationship between individuals and social structures. Like those approaches considered thus far, it follows a rational choice logic, and recognizes the pervasiveness and importance of trust and public good problems in societies.

> *The term* capital, *as part of the concept, implies a resource or factor input that facilitates production, but is not consumed or otherwise used up in production ... social refers in this context to aspects of social organization, ordinarily informal relationships, established for non economic purposes, yet with economic consequences (Coleman, 1993: 175).*

A key concept in Coleman's formulation (1990: Chapter 12) is that social capital is an intangible resource to be found in relations between people – networks – rather than in inanimate objects (physical capital) or individuals (human capital).[2] Yet networks, and the trust they can facilitate – which, it is argued, constitute a vital element in cooperation – are clearly not uniquely associated with the voluntary sector. However, participatory voluntary organizations *qua* networks do feature explicitly in his discussion of forms of social capital. Peoples' creation and subsequent involvement in them is seen either to represent social capital per se, or to create it as a by-product. This by-product can be spatial in the classic public good sense in the case of intentional organizations (Coleman's example is a Parent Teacher Association, from which non-participating parents benefit); or can be usable over time in the case of appropriable organizations.[3] If one further assumes that the other forms of social capital that he highlights – including obligations and expectations, information potential, and norms and sanctions – are particularly associated with the presence of voluntary organizations (as opposed to informal networks or other formal groups), then a further link can be made between the voluntary sector and social capital.[4,5] A major implication of Coleman's argument (and particularly Putnam's interpretation of it) is that involvement in voluntary organizations can be a creative process, changing participants through the very act of taking part, in an analogous fashion to the way in which people's acquisition of human capital through education and training enhances their capabilities. (For Putnam, following Toqueville, this is argued to make them better, community-aware or other-regarding citizens.)

Theories Departing from Rationalist Precepts

All the approaches discussed thus far imply that the voluntary sector represents a rational response to demands or problems which would otherwise be unmet or remain unresolved. The tendency to interpret what is observed as efficient is also implicit in a sixth, voluntary failure theory (Salamon, 1987), although here the focus is on partnership between the voluntary sector and government. Indeed, the whole thrust of the voluntary failure argument is that the voluntary sector in isolation has certain inherent weaknesses, as do the market and the state. The partnership that we observe is then viewed as an effort to secure the best of both worlds, avoiding the problems of insufficiency (stemming in part and perhaps primarily from free-riding problems), particularism, amateurism and paternalism that would otherwise plague a system relying solely or predominantly on the voluntary sector, while reaping the latter's advantages in terms of voluntary inputs, perceived trustworthiness and so on.

The second broad class of theories that we consider in the remainder of this section have in common that they depart from this rationality assumption in a number of ways. Four can be summarized. The first comes from Romo and Anheier (1992) who portray voluntary organizations as value-rational rather than means-rational.[6] They recognize the significance of trust, but suggest that Hansmann's and Coleman's models confuse trust with risk, between which, they suggest, a sharp distinction must be drawn.[7] Risk, it is argued, can best be dealt with through insurance traded in secondary markets, or by the state. But donors' (or consumers') preferences for voluntary organizations are said to be predicated on these organizations' unique abilities to access 'assumed-without-question, taken-for-granted trust ... deeply embedded in long-standing structural and cultural arrangements of the society' (11, 12). Such pre-rational, pre-existing trust is most obviously associated with organizations which share a common culture with their stakeholders, and which are acknowledged a priori to be competent in meeting need. These organizations create (and re-create) trust through repetitive ceremony and ritual – religious organizations are taken to be prototypical. But trust can also be a feature of other value-rational groups which pursue altruistic goals, and are thought of as adept and experienced in meeting need. Notwithstanding their expertise, it is argued that voluntary organizations may well not operate efficiently or responsively since 'they are inert because trust is. Because trust is not a commodity, it cannot be purchased or sold in markets ... Low-performing organizations persist over extended periods of time ... Trustworthiness does not imply efficiency' (17). Thus, while the approach suggests that voluntary organizations may be well positioned and perceived as competent in meeting need by those sharing the worldview created by the cultural system in question, the arrangement is anticipated to be inefficient by some other (objective, external) standards (see also Seibel, 1990).[8]

The remaining three approaches that we will outline in this section explicitly attend to the political context of voluntary sector activity, but take it into account in different ways and at different levels. First, Wolch (1990) has developed a complex and sophisticated 'state-centred' model drawing on the Marxian tradition of social analysis, new institutionalism and Giddensian social theory (see Kendall, 1992, for a critique). She identifies (24) three continua along which, it is argued, the output of voluntary organizations can be located:

commodified —— noncommodified
direct service —— advocacy
elitist —— participatory

The first dimension is primarily concerned with the possibilities of public good aspects, and the third dimension directs our attention back to voluntarism and social capital (while usefully reminding us that meaningful participation is a possibility in voluntary organizations as we have defined them, rather than a defining feature). Wolch explains the contrast between these aspects and the second element:

> *It is important to note that various types of output can generate social change, but some are* more directly designed *to produce social change than others.* Advocacy output *seeks to direct or create social change by influencing public policy or corporate practices (1990: 25; emphases added).*

Evers (1993; 1995) has also tried to develop a framework capable of taking this aspect into account, labelled the welfare mix approach. Like Romo and Anheier (1992), Evers treats rationality as a variable rather than an assumption. Orthodox economists' interpretation of rationality (in his terminology 'instrumentalistic values': 15) is regarded as representing the logic of the market (for-profit sector), but not the state or the community, which are portrayed respectively as the realms of 'strong universalistic orientations', and 'norms and traditions of personal obligations'. Unlike Romo and Anheier, however, Evers does not suggest that the voluntary sector is dominated by a single form of rationality, but prefers to conceptualize it as part of the 'tension field' of civil society, in which the logics of the other three sectors are played out ('co-exist and mix'; see also Billis, 1993; Wuthnow, 1991). Thus, while it is true that associations bring specific values into this arena – reflecting the imprint of, for example, the churches, or new social movements, or demographic or cultural minorities from which they grow – it is emphasized here that these values influence rather than determine their goals and actual behaviour, since they must respond to economic and political pressures too. The model admits that these tensions may be resolved successfully (from the point of view of participating actors) through the achievement of a synergetic outcome (which can be interpreted as an efficient outcome). But it also admits that this is not *necessarily* the case, since tensions can go unresolved, or at least not be resolved to the satisfaction of all stakeholders.

The final perspective we consider shares with Evers a concern to take seriously tensions and potential conflicts between stakeholders. However, the unit of analysis is the individual organization rather than the sector as a whole,[9] and there is no particular desire to privilege the advocacy function as an output at the organization level; rather, the low politics of intra-organizational conflict is an important element of the analytical approach. In this approach, voluntary groups are portrayed as multiple constituency organizations, where the players tend not to be seen as the abstract state, community and marketplace with their respective logics, but rather as functional departments, or individuals with roles thus defined. Kanter and Summers (1987) suggest that this approach is particularly appropriate for voluntary organizations because they lack an overarching measure of organizational performance, and because their stakeholders tend to judge them by different standards. This is over and above the argument for analysing organizations in general as

> *complex entities, the specification of whose goals is problematic. Organizations may have many goals, and they can be inconsistent, contradictory or incoherent; it is often unclear at what level or with respect to what units the goals should be measured ... Goals may even be a mystification (155).*

We draw this section to a close by noting the social constructionist inter- pretation of this approach which would go one more, deconstructing step by emphasizing that it is misleading to freeze by assumption or take as given this range of (different) stakeholder judgements. Rather, they must be understood as created 'in an ongoing process of sensemaking and implicit negotiation' (Herman and Renz, 1997: 188).

IMPLICATIONS OF THEORY FOR EVALUATION

We now turn our attention to some of the most important implications of these theoretical insights for evaluation. We shall see that in some cases the perspectives raise questions for which preliminary answers can be sketched, and efforts have been and are being made to evaluate or cost voluntary activity; while in others, it is much less clear how to respond. Some of the theories also appear to hold lessons for how we might inter- pret the evaluation process itself.

We begin by considering some of the implications for evaluation of voluntary associations' character as the primary organizational conduits for volunteerism – an issue which we have seen in some shape or form cuts across many of the theories discussed – and then consider in turn the implications of asymmetry and trustworthiness; new institutional arguments; and the involvement of multiple stakeholders. In using these headings, and in the interests of brevity, we collapse some of what clearly are distinctive theories into groups in a way that inevitably does violence to some of the more subtle distinctions between them.[10]

As we proceed, we also refer to some relevant empirical evidence. In the first two subsections, following directly from the rationalist character of the theories that underpin them, this implies a broadly positivist mode of empirical analysis and evaluation. The assumption here is that some, and perhaps all, relevant actions and their associated costs and benefits can be meaningfully identified, measured and valued objectively. One helpful way of characterizing this approach is to use the language of production to elucidate and simplify the relevant concepts and relation- ships between them. From this perspective, voluntary activity is represented as involving the deployment of resources which, mediated through technology (which itself summarizes a host of often complex and usually non-mechanistic processes), generate outputs and outcomes. A

BOX 10.1 THE PRODUCTION OF WELFARE APPROACH

- The *resource inputs* to an organization or activity, mainly paid staff, volunteers and capital.
- The *costs* of those resource inputs expressed in monetary terms (alternatively this could be the budget for an agency, which is used to purchase resource inputs, plus recognition of opportunity costs associated with, for example, the efforts of volunteers).
- The so-called *non-resource inputs* to the production or provision process, these being the influences on the achievement of outcomes (see below) which do not have an identifiable price or are not currently marketed (such as the social milieu of a community care setting, or staff attitudes and patient histories in a health care setting).
- The *intermediate outputs* or *intermediate outcomes*, which are the volumes of service output, probably with a quality requirement, and perhaps weighted in some way for user characteristics (casemix), produced from combinations of the resource and non-resource inputs.
- The *final outcomes*, which are changes over time in the welfare, quality of life and status (such as educational attainment or health) of service users and others.

---

variant developed primarily for application in health and social welfare contexts is the production of welfare approach (Davies and Knapp, 1981; Knapp, 1984), which distinguishes the elements shown in Box 10.1.

The approach assumes that final outcomes are influenced (produced) by the nature of the voluntary activities, the types, levels and mixes of resources employed, and the non-resource inputs (an essential part of the process). Clearly the terminology and its arrangement draws on economics, but the framework itself draws on analogies not only with production functions, but also with a range of other perspectives in social policy, psychology, medicine, sociology and elsewhere. As a simple organizing framework, the production of welfare can therefore contain a number of different concepts and evaluative approaches.

Volunteerism

The theories reviewed above suggest that volunteers are involved in production in perhaps two primary ways: first, they represent a significant input, an effect to which supply side and voluntary failure perspectives in particular alert us (in the latter case, this primarily stems negatively from the amateurism characteristic). Second, volunteering, and especially that of a participative character which verges on or overlaps with membership, may also represent a final outcome in its own right – a possibility suggested by social capital arguments among others.[11] That is, people who volunteer may emerge as more socially and politically skilled and better socially and politically positioned; happier and more fulfilled individuals; and generally more rounded citizens than people who do not. This represents a final outcome because it is ultimately individual and societal welfare which, it is suggested, are enhanced. There is certainly empirical evidence in the UK that people are often motivated to volunteer by the expectation that this will enable them to enhance their social networks, and to fit better with the expectations and norms of society at large (Knapp et al, 1996). Other international evidence showing that volunteers and/or members tend to be more participative and perhaps trusting citizens than non-volunteers/members is also suggestive (Barker, 1993; Dekker and van den Broeck, 1998).

At the same time, we should also note the possibility of the reverse effect: the production facilitated by participation is detrimental to society at large, even if it advances the cause of those involved from their own perspective. If voluntary groups are themselves regarded as constituting social capital, then the Ku Klux Klan and the Mafia are perhaps the best known example of this problem. More generally, Onyx (1996: 8) refers to the possibility that membership of some groups might perpetuate the 'potential for narrow-mindedness and enforced conformity'. The fostering of particularistic and paternalistic values (Salamon, 1987) amongst volunteers is another way in which social welfare production could be hampered.

Returning to volunteers as inputs, the market for volunteers has certain unusual characteristics – including, of course, a lack of financial remuneration (other than expenses under most definitions) for those involved. There is also the peculiar relationship between employer and employee to take into account. Because the latter is participating, to some extent, non-contractually and voluntarily, the former could be argued to lack the control rights conventionally associated with the factor market. Should they therefore be treated as resource or non-resource inputs? If we assume the former, it is still far from straightforward either to calculate the costs or indeed (to return to the question of outcomes) to estimate the benefits. Many of the economic issues raised by volunteering were reviewed in a lecture some years ago (Knapp, 1990), and there has been progress in the meantime. Despite the conceptual obstacles, Gaskin (1997) has taken volunteer research a useful step forward with her pilot work on the costing of volunteers and the valuation of their efforts. In addition, Foster (1997) has shown how three different methods for the valuation of volunteers can produce rather different results, depending on the stakeholder perspective adopted: an opportunity cost estimate (the volunteer's own perspective), a replacement cost perspective (the volunteer-using organization's perspective) and an output-based approach (the beneficiaries' perspective). The approaches are not mutually exclusive or competitive, but should be seen as building up to the cumulative value of volunteer inputs.

Information Asymmetry, Trustworthiness and Overall Performance

Taken together, the stream of theorizing which highlights information asymmetries and stresses the centrality of trust suggests perhaps two key messages for evaluation. First, it will be important to take into account the extent to which trust operates to enhance the relative efficiency of voluntary activities. If trust is cultivated legitimately and appropriately, then monitoring and regulation costs could clearly be saved; however, if the trust is misguided or misplaced because providers are not acting as anticipated, then while transaction costs are low, by definition desired outcomes are not being achieved. Second, it will be important – but very difficult – to take into account the true outputs and outcomes of voluntary organizations, or at least to seek out proxies for them. Without such measures it will not be possible to demonstrate whether trust is well placed or otherwise.

In fact, in the economic literature, evaluations have yet to be undertaken which have managed to take into account the factor input/ production cost, transaction costs and outcome/effectiveness sides simultaneously (ie to perform full cost-effectiveness analyses). Instead, two broad approaches can be discerned. First, Ortmann and Schlesinger (1997) have recently critically reviewed both the theoretical and empirical literatures. Inter alia, their review reports that some consumers evidently place more trust in voluntary providers than their for-profit counterparts in some industries (including health, day care for children); in some cases voluntary organizations perform relatively well on directly evaluated (by the researcher) hard-to-measure aspects of quality output; and, if the volume of complaints is used as a proxy for quality of output, other things being equal, their performance can be better than other providers in this sense too. But the evidence is sparse and uneven, to the extent that these authors conclude that the 'trust hypothesis stands on shaky ground as a general proposition. It can be sustained only under particular conditions that have been neither carefully described in theory nor subject to empirical assessment' (97).

Another, pragmatic approach has been to try at least to measure what is relatively easy to measure: costs and intermediate outputs. If there is evidence that the relationship between final outcomes and intermediate outputs is reasonably stable, then findings regarding voluntary organizations' performance measured in terms of cost per unit of intermediate output would at least suggest how they may be performing in terms of cost per unit of final outcome. For example, if cost per (quality and casemix adjusted) place were lower in the voluntary sector than for other providers in a particular service area, and if other, less formal (perhaps softer) data from users and/or professionals indicated that the quality of service was at least as good in this sector, then we could conclude that overall the sector was, perhaps, a more efficient provider in these cases.

For example, two industries in which voluntary services involve hard-to-measure and complex outcomes – in the sense that what is at stake is ultimately the welfare of vulnerable people – are community social and health care. One Personal Social Services Research Unit (PSSRU) study looked at public and voluntary sector day care services for elderly people, standardizing cost differences for a number of factors and for (some) user characteristics (Knapp and Missiakoulis, 1982). Voluntary sector providers were found to be more cost-effective than their public sector counterparts in intermediate outcome terms (but it was predicted that they would lose this advantage if they moved closer towards the public sector level of operation). There were many reasons for this, including a lower supply of volunteers. A second example compared voluntary sector, local government and private providers of residential child care services, looking at costs before and after their standardization for factors beyond the control of providers and also for differences in the characteristics of children accommodated (Knapp, 1986). Again the voluntary sector emerged from the evaluation in a favourable light. Careful account had to be taken of a number of features of the homes which would perhaps not get considered in a narrower financial audit, such as the quality of the care environment (important non-resource inputs). A third, recent study found that voluntary sector providers of residential mental health care for adults were more cost-effective than their public and private sector counterparts, again in intermediate output terms but again standardizing for intersectoral differences in the characteristics and needs of users (Knapp et al, 1998). Of course, none of these studies *proves* that the perceived voluntary sector cost and quality advantages work through to impact upon the long term welfare and personal development of individual service users, but they certainly provide a useful first step in attempting to evaluate the issues at stake.

New Institutional Insights

In contrast to the foregoing, the discussion of implications and empirics of this and the next subsection demonstrates a tendency to go down a more constructionist route, reflecting the theoretical predilections of this group of scholars. These seek to avoid aggregation or discussion of causation. Rather, the emphasis is upon exploring the sensitivities around the process of undertaking evaluation, and the subjective meanings attached by stakeholders to the idea of effectiveness: no attempt is made to reach an overall objective judgement.

Perhaps two implications for evaluation flow most obviously from the so-called new institutional approach. First, the theory affects our expectations of what we will actually find when we come to assess performance. At the broadest level, the net effect of voluntarism is usually taken to be enhanced efficiency, and the rational choice approaches we have outlined raise similar expectations of net gains in productivity. Economists have also suggested why inefficiency might be found,[12] but Romo and Anheier (1992) and Seibel (1990) suggest that inefficiency might be a pervasive feature particularly of those voluntary organizations which have historical roots in geographical or other communities (Evers's 1995 model is more open). An overarching theme is perhaps that voluntary organizations may survive or go under, not only because of comparative advantages in terms of efficiency, but because of their ability to satisfy their stakeholders that their activities are legitimate.

A second implication of these and broader new institutional organizational perspectives concerns the dangers and difficulties of the process of evaluation:

> evaluation and inspection [are] public assertions of societal control which violate the assumption that everyone is acting with competence and in good faith. Violating this assumption lowers morale and confidence. Thus, evaluation and inspection undermine the ceremonial aspects of organisations (Meyer and Rowan, 1977: 59).

This argument helps to explain why and how evaluation may take on ritualistic qualities, with neither evaluator nor evaluated wishing to know the truth. Through this theoretical lens, evaluation can be seen as something likely to be manipulated by interested parties so as to create the right impressions. This allows for the continuation of politically useful, but economically and socially ineffectual or unproven, programmes of support for the voluntary sector. But it also reminds us that evaluation may have a light touch because it is recognized by evaluators that heavy-handedness could undermine the very taken-for-granted trust which programmes may be established to capitalize on in the first place.

Multiple Constituents

At the organization level, an implication of the multiple constituency perspective is that evaluation, like other organizational activities, should be thought of as constituted by active players with their own strategies and interests – an argument that reinforces the thrust of the previous section – that it is misleading to represent the voluntary sector as passive subject matter in evaluations. In the absence of agreed objective measures of performance, key players may attempt to manipulate the process so that evaluated organizations are protected from unwanted intrusion. One way is through the active cultivation of goal ambiguity, so that 'the production function associated with ... services is *actively hidden* by the supplier and cannot easily be detected and controlled from the outside' (Frey and Pommerehne, 1980, cited in Di Maggio, 1987: emphases added).

One could also argue for more subtle variants of essentially the same point. Since complete concealment is unlikely to be sustainable, exaggeration and obfuscation may well present the next best strategies, particularly when information holdings are asymmetric. The difficulty is that because voluntary sector outputs and technological relationships *are* often complex, intangible and difficult to measure, there is plenty of scope for suppliers to do just this. The problems multiply when we move beyond the dyadic relationship between a single supplier and their evaluator to consider the more realistic scenario of multiple stakeholders, each with their own interests and opportunities for strategic misrepresentation.

There is now some empirical evidence to demonstrate that perceptions of effectiveness vary between different stakeholders in voluntary organizations, and that they also attach different meanings to evaluation. Herman and Renz (1997) found a good deal of variation between stakeholders (staff, board members, funders) concerning the extent to which the same health, welfare and disability charities were judged effective or not in terms of internally developed criteria, and interpret this as consistent with the subjective (socially constructed) character of these judgements. Another recent study – this time focusing on child care and community development providers – provides evidence on the complexity of the evaluation game (Murray and Tassie, 1994) between funders and fundees in particular, but also suggests that organizations can and do manipulate relevant information for their own strategic advantage. They found that:

> agencies received contradictory messages from funders, contradictions that are difficult to resolve. Funders are constrained in their ability to co-ordinate their evaluation activities due to differences between them in the nature of their evaluations, and agencies may find it difficult to satisfy more than one funder's definition of what constitutes a good agency due to these differences (Tassie et al, 1998).

The authors interpret these organizations' abilities to survive in this apparently fraught and contradictory environment as consistent with the emphasis given by new institutional theorists to the importance of ceremony in evaluations.

SOME OVERALL CONCLUSIONS

In conclusion, we reiterate the considerable complexity of the topic given to us for this chapter – the evaluation of voluntary organizations. We have tried to make clear some of the challenges which this complexity generates. Would-be evaluators have sought to overcome the complexities either by ignoring them (a common but rarely defensible approach) or by building their empirical endeavours on one or more simplifying models (implicitly, and sometimes explicitly, one or more theories) of voluntary sector existence, operation or performance. The ways in which people simplify the evaluation task will depend upon their disciplinary backgrounds. As we have demonstrated, this can lead to different questions, as well as different answers, in part because each involves different frames for 'selecting, organising, interpreting and making sense of a complex reality to provide guideposts for knowing, analysing, persuading and acting' (Rein and Schon, 1993: 146). The most clear difference in how the question has been framed seems to lie between those with a rationalist, positivist tendency who seek objective answers, and those constructionists who seek to explicate the multiple meanings and perhaps logics at stake.

In our view, normatively, because reality is evidently so complex, and with the existing state of knowledge, evaluation should be a multi-framed activity (Parsons, 1995). However, no evaluations of which we are aware have simultaneously handled all the properties of voluntary organizations that our review of theory and its implications suggests they ideally should – even within each of these two broad frames of reference. To do so would be an enormous task, but it is certainly fair to suggest that too many evaluations are based on theoretical or conceptual bases that are too narrow and perspectives that are too particular.

To keep an evaluation task manageable, the evaluator would need to focus on those features of the specific field under consideration. For a start, priorities for addressing the various dimensions of resource, process and outcome that we have discussed are likely to vary according to the field in which the sector or individual organization is situated. For instance, attending to participation as an output may be crucial in sports and social clubs, but less so in acute health care; focusing on advocacy is likely to be more important for environmental groups, but less so for philanthropic intermediaries. Secondly, there may be prior evidence to suggest that one theoretical perspective has greater face (or other) validity than others in the particular context under study. One should beware premature selection of conceptual base, but pragmatically something of this kind is almost imperative in order to make discrete field studies more manageable.

Whatever choices are made, there is clearly a need for full and frank explication of assumptions and value judgements, and ideally also some examination of the sensitivity of findings to the starting assumptions, the data collection techniques and the modes of analysis.

ENDNOTES

1 For example, we do not discuss here entrepreneurship theories (Badelt, 1997) or 'social origins' theory (Salamon and Anheier, 1998).
2 There is a major specialist literature on networks within sociology (McPherson et al, 1992), but an exploration of this field is beyond the scope of this chapter.
3 For example, the utility of a residents' association formed to address a particular problem does not evaporate when that problem is solved, because participation within it has enriched members' social networks, and these now constitute a durable resource which can be drawn upon for other purposes (whether mediated through this voluntary group, or otherwise).
4 For a very useful review and critique of the social capital idea, see Foley and Edwards (1997) and the accompanying papers.
5 This assumption is not made by Coleman himself, but does appear to be made by some who have employed the concept empirically. For example, Putnam (1993: Chapter 4) considers 'scarcity of sports and cultural associations' to be a major (negative) ingredient in constructing his 'civic community index', and no

attempt appears to be made to measure participation in wholly informal networks. Of course, arguing from perspectives long pre-dating the development of the social capital approach, both sociologists (Van Til, 1988) and economists (James, 1987; James and Rose-Ackerman, 1986) have noted that voluntary organizations are important vehicles for socialization or the performance of 'integrative functions'.

6   The idea of value-rationality was developed by Max Weber. Value-rational organizations are those in which the aims of founders, subsequently substantively imprinted on succeeding controllers, may not be instrumental in the sense of choosing a means to an end, but instead are 'determined by a conscious belief in the value for its own sake of some ... form of behaviour, independent of its prospects of success' (Weber, cited by Hughes et al, 1995: 106).

7   This controversial distinction between 'risk' and 'trust' (see also Williamson, 1993: 97) is just one of many ways of trying to deconstruct trust. In fact, more recently writers on the subject have rarely been content to make such a simple distinction, but have instead developed ornate typologies and multiple classifications. Two recent complementary accounts are by 6 (1994) and Mitzal (1996).

8   However, because these authors position themselves theoretically with new institutional theorists who ultimately deny the possibility of efficiency existing objectively as a property independent of the subjective views of actors, it is not clear how agencies can be logically categorized as efficient or inefficient.

9   In fact, Evers argues that tensions, resolved or otherwise, may also be evident in individual organizations, which can then be seen as 'hybrid' or 'polyvalent'. By this, Evers means that the multiple logics under which they operate can impel them to engage simultaneously in service provision and campaigning, the balancing of which can be 'a difficult and often conflict-laden issue' (1995: 171). However, most of Evers's analysis is at a macro-structural level.

10 We do not discuss the general problem of taking into account public good and externality attributes of service in evaluation; this is exhaustively treated in welfare economics (see, for example Barr, 1993). We also give short shrift to the sector's political and advocacy roles, for the opposite reason; there is virtually no theoretical argument or empirical evidence beyond case studies of individual organizations (Jenkins, 1987). The one serious attempt to address this question, by 6 and Forder (1996) spends a good deal of time pointing to the huge difficulties of attempting to measure the 'outputs' of this activity (229–230) and judging them insurmountable, and then opts to 'assess performance by appraising strategy' instead.

11 At the crudest level, volunteering could be distinguished from membership on the basis that the latter involves activities with others for joint benefit, while the former involves activities for others, perhaps of a more public or altruistic character. However, activities, like the organizations which undertake them, are notoriously difficult to categorize into public and private pigeonholes (Knapp and Kendall, 1990). See Taylor and 6 (1994) and Lynn (1996) for detailed discussions of the (overlapping) complications of defining membership and volunteering respectively.

12 Economists have also outlined a number of reasons why we might expect to find inefficiency in these contexts. Most obviously, voluntary organizations are usually thought to suffer from free-rider problems impairing allocative efficiency (transaction costs and stakeholder theory arguments concerning the availability of countervailing mechanisms notwithstanding). Others have argued that they benefit from an unhealthy amount of insulation from market

forces, and that the attenuation of property rights is always problematic, leading to productive or x-inefficiency; see Steinberg (1987). However, the overall thrust of the dominant theoretical formulations, as described earlier, runs in the opposite direction.

BIBLIOGRAPHY

Ashford, K and Clarke, J (1996) 'Grant monitoring by charities: the process of grant making and evaluation', *Voluntas*, Vol 7, pp279–299

Badelt, C (1997) 'Entrepreneurship theories of the non-profit sector', *Voluntas*, Vol 8, No 2, pp162–178

Barker, D (1993) 'Values and volunteering', in Davis Smith, J (ed) *Volunteering in Europe: Opportunities and Challenges for the 90s*, Voluntary Action Research Second Series No 4, Volunteer Centre UK, Berkhamsted

Barr, N (1993) *The Economics of the Welfare State*, Weidenfield and Nicholson, London

Ben-Ner, A, and Van Hoomissen, T (1993) 'Nonprofit organisations in the mixed economy: a demand and supply analysis', in Ben-Ner, A and Gui, B (eds) *The Nonprofit Sector in the Mixed Economy*, The University of Michigan Press, Michigan

Billis, D (1993) *Organising Public and Voluntary Agencies*, Routledge, London

Coleman, J S (1990) *Foundations of Social Theory*, Belnap Press of Harvard University Press, Cambridge, MA

Coleman, J S (1993) 'A rational choice perspective on economic sociology', in Smelser, N J and Sweberg, R (eds) *The Handbook of Economic Sociology*, Princeton University Press, Princeton, New Jersey

Davies, B P and Knapp, M R J (1981) *Old People's Homes and the Production of Welfare*, Routledge and Kegan Paul, London

Dekker, P and van den Broeck, A (1998) 'Civil society in comparative perspective: involvement in voluntary associations in Northern Europe and Western America', *Voluntas*, forthcoming

Di Maggio, P (1987) 'Nonprofit organisations in the production and distribution of culture', in Powell, W W (ed) *The Nonprofit Sector: A Research Handbook*, Yale University Press, New Haven

Evers, A (1993) 'The welfare mix approach: understanding the pluralism of welfare systems', in Evers, A and Svetlik, I (eds) *Balancing Pluralism: New Welfare Mixes in Care for the Elderly*, Avebury, Aldershot

Evers, A (1995) 'Part of the welfare mix: the third sector as an intermediate area between market economy, state and community', *Voluntas*, Vol 6, No 2, pp159–182

Foley, M and Edwards, M (1997) 'Editors' introduction: escape from politics? social theory and the social capital debate', *American Behavioral Scientist* (special issue devoted to social capital, civil society and contemporary democracy), Vol 40, No 5, pp550–561

Foster, V (1997) 'What value should be placed on volunteering?' in Pharoah, C (ed) *Dimensions of the Voluntary Sector*, Charities Aid Foundation, West Malling

Frey, B S and Pommerehne, W W (1980) 'An economic analysis of the museum', in Di Maggio, P (1987) op cit

Gaskin, K (1997) 'Assessing the economic value and cost of volunteers', in Pharoah, C (ed) *Dimensions of the Voluntary Sector*, Charities Aid Foundation, West Malling

Hansmann, H B (1980) 'The role of nonprofit enterprise', *Yale Law Journal*, Vol 89, pp835–898

Herman, R D (1990) 'Methodological issues in studying the effectiveness of nongovernmental and nonprofit organisations', *Nonprofit and Voluntary Sector Quarterly*, Vol 19, No 3, pp293–306

Herman, R D and Renz, D O (1997) 'Multiple constituencies and the social construction of nonprofit organizational effectiveness', *Nonprofit and Voluntary Sector Quarterly*, Vol 26, No 2, pp185–207

Hughes, J A, Martin, P J and Sharrock, W W (1995) *Understanding Classical Sociology: Marx, Weber, Durkheim*, Sage Publications, London

James, E (1987) 'The nonprofit sector in comparative perspective', in Powell, W W (ed) *The Nonprofit Sector: A Research Handbook*, Yale University Press, New Haven

James, E (1989) 'Introduction' in James, E (ed) *The Nonprofit Sector in International Perspective: Studies in Comparative Culture and Policy*, Oxford University Press, Oxford

James, E and Rose-Ackerman, S (1986) *The Nonprofit Enterprise in Market Economics*, Harwood, New York

Jenkins, J C (1987) 'Nonprofit organisations and policy advocacy', in Powell, W W (ed) *The Nonprofit sector: A Research Handbook*, Yale University Press, New Haven

Kanter, R M and Summers, D V (1987) 'Doing well by doing good: dilemmas of performance measurement in nonprofit organisations and the need for a multiple constituency approach', in Powell, W W (ed) *The Nonprofit Sector: A Research Handbook*, Yale University Press, New Haven

Kendall, J (1992) Review of Jennifer R Wolch, *The Shadow State, Voluntas*, No 3, pp247–256

Kendall, J and Knapp, M R J (1995) 'A loose and baggy monster: boundaries, definitions and typologies', in Davis Smith, J and Hedley, R (eds) *Introduction to the Voluntary Sector*, Routledge, London

Kendall, J and Knapp, M R J (1996) *The Voluntary Sector in the UK*, Manchester University Press, Manchester

Knapp, M R J (1984) *The Economics of Social Care*, Macmillan, London

Knapp, M R J (1986) 'The relative cost-effectiveness of public, voluntary and private providers of residential child care', in Culyer, A J and Jônsson, B (eds) *Public and Private Health Services*, Blackwell, Oxford

Knapp, M R J (1990) *Time is Money: The Costs of Volunteering in Britain Today*, Volunteer Centre UK, Berkhamsted

Knapp, M R J and Kendall, J (1990) *Defining the British Voluntary Sector*, paper prepared for 1990 Independent Sector Spring Research Forum, Boston, MA, March

Knapp, M R J and Missiakoulis, S (1982) 'Inter-sectoral cost comparisons: day care for the elderly', *Journal of Social Policy*, Vol 11, pp335–354

Knapp, M R J, Koutsogeorgopoulou, V and Smith, J D (1996) 'The economics of volunteering: examining participation patterns and levels in the UK', *Non-Profit Studies*, Vol 1, No 1, pp38–55

Knapp, M R J, Chisholm, D, Astin, J, Lelliott, P and Audini, B (1998) 'Public and private residential care: is there a cost difference?' *Journal of Health Services Research and Policy*, forthcoming

Krashinsky, M (1986) 'Transaction costs and a theory of the nonprofit organisation' in Rose-Ackerman, S (ed) *The Economics of Nonprofit Institutions*, Oxford University Press, Oxford

Leat, D (1992) *Trusts in Transition*, Joseph Rowntree Foundation, York

Lynn, P (1996) 'Measuring voluntary activity', *Non-Profit Studies*, Vol 1, No 2, pp1–11

McPherson, J M, Popielarz, P A and Drobnic, S (1992) 'Social networks and organizational dynamics', *American Sociological Review*, Vol 57, pp153–170

Meyer and Rowan (1977, reprinted 1991) 'Institutionalised organisations: formal structure and myth and ceremony' in Powell, W W and Di Maggio, P (eds) *The New Institutionalism in Organizational Analysis*, University of Chicago Press, Chicago and London

Mitzal, B (1996) *Trust in Modern Societies*, Polity Press in association with Basil Blackwell, Cambridge

Murray, V and Tassie, B (1994) 'Evaluating the effectiveness of nonprofit organisations', in Herman, R D (ed) *The Jossey-Bass Handbook of Nonprofit Leadership and Management*, Jossey-Bass publishers, San Francisco

Onyx, J (1996) 'Social capital: theory and measurement', Working Paper No 34, Centre for Australian Community Organisations and Management (CACOM), University of Technology, Sydney

Ortmann, A and Schlesinger, M (1997) 'Trust, repute and the role of nonprofit enterprise', *Voluntas*, Vol 8, No 2, pp97–119

Parsons, W (1995) *Public Policy: An Introduction to the Theory and Practice of Policy Analysis*, Edward Elgar, Aldershot

Putnam, R (1993) *Making Democracy Work: Civic Traditions in Modern Italy*, Princeton University Press, Princeton, New Jersey

Rein, M and Schon, D (1993) 'Reframing policy discourse', in Fischer, F and Forester, J (eds) *The Argumentative Turn in Policy Analysis*, UCL Press, London

Romo, F P and Anheier, H K (1992) 'The triadic transaction: a socio-economic approach to nonprofit organizations', unpublished manuscript

Salamon, L S (1987) 'Partners in public service: the scope and theory of government–nonprofit relations', in Powell, W W (ed) *The Nonprofit Sector: A Research Handbook*, Yale University Press, New Haven

Salamon, L S and Anheier, H K (1996) *The Emerging Nonprofit Sector: An Overview*, Manchester University Press, Manchester

Salamon, L S and Anheier, H K (1997) *Defining the Nonprofit Sector: A Cross-National Analysis*, Manchester University Press, Manchester

Salamon, L S and Anheier, H K (1998) 'Social origins of civil society: explaining the non-profit sector cross-nationally', *Voluntas*, forthcoming

Saxon-Harrold, S (1993) 'Attitudes to charities and government', in Saxon-Harrold, S and Kendall, J (eds) *Researching the Voluntary Sector*, volume 1, Charities Aid Foundation, Tonbridge

Seibel, W (1990) 'Organizational behavior and organizational function', in Anheier, H and Seibel, W (eds) *The Nonprofit Sector: International and Comparative Perspectives*, de Gruyter, Berlin

Steinberg, R (1987) 'Nonprofit organizations and the market', in Powell, W W (ed) *The Nonprofit Sector: A Research Handbook*, Yale University Press, New Haven

Tassie, B, Murray, V and Cutt, J (1998) 'Evaluating social service agencies: fuzzy pictures of organizational effectiveness', *Voluntas*, forthcoming

Taylor, M and 6, P (1994) 'Membership in voluntary organisations: do we know what we mean by it?', unpublished manuscript

Van Til, J (1988) *Mapping the Third Sector*, Foundation Center, New York

Weisbrod, B A (1975) 'Towards a theory of the nonprofit sector', in Phelps, E (ed) *Altruism, Morality and Economic Theory*, Russell Sage, New York

Weisbrod, B A (1988) *The Nonprofit Economy*, Harvard University Press,

Cambridge, MA

Williamson, O E (1993) 'Transaction cost economics and organization theory', in Smelser, N J and Sweberg, R (eds) *The Handbook of Economic Sociology*, Princeton University Press, Princeton, New Jersey

Wolch, J (1990) *The Shadow State: Government and the Voluntary Sector in Transition*, The Foundation Center, New York

Wuthnow, R (ed) (1991) *Between States and Markets: The Voluntary Sector in Comparative Perspective*, Princeton University Press, Princeton, New Jersey

6, P (1994) 'Trust, social theory and public policy', unpublished manuscript

6, P and Forder, J (1996) 'Can campaigning be evaluated?' *Nonprofit and Voluntary Sector Quarterly*, Vol 25, No 2, pp225–247

6, P and Kendall, J (1997) *The Contract Culture in Public Services*, Arena, Aldershot

11

Evaluating NGO Development Interventions

Roger C Riddell

INTRODUCTION

It is not possible in the space of a short chapter to capture all aspects of NGO development evaluations because of the difficulty of obtaining information. Much of the experience with evaluation is not written down or is contained in 'grey' literature which is not easily accessible. The evaluation of NGO development interventions is also a very fast changing area. This chapter has a more limited purpose. It summarizes the main results and findings of a draft report commissioned by and produced for the Expert Group on Evaluation of the Development Assistance Committee (DAC) of the Organisation for Economic Cooperation and Development (OECD) entitled *Searching for Impact and Methods: NGO Evaluation Synthesis Report* (Kruse et al, 1997) which focuses on evaluation methods. The main focus of the report is on the methods used in the major NGO evaluations commissioned by donors, using this as a backdrop against which to discuss approaches to evaluation conducted by NGOs themselves. However before this summary of the report is presented some introductory remarks are made about concerns (of NGOs and others) about the links which are commonly made between evaluation and impact assessment.

FROM ASSESSMENT TO IMPACT ASSESSMENT: DOUBTS ABOUT THE JUMP

Judging the effects of NGO development interventions is critically influenced by – some would argue predominantly determined by – the methods used to assess those interventions. The conference session at which the ideas in this article were presented was called 'Impact, Evaluation and

Effectiveness?' whose title would appear to be built on a number of assumptions. Most directly, it is assumed that the most important criteria against which NGO development interventions should be judged is the (development) impact that they have. This in turn should help to inform us about their effectiveness, or the effectiveness of the development interventions. This raises a series of questions: are there not other criteria against which to judge NGO development interventions and thus to help assess the effectiveness of NGOs in development? The following paragraphs provide seven different sorts of reasons which question the link often made automatically between assessment and evaluation on the one hand and impact on the other, or which raise more fundamental questions about evaluation methods. The first few arguments challenge the need for evaluations to be conducted at all; the second group focus more on different types of evaluation and assessment and fears about the use or potential use to which the results of such evaluations might be put. What all the points share is that they either have been in the past or are today used by NGOs to question the impact–evaluation–effectiveness links.

Not Interested in Evaluation

The first challenge to impact assessment comes from NGOs who are not interested in evaluation at all. This is really an overarching position which can subsume very different perspectives about evaluation, a number of which are discussed further below. What is important to note here is that while there has been an enormous growth in interest in evaluation and evaluation methods among and across NGOs over the past ten years, one needs to be cautious in making the assumption that all NGOs now subscribe to the view that evaluation is important and should be carried out. In a book published as recently as 1995, Edwards and Hulme maintained that 'Most NGOs are not concerned with accountability at all' (1995: 260). Even if the percentage share of NGOs not interested in evaluation is far lower – and we are all in the game of guesswork when it comes to trying to provide a precise figure – it is not negligible or insignificant.

Helping and Providing Aid Is the Sole Basis for Legitimizing Development Activities

One reason given by some NGOs for their lack of interest in, and sometimes hostility towards, evaluation, can be traced back to what they view as their legitimacy – the reason for their existence and for undertaking the activities they perform. One group of Northern NGOs – it seems often to be smaller organizations – argue that the reason they exist is to respond to the cry for help from poor people and poor communities in developing countries. Responding to that call, by providing money, sending medicines, blankets, hoes or cows, provides the sole basis for judging the activities of these organizations, it is argued. What those helped do with the funds or goods provided is an issue for the recipients, not for the NGO in the North sending them; hence, it is argued, it is wholly inappropriate – even morally wrong – to judge the NGO concerned by the impact of the funds provided. In some senses, to ask about impact is to betray a trust between the donor and the recipient. A linked, and probably more widespread, view is heard by some people providing donations to development NGOs; don't waste precious and scarce funds undertaking expensive evaluations to assess effectiveness, spend it on helping those who are clearly in need and clearly have greater needs than the funds available can provide.

NGO Development Interventions are Unique

Linked in some ways to the previous argument is the view that evaluations to assess impact are of little value (at the extreme are of no value) because, it is argued, both the results achieved and the reasons why such results were achieved are bounded, based and rooted overwhelmingly in unique conditions and circumstances which are highly unlikely to be repeated or replicated elsewhere. On the one hand, few if any lessons can be transferred from a particular sectoral project implemented with and by one community to the very different context of a different community in a different socio-economic, political and cultural setting. On the other hand, once a particular project has been implemented in a particular community, providing clean water, agricultural extension advice or a primary school, the lessons learnt for that community will immediately be redundant as that community will no longer need what has already been provided.

Difficulties of Isolating Project Outputs

A variant on this theme is an argument about the difficulty/impossibility of assessing impact based on the important distinction between output and outcome – one which, it should be acknowledged, is more often raised by theoreticians than by practitioners and applies to any activities, particularly those concerned with social and human development, and not only NGO development activity. Here it is argued that if one is trying to assess the impact of a particular project it is essential to assess and thus isolate the contribution of the project, and only the project – the project's outputs – on the beneficiaries and be careful not to attribute to the project wider outcomes which occur either directly or indirectly as a result of other factors, causes and influences. For example, if an NGO project consists of providing agricultural advice to poor farmers to raise their yields, and yields then rise, it is important to know what other factors (access to credit for input purchases, rainfall patterns, availability of seed and fertilizer) have contributed to the yields achieved in order to isolate the contribution of the NGO's particular project to the overall and wide outcome achieved. In practice, while it is more common for NGOs to point to external factors when they have influenced a project adversely, it is far less common for them to try to factor out and acknowledge those external factors which place their project activities, and the links between inputs and overall outcome, in a far better light. It is argued that the quite widespread practice of evaluations of NGO activities failing to trace through the narrower link between project inputs and project outputs suggests that a not inconsiderable number of impact assessments are of little value.

The Disjuncture Between Project Impact Evaluation and Development Processes

A common concern, and criticism, made by NGOs, often those who undertake impact evaluations, is rooted in different views about development. On the one hand, it is argued, development evaluations are focused overwhelmingly on discrete projects and assessing their impact, whereas, on the other hand, development needs to be viewed more as a long term process which can often be distorted by being packaged up into separate projects with artificial objectives. What are the consequences? An extreme view is that it is not possible to assess the impact of (the more important) development processes. A less extreme view is that while it might be possible to develop impact assessment methods appropriate and relevant to monitoring and assessing the progress of development processes, current impact assessments and impact assessment methods have developed tools relevant and appropriate only to discrete projects. Here the criticism is rooted in the methods used and is not, like the more extreme view, one based on a priori principles.

Assessing Impact Encourages Funding on the Basis of Impact

The criticisms made here focus not so much on forms of assessment which concentrate solely or exclusively on the impact of the development intervention, but more on what is done with the data and information obtained from such impact assessment. The major focus here is on the donors and those who influence the funding of NGO development interventions, and the worry/criticism/concern is when funders use the results of impact assessments to alter funding decisions. The specific concern is that the greater is the focus on impact, the greater is the likelihood that funds will be shifted towards those development interventions (projects) which achieve better results (so judged) and away from those whose results are judged as poor to (in the extreme case) failure. At first sight, the criticism seems odd: if it is accepted that there is merit in assessing impact then surely it should be accepted that funds *should* be channelled towards successful projects and away from those not succeeding, especially those that are clearly outright failures? Surely few (if any) NGOs would be advocates of allocating funds towards development failures?

The point being made is both more subtle and more profound in its implications. It is argued that if donors (and other funders) were to judge NGO development activity solely by results achieved, and especially – as is common – cost-effectiveness which is an influential factor in coming to judgement, then there is a high risk that this would fundamentally alter the nature and purpose of NGO development interventions. Specifically:

- it would encourage NGOs to move away from experimental and innovative activities because of the uncertainty of the results and the low priority given to tangible and immediate impact on beneficiaries;
- it would encourage NGOs to move away from risky initiatives where the results are likely to be uncertain and costs may be high in relation to results obtained;
- it would encourage NGOs to move away from projects focused on poorer people because the costs are likely to be greater and the prospects of achieving financial sustainability poor; and
- it would encourage NGOs to implement projects which minimize inputs or processes that add to the time taken for implementation; this would be likely to lower the emphasis given to partnership and participation, to learning, and to developing and strengthening trust and the cement of social capital.

As performance is increasingly influenced by cost-effectiveness criteria, work with poorer groups risks being rated lower than work with higher income strata groups. Working with poor and more marginalized groups may be seen as a less effective use of limited (and perhaps shrinking) funds because of the higher risk of failure. In short, to the extent that resources channelled to NGOs are provided on the basis of results achieved, this process is likely to have two results. On the one hand, it is likely to encourage NGOs to play safe and not expose themselves to the higher risks of failure for fear of putting a self-imposed break on funding channels. On the other, to the extent that NGOs decide to resist such pressures there is growing risk either that the funds available will be channelled to the more compliant NGOs, or that new NGOs will rise up to try to take the place of these resisting NGOs and take their funds.

Is all this a theoretical fear? The evidence both supports and challenges the reality of these fears. A major Canadian report on NGO effectiveness argued thus (Fortin et al, 1992: xiv):

> *The quality of work done by NGOs should a be major concern behind NGO funding. Funding should be based on a performance measurement system using specific performance indicators and each NGO should be provided on a confidential basis with the results of its evaluation.*

In contrast, the recent Australian study revealed an awareness of the dangers of funding solely by results (Kershaw et al, 1995: 44–45):

> *... if NGOs were to lose their autonomy in programming and policy dialogue, they might become increasingly like government agencies. While this might make the relationship more harmonious, the Review Team believes that in time NGOs would come to offer the Government LESS as development partners ... NGO capacities for innovation and developing new areas and new forms of development cooperation may diminish as they increasingly follow the requirements and objectives set by Government. AusAid does not expect private companies to harness the voluntary resources of the Australian community, to represent the interests of the wider community in policy development processes, or to undertake a third sector role. It doesn't expect private companies to provide community-to-community links.*

The Effects of Adopting Evaluation Methods on the Nature of the Organization

A final concern focuses on the ways in which methods of evaluation influence the organization using the methods selected (or imposed). It is often argued that one of the benefits of NGOs (and other organizations) undertaking evaluations is that the process of doing evaluations, reflecting on the results obtained and trying to alter processes and practices to enhance performance is itself beneficial. In this view, the process inculcates a more rigorous approach and attitude to work which ripples through the organization well beyond those immediately involved in evaluation. This is viewed as something positive and beneficial. However, the results may not always be beneficial. In particular it is argued, on the one hand, that smaller NGOs with few resources and even more limited staff skills and staff time simply do not have the time, space and resources to undertake impact evaluations to the depth required to achieve meaningful results. On the other hand, and more profoundly, it is also argued that even if time, space and resources *were* available, undertaking even a simple impact evaluation would be such a large event in relation to the size of the (small) NGO that the process of doing the evaluation would risk changing the nature of the very organization whose activities are being assessed. At the extreme, the policy conclusion is to wish to resist all evaluations. Less radically, it is argued that new/different/simpler evaluation methods need to be applied to smaller NGOs. And within that context it is argued that the starting point should be the preservation of the attributes of the small NGO, suggesting that the methods adopted need to emerge from the organization, and thus rejecting an approach which begins with and tries to trim down and latch the methods used by larger organizations on to the smaller NGO.

THE EVOLUTION OF METHODS USED BY DONOR-COMMISSIONED STUDIES TO ASSESS THE IMPACT OF NGO DEVELOPMENT INTERVENTIONS

Current methods and approaches of assessing the impact of NGO development interventions have been influenced profoundly by three interrelated factors: the past (and reasonably short) history of NGO evaluation; the influence of official donors in encouraging NGOs to undertake evaluations in a systematic way; and, in that context, the early dominance of the US in NGO evaluation. This section focuses on the evolution of methods used in many donor-initiated or donor-commissioned studies of the impact of NGO development interventions. The OECD/DAC study (Kruse et al, 1997) reviewed some 20 major evaluation studies commissioned by 10 different donors in the past 20 years (see Box 11.1). The purpose of this section is to try to assess how the methods used in these studies evolved. The discussion is intended to highlight some general trends and influences; clearly not all the generalizations made apply to all the studies undertaken.

BOX 11.1 LIST OF DONORS WHOSE STUDIES ARE INCLUDED IN THE OECD/DAC STUDY

Donor	Year of Major Studies (publication date)
Australia	1995
Canada	1992
Denmark	1988*, 1989, 1994[1], 1995
Finland	1994, 1995*
New Zealand	1987, 1989, 1990, 1991, 1993
The Netherlands	1991[2]
Norway	1994, 1995
Sweden	1995[3]
UK	1992/5[4], 1995
US	1979, 1995, 1996[5]

* Evaluation of volunteer programmes

Notes:
1 Evaluation of framework agreements.
2 In 1995, the Dutch NGOs produced a report on measures taken in response to the 1991 report.
3 From 1987, Sida has commissioned studies on the capacity of the 13 (originally 14) framework organizations.
4 There was an early, very sketchy, UK study in 1986. The 1992 (ODI) study was published in book form in 1995, the year the second UK study's findings were published.
5 Besides the 1979 and 1995 studies, USAID has conducted a succession of reviews in 1988, 1994 and 1996, many of which have also addressed the issue of impact.

Source: Kruse et al, 1997: 16

From its earliest days, the United States Agency for International Development (USAID) required its major aid projects to be evaluated; end of project evaluations were required of all major projects, and mid-term assessments were commonplace. As USAID began to expand its funding of private voluntary organizations (PVOs), it became an (automatic) requirement that PVO projects should also be evaluated. This link, in turn, was reinforced by the closeness with which the work (aims and objectives) of US PVOs was viewed vis à vis the aims and objectives of USAID; for many years it has been a requirement that US PVOs ensure that any project proposal they put forward for funding adequately supports achievement of USAID mission objectives. Indeed it is this sort of requirement and restriction which has led some PVOs in the US, such as Oxfam America, to refuse to take official aid funds.

Given both the overall requirements of USAID to evaluate all projects and PVO initiatives being seen if not as similar to, at least in a continuum with, official aid projects, it is not surprising that the methods used in evaluating PVO projects have been similar to those used in official aid projects. The earliest multi-project evaluation of US PVO development activities was commissioned (by USAID) in the late 1970s and published in 1979, almost ten years before other (European and multilateral) donors began to focus systematically on the evaluation of NGO development projects (Barclay et al, 1979). In retrospect it would appear that this study had a profound impact on subsequent donor-initiated and donor-funded evaluations of NGO development projects, as well as on developments within the US itself. It focused on four questions:

1) Are PVO activities resulting in development benefits?
2) Are these benefits accruing primarily to the poorest members of the population?
3) Will project benefits be sustained when PVO activities are phased out? and
4) Are PVO activities cost-effective in terms of potential spread and replicability?

In practice, the cost-effectiveness aspects were all important; indeed, one of the two objectives of the evaluation exercise was to test and develop a cost-effective methodology for documenting and explaining the development impact of PVO projects. The concept of developmental impact was divided into three dimensions:

1) direct benefits generated by the commitment of PVO resources, standardized for differences in project costs;
2) the potential that these benefits would be sustained after the donor's resources were exhausted or withdrawn; and
3) the prospects for future development in related activities by the same participant population, based upon the success of the original project.

These variables were categorized as direct benefits, benefit continuation and benefit growth. Direct benefits were quantified by converting benefits in kind into monetary equivalents based on the assumptions of evaluators, in order that costs per beneficiary could be estimated and a cost-benefit ratio derived. In other words, impact was viewed predominantly through the prism of cost-effectiveness. The continued, if not growing, importance of cost-effectiveness issues in PVO evaluations is illustrated by the funds USAID allocated to, and the prominence given to, developing a cost-effectiveness manual during the early to mid–1980s: see Nathan and Associates, 1983; 1986.

Like so many subsequent NGO evaluations, the 1979 study was hampered by the absence of baseline data, so judgements on impact had to be based on crude and proxy data and information, while assessments of benefit growth and benefit continuation were little more than projected guesses into the future.

Since the 1979 US study, and especially since 1988 (see Box 11.1), other donors (bilateral and multilateral) have funded and commissioned a series of major evaluation studies on NGO development interventions. What interests us here in particular is what approaches have been used to evaluate these interventions and what influenced the methodological approaches used. Five direct factors have been most influential in determining the methods and approaches used by donors.

The first is the experiences and history of PVO evaluation in the US. In unpacking this history, a series of influences can be identified. Perhaps the most important is an acceptance that it is legitimate to evaluate NGO development interventions in regard to their impact, most notably their impact on the poor. It may seem odd to mention this at all, when the whole purpose of the evaluation of development interventions is to evaluate impact and (as the US approach goes on to confirm) legitimate impact assessment in terms of cost-effectiveness. While no NGO has argued that it is illegitimate to assess their development interventions in terms of the development impact on the poor people helped, a series of issues are being brought forward to question at least the extent to which this should be the sole or even dominant criterion against which such interventions are judged. These include the importance given to processes of development and capacity building, to experimentation and innovation, and finally to risk and questions raised about the growing link between impact and future funding.

The second factor influencing the donor approach to assessing NGO development interventions has been the rapid growth in official aid funds channelled to and through NGOs in the 1980s and at least the first half of the 1990s. This growth has put pressures on donor agencies to provide assurances (ultimately to parliament) that the monies allocated have been put to good use, leading the donors, in turn, to focus on impact and cost-benefit assessments as the means by which to make the value-for-money judgement, again following the practice of assessing official aid projects and programmes.

The third factor influencing the methods employed has been the core and evolving criteria used in assessing and evaluating mainstream development projects. As already noted, cost-effectiveness and sustainability were issues of concern to mainstream evaluations as long ago as the 1970s. To these have been added assessment in relation to gender and environmental impact. More recently, one is beginning to see signs of donor assessments asking about impact or influence in relation to democratic forces and civil society.

A fourth factor influencing the methods by which NGO development interventions have been judged has been the incorporation of some (though not all) of the factors which NGOs and PVOs have claimed constitute if not the uniqueness, then at least the comparative advantage and particular strength of NGOs. The ones picked up by donor evaluations are the following:

- ability to reach down to (and have an impact on) the poor;
- the innovative nature of NGO development interventions;
- the replicability and/or scaling-up potential of NGO projects; and
- the participatory nature and/or strength of NGO development interventions.

By far the most important factor has been the claimed impact/poverty aspect of NGO interventions. Thus, not only have all donor evaluations of NGO development interventions sought to assess these interventions against the impact/poverty group attribute but this has usually been given a dominant position in the evaluation. In contrast, innovation, replicability and scaling-up have not been universally used, while poor performance on these scores is not viewed as challenging the legitimacy of the development intervention being scrutinized as much as failure against the impact/poverty criteria. While the issue of participation has been given increasing prominence, it has generally not been seen as a legitimizing characteristic; rather it has more commonly been assessed within the impact/poverty group context. Mention should also be made here of cost-effectiveness issues. It would be incorrect to argue that it has only been donors who have highlighted cost-effectiveness issues. Perhaps, in part, because of the importance which donors give to cost-effectiveness issues when distributing funds, NGOs have become increasingly vocal in claiming that channelling funds to them and their development projects is a cost-effective way of utilizing aid funds.

The fifth, and final, factor influencing evaluation methods for assessing NGO development projects has been the logical framework and linked log-frame techniques of undertaking evaluations. The formal requirement to use log-frame approaches in both drawing up project proposals and undertaking monitoring and evaluation activities is both comparatively new and far from a universal requirement of all donors. Yet what has become more common is for donor evaluations to focus quite explicitly on the question of whether the projects funded have achieved the objectives set. This has had importance at different levels. At one level, giving

---

**BOX 11.2 CHECKLIST ISSUES ASSESSED IN
DONOR-BASED IMPACT ASSESSMENTS**

The achievement of objectives
Impact: livelihoods, poverty reach, alleviation of poverty and degree of
    participation
Sustainability (financial and institutional)
Cost-effectiveness
Innovation and flexibility
Replicability and scaling-up
Gender impact
Environmental impact
Democracy, pluralism and civil society

Source: Kruse et al, 1997

---

prominence to assessment against objectives provides acknowledgement
(even if indirect) of the diversity, range and complexity of NGO development interventions, not least by highlighting that by no means all
interventions aim either to reach poor groups or to raise living standards
(at least directly). At another level, the importance attached to focusing on
assessment against objectives – and little apparent opposition by NGOs
has been observed to such an approach – has had an important influence
on the way that NGOs perceive their approach to development. In particular, the growing emphasis given to objectives, and the articulation of
objectives, has reduced both the number and share of total NGO interventions initiated with vague and/or open-ended objectives.

Thus, the majority of donor-initiated studies of NGO development
interventions have based their assessments on the headings and issues
listed in Box 11.2.

The evolution of an apparently more complex and systematic approach
to evaluation needs to be placed alongside the problems of obtaining
accurate data and information with which to draw conclusions about
impact. A common theme running through most of the donor-initiated
evaluations has been comments on the inadequacy and even absence of
data – often quantitative, but not uncommonly qualitative data – with
which to draw firm conclusions on many, if not most, of the areas listed
above. Indeed, the Norwegian study stands in marked contrast to all the
other studies by arguing forcefully that the evidence available and the tools
with which to make a firm assessment are simply insufficient to make any
reliable and generalized comments about the impact of NGO development
interventions (Tvedt, 1995).

For the other studies, a repeated and consistent conclusion drawn
across countries and in relation to all clusters of studies is that the data are
exceptionally poor. There is a paucity of data and information from which
to draw firm conclusions about the impact of projects, about efficiency and
effectiveness, about sustainability, the gender and environmental impact

232

of projects and their contribution to strengthening democratic forces, institutions and organizations and building civil society. There is even less firm data with which to assess the impact of NGO development interventions beyond discrete projects, not least those involved in building and strengthening institutional capacity, a form of development intervention whose incidence and popularity have grown rapidly in the last five years.

Three major reasons why such large data gaps exist are given: the first is that little to no baseline data has been produced or systematic records kept; the second is the absence or paucity of ongoing monitoring of projects; and thirdly that where emphasis has been given to assessment it has tended to focus on project outputs and not on wider impacts and outcomes. The reason for these data gaps lies in the fact that no priority was given to evaluation; the emphasis has been on doing rather than assessing. As a result, evaluation methods used in donor-initiated studies have often been based on a rather ad hoc mixture of the following: reviewing (usually inadequate) data sources; conducting interviews with the implementing agency, beneficiaries and other relevant stakeholders, often using variants of rapid and participatory methods and verification (triangulation) techniques; and the utilization of relevant research and official reports and data sources. It is partly because of the gaps just mentioned that most donor-commissioned studies have focused on whether the projects reviewed have achieved their objectives.

It is important, however, to make two additional points. The first is that as the studies reviewed have tended to focus on projects which often began five or more years ago, they do not provide an accurate representation or cross-section of current projects, especially those of larger NGOs. Thus in the last five or so years, there has been a rapid increase in the numbers of NGOs who are trying to undertake baseline studies, incorporating monitoring procedures into project cycles and agreeing at the outset (and often planning for) mid-term and end-of-project evaluations. The second is that the generalized view about the paucity of data needs to be placed alongside major advances which have been made in developing indicators for assessment of more narrow sectoral and sub-sectoral interventions. The greatest advances have been made in relation to micro-enterprise and linked activities and in some primary health care projects.[1]

METHODS OF EVALUATION BEYOND THE DONOR-INITIATED STUDIES

Having looked at the methods used in the donor-initiated evaluations, the synthesis study tried to review approaches used in evaluations undertaken by the NGOs themselves. These are discussed in detail in 13 case studies which form Volume II of the study covering the following countries/donors: Belgium; The European Community; Finland; France; The Netherlands; Norway; the UK; the US; Bangladesh; Brazil; Chile; Kenya; and Senegal. Three general observations were made.

The first is that there is both a growing interest among NGOs over the issues of evaluation, and growing recognition of the need to undertake evaluations. Most work would appear to be initiated by larger NGOs in both the North and the South, and medium-sized NGOs in the North; it is these who are most heavily involved in trying to develop evaluation methods. Secondly, however, the study was able to confirm that evaluations are undertaken by both smaller NGOs and by community-based organizations (CBOs), including often quite lengthy self-evaluations. It found evidence of quite sophisticated as well as quite lengthy methods and approaches used, though it also confirmed that there remains a particularly large gap between what is done by small NGOs and what is known about these approaches outside the NGO or CBO. A third observation is that many of the issues raised in the donor-commissioned studies as appropriate for examination are raised and addressed in project evaluations undertaken or commissioned by NGOs. Thus it is not only donor-commissioned evaluations of NGO development interventions, but evaluations conducted by the NGOs themselves, which focus on assessment against objectives and assessment of impact in terms of efficiency, effectiveness and sustainability. Additionally many (though a smaller number) of evaluations assess impact in relation to gender and environmental issues.

However, the synthesis study tried to analyse and isolate differences between donor-initiated and NGOs' own evaluation studies. In terms of approach, five differences or differences in emphasis and/or approach are highlighted.

1) In many NGO evaluations, major emphasis is placed on the need to incorporate participatory methods into evaluations, including especially the need to incorporate the beneficiaries in the evaluation process, though there remains still a considerable gap between intention and practice, as illustrated in Box 11.3.

2) Relatedly, many NGO approaches to evaluation focus not so much on accountability upwards but on accountability downwards – in some cases to the organizations implementing the project, in most cases to the beneficiaries. In this context, and linked to participatory approaches, there is much talk of stakeholder analysis.

3) In a growing number of NGO approaches to evaluation, major emphasis is placed on evaluation as a learning tool, thus the feedback of results to enhance future interventions is often seen as of far greater importance than reporting on the impact of current or past projects.

4) Within this context, NGOs often tend to view evaluation more as one of many tools to be used for improving the lives of the beneficiaries over the longer term than as a distinct, separate and stand alone exercise or activity. In this context, for many NGOs, evaluation is not merely seen as an integral part of appraisal and monitoring, but it is also seen as a sub-part of overall strategic planning. Relatedly, evaluation is often viewed as part of a process of strengthening internal capacity to engage more effectively in development activities.

Box 11.3 NGO Approaches and Debates on Participatory Evaluation

NGOs place high value on the importance of participation in evaluation but the evidence suggests that in many cases there is still a wide gap between theory and practice. Thus, while almost all NGOs speak of the importance of participation, and often criticize donor-commissioned studies for the absence or low priority given to participation, there is far less evidence of participation in NGO evaluations than these comments would suggest. The Chilean country case argues that 'it is not entirely clear' why there is so little evidence of NGOs working with participatory approaches to evaluation. Yet it found some examples such as the CIDE (*Centro de Investigacion y Desarrollo de la Educacion*, or Centre for Education, Research and Development). Today, CIDE requires that all its own projects have a strong evaluation component, and that this assessment be based in considerable measure on client participation. Interestingly, however, while CIDE has developed these approaches to evaluation, few NGOs have approached it for assistance in evaluating their work (see Bebbington et al, 1997).

The second general point to make is that the discussion of participation often confuses two different issues: whether (all) evaluations should be participatory evaluations, and the precise role that the main beneficiaries (as well as other stakeholders) should play in the evaluation process. There is an important difference between beneficiary participatory evaluation when the beneficiaries are involved in the evaluation process and seeking out the views and opinions of the beneficiaries as a necessary part of the evaluation process. It is in terms of the latter that NGOs are largely in agreement. However, differences remain as to the importance to be attached to their views. At one extreme, it is argued that the views of the beneficiaries should always take precedence over the views of everyone else. Though this is held extremely strongly by some NGOs, the evidence gathered would suggest that among NGOs this is very much a minority view. A more commonly held view is that the opinions of the beneficiaries are extremely important but that they should not necessarily, and always, be dominant.

Concerning participatory evaluation, there seems to be a growing consensus among many NGOs that there are limits to the extent to which it is possible to undertake participatory evaluations involving the beneficiaries. In particular, it is argued that it is far too ambitious to hope to involve the beneficiaries in evaluations especially if they have not been involved in either appraisal or ongoing monitoring, and especially if they have been involved in neither. What is more, the available evidence (though it is certainly partial) suggests that this still seems to be the norm. For instance, a recent survey of project applications undertaken by the Swedish NGO Forum Syd found that in 43 per cent of the cases examined the beneficiaries had played no role whatsoever in discussions involved in drawing up the project plans (1996). One example of a form of participatory evaluation is the Oxfam project in Wajir, northeast Kenya. While the process was certainly participatory, the implementers conclude that it would be inappropriate to even attempt to undertake evaluations dominated by the beneficiaries, arguing rather that an effective process of self-evaluation is one which 'explicitly recognises and grows out from an acknowledgement that both the project staff and the intended beneficiaries are stakeholders in the activities being undertaken and both need to be involved in the process of assessment' (see Riddell, 1997: 17).

Source: author's own material

5) Linked to the previous characteristic, there is considerable evidence to show the extent and number of different NGO initiatives embracing experimentation with and linked to research into evaluation methods. Especially important is work focused on trying to find appropriate indicators with which to assess the different dimensions of impact. And it is here that often one sees and reads of NGO concerns with using and attempting to develop appropriate indicators with which to judge impact and assess performance. Yet it should also be noted that this concern to try to develop indicators is not universal; thus there would appear to be less concern among many US PVOs with these issues than among NGOs in most other countries.

The degree of unanimity and/or tension between NGOs and donors over approaches to assessment differs quite markedly across donor countries. At one extreme, as already noted, are the US PVOs which have quite tight requirements concerning both the sort of project which the government will fund and the way that project is assessed; most US PVOs comply, some grudgingly, while others have opted out of the system. At the other extreme come the Scandinavian countries which tend to be characterized by relatively little tension between donors and NGOs over approaches to evaluation, because of a more liberal approach to how NGOs should assess their development work. This in turn is rooted in relatively few donor requirements about how development work should be undertaken by NGOs. By contrast in the UK increasing official funds allocated to NGOs have brought with them increasing requirements at both appraisal and project completion stage. Some NGOs (and especially larger ones) have seen these requirements as unduly interfering in what are considered by them to be their own territory and their own decisions.

Where this has occurred, however, the distinction between donors and NGOs, and between donor views and NGO views – about development approaches and about evaluation methods and approaches – has tended to become far more blurred in recent years, in large part as a result of the rapid expansion in state funding of NGO development projects. Thus one of the consequences of the rapid expansion in state funding of NGO activities has been not only the growth of smaller NGOs and the growth of small into bigger projects, but also the creation of new NGOs both in the North and the South. Indeed, one of the purposes of the expanded amount of USAID funds going to US PVOs has been to create new NGOs in Southern countries. It is thus not surprising that many of the NGOs (and PVOs) created at least as an indirect result of the expansion in funds will tend to have a less critical view of requirements made for spending money and assessing how it has been spent than some of the older, more independent NGOs. The result is that it is becoming increasing difficult to talk, even at the level of individual countries, about NGO views, about development and about assessment methods. Though it was always dangerous to talk sweepingly about the characteristics and approaches of all NGOs working in development, it is becoming even less possible to do so today.

VERIFICATION APPROACHES OF ASSESSMENT

One of the underlying concerns NGOs have had about donor initiated assessments of their work is with the judgements made. When non-quantifiable data and information are used to make assessments, and form value judgements, there is often a fear that subjective factors will influence the judgements made, especially if it is believed that outsiders are not sufficiently knowledgeable about, or sympathetic to, the organization whose project is being assessed. It is within this context that the verification methods used by two donor studies – the Canadian and Australian studies – are of particular interest. Though these differed in the details, both studies undertook assessments of NGO projects using external experts; they then asked the NGOs whose projects were being evaluated to assess these projects for themselves. They then compared the results, noting where and when the NGOs and experts broadly agreed in their assessments (in some cases both providing a positive assessment, in others, both providing a negative assessment) and where and when the experts and NGOs differed in their assessments, ironing out the (smaller) differences within these two groups. The results were as follows:

Areas where NGO self-assessment was verified:

self-reliance
sustainability
impact on women
meeting women's needs
environmental impact

Areas where NGO self-assessment was not verified:

poverty alleviation
financial viability
involvement/participation of women
cost-effectiveness

CONCLUSION: WHERE TO NOW?

A final methodological issue which the OECD/DAC study raises is the extent to which there is merit in donors continuing to commission mega evaluation studies focusing on the impact of discrete NGO projects. The thrust of this final section is to suggest that this is unlikely to happen.

One of the report's recommendations is that donor funds would probably be better spent in helping NGOs develop and experiment with different methods of assessment than in undertaking a large number of impact studies based on methods used to date. One reason for this is clearly based on the view that NGO evaluation of projects is still very much in its infancy; a second (already noted) is that project evaluations will continue to provide extremely limited information so long as baseline data and ongoing monitoring remain so inadequate. A third reason – originating predominantly from NGOs rather than (most) donors – is that there is a discernible and, in some cases, quite pronounced shift away from discrete and time-bound stand alone projects aimed at achieving more concrete objectives, not least an improvement in living standards of the beneficiaries being assisted. Replacing this is a more open-ended process form of engagement, a core component of which is often to strengthen the capacity of the organization being assisted. What is therefore of particular interest is that an analysis of many of the most important factors found to be contributing to project success in the donor-initiated studies can be traced back to capacity building, institutional and managerial issues. These are illustrated by Box 11.4 which summarizes information from the donor studies which explain the differing performance of differing NGO projects in terms of the factors said to be most important.

BOX 11.4 THE FACTORS CONTRIBUTING TO OR IMPEDING SUCCESS OF NGO DEVELOPMENT PROJECTS OR PROGRAMMES

Cluster A: Mentioned in Four or More Donor Studies

Order of Importance	Name of Factor	Frequency: Number of Donor Studies
Importance		
1=	External factors and links outside the project	7
1=	Competent/professional staff	7
3	Involvement of the beneficiaries/responding to local need	6
4=	Overall vision	5
4=	Good project design and good planning	5
4=	Adequate management, including finance and administration/adequate local capacity	5
7	The sector	4
8	Knowledge of other experiences/documentation and research/the ability to network	3

Cluster B: Mentioned in One or More Donor Studies

9	Sufficient funds	2
10	The ability to stay small	1
11	Sufficient time to achieve objectives	1
12	The heterogeneity of different NGO interventions	1
13	Religious/membership or other affiliation	1
14	In-country presence	1

Source: Kruse et al, 1997: 31

It is partly linked to the growing importance given to management and institutional and capacity building initiatives that one can understand another growing trend across donor countries in relation to the evaluation of NGO development projects. This is the new evidence of a shift away from donors undertaking and even monitoring evaluation results to ensuring that NGOs have in place mechanisms which allow them to verify and assess their own performance – and ensuring that donors are sufficiently confident in the reliability of the result obtained. The best examples of this type of thinking come from Denmark and the US. For Denmark, a recent paper from the NGO Unit argues unequivocally that 'the responsibility for evaluation of projects implemented by NGOs rests with the NGOs themselves' (DANIDA, 1996: 4). For the US, a 1993 study is highly critical of donors imposing unnecessary burdens on NGOs in terms of providing information (to them) at the project level, notably in terms of inputs. Thus, it argues that

> *The USAID approach (project implementation) establishes a burdensome system of surveillance which stifles creativity and diverts energy from important long term program goals ... Audit requirements tend to be burdensome, expensive and preoccupied with trivia. They discourage small PVOs and act as a disincentive to United States organisations in working with indigenous organisations ... The preoccupation with INPUT management and the detailed review and approval of inconsequential management decisions needs to be replaced with a substantive concern for the achievement of fundamental goals (USAID, 1993).*

This perspective needs to be viewed in conjunction with the New Partnership Initiative (NPI), an agency-wide effort to make local capacity building a central concern of all agency programmes (USAID, 1995). The thrust of the NPI is not only to increase and expand the role and importance of PVOs and NGOs in the overall aid programme but to alter the nature of the relationship between USAID and PVOs. This suggests that USAID is moving away from a focus on discrete projects, and placing emphasis on management of the aid programme, focusing on ways to enhance capacity and strengthen the capability of institutions utilizing USAID funds. Relatedly to the extent this becomes the driving force of policy, it would suggest a shift in focus away from micro-management and monitoring, with the aim of transferring the assessment of impact onto the NGOs and PVOs themselves. This suggests that (eventually) USAID will not concern itself directly with monitoring and assessing the extent to which most benefits are achieved at least cost. Thus,

> *NPI is a challenge to the nongovernmental community to share the risks and responsibilities of full partnership with USAID. This is not business as usual. Partners in the initiative will as is the case elsewhere within USAID be responsible for their own results-based performance (USAID, 1995: 5).*

More explicit still is the following statement from the March 1995 Policy Guidance, USAID US PVO Partnership:

Within the context of USAID's commitment to managing for results, PVOs receiving USAID funds are responsible for tracking the progress of approved activities, adjusting those activities as needed, and ultimately achieving agreed upon objectives (5).

If USAID follows through on the thrust of this new orientation, and if it continues to be as influential in the future development of methods of analysing NGO development projects as it was in the past, it may be that one will be seeing new interactions between NGOs and donors which will influence, perhaps quite profoundly, the way in which donors wish to see NGO evaluations undertaken. And if the past is also a guide to the future, this, in turn, will influence the way in which NGOs themselves approach impact evaluation.

ENDNOTE

1   The US case study in the OECD/DAC evaluation report provides a quick summary of some of the approaches used (see Mansfield, 1997).

BIBLIOGRAPHY

Barclay, A H et al (1979) 'The development impact of private voluntary organisations: Kenya and Niger', report to the Office of Private and Voluntary Cooperation, Contract AIDS/otr-C–1383, Work Order No. 39

Bebbington, A et al (1997) 'The Chile case study: NGO evaluation policies and practices', Appendix 11 of Volume II in Kruse, S-E et al (eds) *Searching for Impact and Methods: NGO Evaluation Synthesis Report*, prepared for the OECD/DAC Expert Group on Evaluation, Department for International Development Cooperation, Ministry for Foreign Affairs of Finland, Helsinki (draft, May)

DANIDA (1996) 'Status of NGO evaluations in Denmark', paper presented to the Nordic NGO Evaluation Seminar, Helsinki, DANIDA: NGO Unit (March, mimeo)

Edwards, M and Hulme, D (1995) *Beyond the Magic Bullet: NGO Performance and Accountability in the Post-Cold War World*, Kumarian Press, Hartford, CT

Fortin, J L et al (1992) *Evaluation of CIDA's* [Canadian International Development Agency] *Non-Governmental Organization Program*, Secoma Ltd, Ottawa

Forum Syd (1996) 'A checklist for measuring the performance of development projects: a method adopted by Forum Syd to promote an evaluation system', Forum Syd (mimeo), Stockholm

Kershaw, I et al (1995) *Review of the Effectiveness of NGO Programs*, AusAid, Canberra

Kruse, S-E et al (1997) *Searching for Impact and Methods: NGO Evaluation Synthesis Report Volumes I and II*, a report prepared for the OECD/DAC Expert Group on

Evaluation, Department for International Development Cooperation, Ministry for Foreign Affairs of Finland, Helsinki (draft, May)

Mansfield, D (1997) *The United States Case Study: NGO Evaluation Policies and Practices*, Appendix 8 of Volume II of Kruse et al (op cit)

Nathan, R and Associates (1983) 'Assessing the cost-effectiveness of PVO projects: a guide and discussion', prepared for the Office of Program Management Support, Bureau of Food and Voluntary Assistance. Washington, DC: USAID (August)

Nathan, R and Associates (1986) *The Cost-Effectiveness Analysis Field Manual*, prepared for the Office of Program Management Support, Bureau of Food and Voluntary Assistance, Washington, DC: USAID (November)

Riddell, R (1997) 'The Kenyan case study: NGO evaluation, policies and practices', Appendix 12 of Volume II of Kruse et al (op cit)

Tvedt, T (1995) *NGOs as a Channel in Development Aid: The Norwegian System*, Royal Ministry of Foreign Affairs, Oslo

USAID (1993) *A Public–Private Partnership that Works*, USAID, Washington, DC

USAID (1995) *Core Report of the New Partnership Initiative*, USAID, Washington, DC (mimeo, draft)

12 Advocacy and Third Sector Organizations: A Composite Perspective

Alan Fowler

INTRODUCTION

This chapter draws on the experience of voluntary organizations to be found in western Europe and North America and of nonprofit, non-governmental organizations involved in international development (NGDOs), to create a composite model of factors conditioning their influence on public policy.[1] First, we explain briefly why policy advocacy has gained, differentially, in importance for voluntary organizations (VOs) and NGDOs. Then, using a dynamic framework, we explore the interplay between four factors which appear to condition the effectiveness of third sector organizations' (TSOs) advocacy initiatives. These are:

1) key organizational characteristics of the TSO;
2) the context set by national and international political economies;
3) the nature of governance, specifically the system of policy formulation to be influenced; and
4) the interrelationship between the institutional interests of the government and the TSO.

We then place this model within the framework of globalization and focus on three issues that arise from doing so: clarifying the notion of TSO autonomy; the problems arising from the dispersal of governance as a result of the erosion of national sovereignty; and the political accountability of TSOs for what they do. The concluding part offers pointers towards areas which would benefit from further research about, and dialogue between, VOs and NGOs on their advocacy roles and strategies.

THE GROWTH OF THIRD SECTOR ORGANIZATIONS IN POLICY ADVOCACY

This section provides a brief review of policy advocacy from the perspectives of voluntary and non-governmental development organizations. The analysis provides part of the input for creating a composite model.

Advocacy and Voluntary Organizations

Voluntary organizations and NGDOs have different historical trajectories in advocating for reform in public policies. In the UK, VOs as public entities date back over 300 years, with roles as diverse and perverse then as they are today, including influencing the government of the day (Whitaker, 1974).[2] For example, it was pressure from VOs in the late 1800s which eventually led to the abolition of the slave trade. In other words, while perhaps biased towards conservative and remedial rather than radical works, VOs have a demonstrable history of trying to influence the acts and omissions of government. The growth of VO advocacy has been essentially endogenous and organic in the sense of producing and being a product of emerging political and economic systems, accompanied by reasonably well formalized and understood policy processes.

In the North, the nature of VOs as advocates has evolved in many ways. Two aspects are important for this discussion. In its infancy, VO advocacy was not an activity undertaken by those affected by disadvantage but was the morally inspired prerogative of politicians, elites and other sections of the better-off classes. But over time in the North, as in politics, VO advocacy has become a job of skilled interest professionals, often closely allied to the mass media. More recently, differences have arisen in the type of VOs adopting policy advocacy as an agenda. As Taylor (this volume) points out, it is increasingly those affected by policy – the poor, the marginalized, the brutalized, the homeless, the disabled, the victims of racial discrimination – self-organized into mutual benefit organizations, who are advocating on their own behalf. They no longer rely on or trust those of the professional or middle classes who, as intermediaries, have been making their case for them. Taylor also identifies a shift in the focus and advocacy agenda of VOs in the UK from charity without rights, to the introduction of rights, to the enforcement and implementation of rights. Corresponding to these eras are transitions in the British political economy. Major transitions moved the UK from political exclusion coupled to economic laissez faire, through full political franchise married to a social welfare economy with a predominant state role, to a polarized polity and 'free', but managed, capitalized market economy.

Irrespective of historical period, the willingness and ability of VOs to engage with governments on issues of policy depended on its mission and autonomy – that is, its reason for establishment and its independence from public funding. Both contribute to a VO's capability to select and promote a policy position. A clear mission sets out the agenda and a negotiating position vis à vis the regime in power. A non-state resource base reduces the likelihood of self-censorship, which is more probable where the object of policy pressure is simultaneously the financier of the advocate's efforts (Pfeffer and Salancik, 1978).

It is common in the North for VOs to receive public funding while maintaining an advocacy role. Evidence suggests that in such cases a government's inclination to constrain or enable a policy advocate is conditioned by two things: first, the degree to which policy advocacy is considered to be a legitimate objective of VOs; and second, the degree to which the interests of the regime in power are furthered or hampered by the position a VO takes and vice versa (Najam, this volume). In the former case, structural differences have been identified between countries' tolerance of VO advocacy, overtly based on law, but more probably just as much a product of political history and political culture.

A 24-country comparative study shows an important division in societies' acceptance or otherwise of advocacy by VOs. In general terms, it would appear that endogenous processes of political and economic development have produced a distinctive pattern in terms of the degree to which VOs may or may not be engaged in advocacy and the political agendas they may or may not pursue. By this I do not mean party politics, but a legitimate right to take a stand on matters of public policy and seek to alter things accordingly, through non-party political campaigns and other means.

> The central finding is that all and only charity law countries have constraints on campaigning which are specific to non-profit bodies (Randon and 6, 1994: 27).

In other words, there is an implicit connotation within the concept of 'charity' (or 'philanthropy' in North America) which excludes politically oriented goals. This is exemplified by the following statement.[3]

> The concept of a 'charitable purpose' is one of service provision, and not one which admits any political campaigning (ibid: 37).

The authors could not identify any 'inner logic of the law' to explain such a division. What they do conclude is that the theoretical treatment of VOs as separate from the state in charity law countries does not appear to be valid. Instead, by providing some form of public good, charity law tradition regards VOs in some nebulous way as public entities, even though not part of the state, which can legitimately be made subject to administrative control.

Put another way, Northern countries applying a charity law perspective regard campaigning as a political purpose, rather than a political activity; the former is not a charitable act, while the second could be within ill-defined limits. Testing these limits in countries where charity law operates – the US and the UK for example – remains an ongoing issue for VOs (and for some Northern NGDOs subject to charity law, such as Oxfam).

The key point to carry forward is that political history is an important variable in the way that states understand and treat campaigning by VOs. And, where this understanding has been 'exported' through colonial[4] or more recent processes,[5] it can constitute a precondition shaping the trajectory of NGDO–state relations and NGDO policy advocacy.

Advocacy and Non-Governmental Development Organizations

For Southern NGDOs, the historical trajectory to today's advocacy role has slight parallels with, but significant differences to, the North. An important distinction must be made between countries with and without a significant history of civic insurrection – commonly expressed through guerrilla movements – against dictatorship and repression. Why? Because extended insurrection creates a setting which shapes the agenda and behaviour of both local and foreign NGDOs. For example, in Latin America, and parts of southeast Asia such as Thailand and the Philippines, military and civilian dictatorship led to an active engagement of NGDOs, or of their future leaders, not just in issues of public policy but also, through armed revolt, in shaping the character of the state and nature of governance.[6] Freedom from dictatorship and the restoration of democracy was the agenda; development could come later.

However, civic insurrection also led dictators and military leaders to tolerate and sometimes create deferential NGOs as well as to allow external aid to finance them. Why? Because the function of these NGDOs was to undermine popular support for guerrillas by ameliorating the dire situation faced by the masses, while at the same time showing a human face to the world. Consequently, through their foreign partners, many local NGDOs became linked to the Cold War foreign policy agendas of Northern governments, mediated through international aid. Despite much rhetoric about empowerment and solidarity in the struggle, NGDO activity was generally palliative and not policy oriented. The bulk of finance went to provision of social and other rural services, albeit with empowerment intentions (Smith, 1990).

Hence, for much of this century, policy advocacy – or, more broadly, influencing governance in terms of civic rights – has been an active, and, on occasion, the sole agenda, for local NGDOs in some countries; while service provision without policy concerns was the remit of others.[7] Be that as it may, the advent of stability, democracy and political pluralism during the 1980s has caused local NGDOs to redirect or expand their attentions towards developmental as well as civic policies.

In non-insurrection settings, typically in sub-Saharan Africa and south Asia, NGDOs' primary concern in the first two-thirds of three-and-a-half decades of development has been engagement in the 'policy downstream'; in other words, working directly with people who are poor and marginalized. In this emphasis, local NGOs are often mirrored by foreign transnationals in providing social and development services (Smillie, 1995). Alternatively, inspired by a Gandhian tradition for example, local NGDOs sought to identify ideologically with, and directly promote, community and national self-reliance. Whatever the case, the NGDO mode and ethos was to engage operationally with people and their struggles for survival. This modality was fed by an ethic of remedial action – in part stemming from Northern NGDO origins in relief and refugee assistance brought about by World War II and natural disasters. An action orientation was also informed by the social welfare and Christian charity perspectives prevalent in the North, by pressures to show rapid disbursement of funds with low overheads, by a moral belief that through dedicated effort NGDOs could and would make *the* difference to poverty and injustice, and by historical association with colonial powers who used NGDO services as one instrument of containment – welfare and social service provision was encouraged, critical activism certainly discouraged. However, the picture of NGDOs as 'doers' rather than 'advocates' over a 25-year period began to shift in the early and mid-1980s.

The serious attention given to advocacy by a greater number of NGDOs began about ten years ago. The phenomenon results from a complex set of factors. First, governments allocating taxes to international development assistance (aka official aid) have changed their policies. Until the late 1970s, recipient governments were seen to be both the engine of and guide for development activity and growth. Under the rubric of struc-tural adjustment, the 1980s saw a pronounced donor shift away from an emphasis on states to a view which prioritized market and non-state actors as the motors for economic growth and social change. In fact, since the early 1980s, conventional wisdom has regarded inefficient, corrupt and undemocratic governments as the cause of, rather than the solution to, low growth and poverty reduction.[8] Consequently, the private sector and NGDOs gained donor attention. Amongst others, this means that NGDOs are now more intensely interacting with bilateral agencies and with multi-lateral development banks (MDBs) which can lend only to governments. Correspondingly, they were drawn into and began forging their own way into policy arenas from which they were previously excluded.[9]

In promoting this type of engagement, official aid applies the language of civil society and good governance. In other words, as part of a concern to pluralize the civic arena and democratize political processes, aid resources with these goals and conditions are being made available to NGDOs. For example, specific funds such as the TACIS Fund in the European Union and the British Know How Fund exist within a number of international aid agencies to pursue civic goals in central and eastern Europe. Thus to some extent the growing involvement of NGDOs in policy work is government resource-led and externally stimulated. Dilemmas of autonomy and co-optation are readily apparent.

A second reason is that for many years some NGDOs, such as D-GAP based in Washington, DC and the Third World Network headquartered in Malaysia, had actively questioned donors' economic and other policies. In the new policy framework, such NGDOs gained greater access and had the track record needed to voice their concerns to a wider audience, and to be heard. Often funded by private foundations to reduce the dangers of co-optation, they spearheaded the '50 Years is Enough' campaign, championing reform of the World Bank. The old boundaries to NGDO policy campaigning were being, and continue to be, expanded and redrawn.

Thirdly, evaluations of 20 years of NGDOs' development efforts show modest, if not disappointing, impact (ODI, 1996). One reason for poor performance was identified to be policy environments which negated NGDO efforts. Another was the less than suitable, low quality funding practices of donor agencies when dealing with NGDOs. As a response, NGDOs saw the necessity to move upstream into processes of agenda setting and policy development, not just dangling on the tail end of policy implementation, picking up the pieces of market, political, trade, debt and aid failures.

Moving upstream took on two tracks. One track was towards governments in the South. Here, where conditions permit, NGOs pursue tactics of domestic participation and argumentation complemented by simultaneous moves to increase pressure from outside via the aid system and MDBs. A second, related, path is towards altering policies of the official aid system itself. In this latter case, MDBs are particularly important because of the disproportionate power they can hold over national policy choices. Even where levels of MDB lending are small, as in Brazil, India, China and South Africa, even a tiny foot in the door enables them to pronounce on economic and other policy areas, such as governance. Commercial lenders pay keen attention to what they say and make investment decisions accordingly. An implication of these strategies is that recipient governments are not sovereign and that policy making is multi-centred.

Fourthly, NGDOs increasingly see the limited extent of what direct action can achieve for their missions when set against commercial and political power and interests. Some are therefore adopting a more complex strategy of using operational work and the situational testimony of the poor to gain leverage on structural forces that maintain inequality and injustice and threaten sustainable development (Fowler, 1997). This involves gaining policy leverage on market as well as state actors, using a wider array of instruments, including mobilizing the general public as citizens and voters.

Fifthly, a concern for sustainability has brought the interconnectedness of different levels of development action into sharper focus. In response, NGDOs are re-appraising their work through multi-level lenses. One outcome is the building of new capabilities to operate at different levels of policy development as well as forging alliances between NGDOs with existing expertise and necessary links to policy makers.

Finally, with nation states arguably no longer the real sovereign units for economic and environmental policy making, NGDOs are increasingly concerned about the lack of public control over the public arena. In other words, in adopting a political analysis of poverty and social justice, they find that governments are less and less able solely to design or implement policies which are technically within their jurisdiction. This realization has given another impulse to finding and interacting with those who really have control in order to alter the way they think and work. Increasing stress on the social and ethical responsibility of businesses is one example of where the NGDO policy agendas now lie.

Together, these factors have both accelerated and shaped the ways in which NGDOs understand and engage with advocacy and the policy arena.

A COMPOSITE MODEL OF THIRD SECTOR ORGANIZATIONS AND ADVOCACY

The foregoing review provides a number of ingredients for creating a dynamic model of TSOs as effective policy advocates. Figure 12.1 is a schematic presentation of the factors which appear to shape TSOs in advocacy roles. Each factor is described in terms of its influence on TSO effectiveness in advocacy.

TSO Characteristics

A number of organizational factors appear to stand out in relation to TSOs as policy advocates. First is their ownership. Specifically, are they established by members principally to serve their own interests, and perhaps others in similar circumstances? Or are they established to serve the interests of others? In other words, are they member-serving or public-serving nonprofits? (Salamon and Anheier, 1994). As alluded to earlier, public-serving VOs and NGDOs must acknowledge the fact that when people speak and advocate in their own interests it usually carries more weight and credibility than when intermediaries do so on their behalf. Governments are increasingly questioning the legitimacy and real interests of policy agendas that are not backed up by demonstrable accountability to those in whose name policy positions are advanced.

An international perspective brings comparable 'who is speaking for whom?' situations. For example, intermediaries from one continent, Africa in this instance, clashed with Northern NGDOs on the stance to be taken towards replenishment of the World Bank's soft lending arm, the International Development Association (IDA) (Nelson, forthcoming). In this case, Northern NGDOs clearly stood without backing from those for whom aid was intended to assist. They modified their position. But, without recognized systems, forums or process to mediate between contending TSO positions, credibility is offered up to opposing interests and useful policy inputs can be dismissed as illegitimate.

Secondly, the source of a TSO's resources can lead to excessive compromise or self-censorship and/or charges from governments that the organization is serving foreign masters and, possibly, anti-national interests. In engaging with the official aid system, many NGDOs try not to use funds derived from official sources. But in many settings, organizational survival derives from aid that comes directly from taxes paid by foreigners. This is particularly the case for TSOs that have arisen in eastern and central Europe with assistance from aid programmes. The dilemma this may pose is less of a problem for domestic VOs that are part of the polity, but, as Taylor shows, reliance on government funding to influence the same government can lead to self-restraint or complex layering. A TSO may find itself accepting funds from one government unit in order to influence other parts of the government.

Thirdly, the agenda an NGO pursues may have more or less resonance with that of the policy maker or political regime in power. Crudely speaking there are three types of TSO agenda: welfare, reform or entrepreneurism. A reform agenda is most likely to lead TSOs into policy advocacy as a significant feature of their work and competence. Their effectiveness then depends, in part, on the degree to which the agenda they want and, more importantly, the beliefs, values and ideology which underpin their position, correspond with or run counter to power holders.

Finally, a TSO needs specific advocacy competencies. Typically these are of two types. First are political dimensions of constituency support: proximity and access to policy makers, inter-NGDO lobby networks and alliances, credibility in the subject area and media 'feeding'. Second are technical skills, including research, analysis, interpretation and appropriate packaging, resource mobilization, detailed insight into the actual practice and process of policy making and implementation, strategic thinking and application, and resilience (anon, 1997).[10]

The Political Economy

A country's political economy has many dimensions. Two stand out in relation to TSO effectiveness in advocacy. First is the extent to which political and economic power are separate or interwoven. Put another way, how much control do political power holders have over the material base from which TSOs must survive and operate? Where control is far-reaching, as in the former Soviet Union, TSO autonomy is essentially a fiction.

Separation between the two types of power implies a division of labour between roles in society that may or may not be firmly institutionalized. Usually TSOs are allotted a place and civic functions which may or may not be contested by them or others. Previous descriptions suggest that in many countries, especially those in transition to market economies and plural politics, roles are still to be institutionalized. While the optimum configuration is a subject of ongoing debate in the North, the path being set out for the South – disputed by China and others – is towards three-sector configuration of plural democratic state, free market and strong civil society (Najam, 1996; Nerfin, 1986).

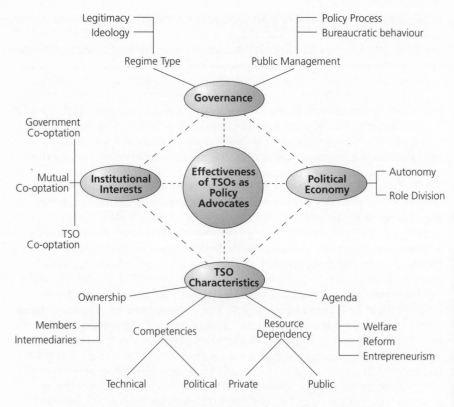

Figure 12.1 *A Composite Model of TSO Policy Advocacy*

An additional feature of role division is the extent to which sociocultural norms make private finance a significant proportion of the domestic TSO resource base. And, even if private giving for the well-being of others is significant, it cannot be assumed that this would be through an intermediary organization (Fowler, 1992). To preserve and reinforce social cohesion, many cultural settings call for person to person, family to family or intra-clan assistance. This type of reciprocity is seen to be essential for maintaining social status and as a safety net for coping with adverse conditions (McCarthy, 1989). In other words, local giving has a necessarily externally informal expression. Within the group concerned, however, the system is regarded as a formal obligation.

Governance

Governance can be defined as the acquisition and application of political power in the management of public affairs. This can be unpacked into two elements: the type of political regime in terms of its ideology and legitimacy, and the way that public affairs are managed, particularly bureaucratic norms and behaviour and the inclusiveness of the policy making process.

Any political regime has a view about the allocation of rights and responsibilities for economic endeavours, for individual and public welfare and for the national interest. In economic terms, there are regimes which believe that assets belong, and that wealth should accrue to, individuals. The state must therefore justify any claim on assets or wealth which individuals own; it is not a right. In contrast are those who believe assets are a common property owned collectively through the state, and that wealth creation is a communal endeavour. Because wealth accrues to and through everyone, individuals have to justify entitlements above a guaranteed minimum for well-being. There are infinite combinations of positions between these two. The issue for TSOs is to set their mission against the ideological makeup of the regime in power and then form strategies which seek to shift policies which flow from the prevailing ideologies. Transitions in regime may work for or against a TSO's advocacy position. Whatever the case, strategies required will depend, inter alia, on the legitimacy enjoyed by the regime.

Legitimacy derives from a transparent, publicly credible process of seeking and obtaining a mandate to govern. Methods employed to obtain a mandate vary between countries. The North has adopted, and is busy propagating, a system of multiple parties based essentially on class interests, tied to periodic elections. Propagation is taking place even if such models are foreign to other political cultures or where necessary preconditions, such as citizenship, do not exist. This is argued to be the case in African states that have been externally imposed and not organically formed. This is important to TSOs for the following reasons.

A distinguishing feature of Northern democratic systems is a structural premise of adversarial or coalition politics. The US and the UK exhibit the former; Canada and much of western Europe the latter. Perhaps, not coincidentally, this roughly accords with the adoption or not of charity law which regulates the political campaigning activities of nonprofits. It can therefore be hypothesized that a TSO's potential for effective policy advocacy is higher in the latter than in the former political system.[11] Indicative support for this proposition can be found in the fact that, in countries with coalition politics, significant levels of overseas aid are channelled through nonprofit foundations with a political signature but without any significant domestic political interference from successive regimes.[12] Similar NGDOs do not exist in the UK or US. Research is needed to extend the work of Randon and 6 with a political systems perspective.[13]

Whether or not the premises of democracy are relevant, in comparing NGDO policy influence between Zimbabwe and Botswana – both ex-British colonies – Alan Thomas concludes that the relative presence or absence of democracy does make a difference to the effectiveness of TSO advocacy (Thomas, 1994). He formulates positive links between five aspects of democratization (including accountability through elections rather than legitimacy) and four main ways of achieving advocacy influence. It is beyond our purpose to detail the working hypotheses he arrives at but, to paraphrase, it can be argued that the greater a regime's legitimacy the more likely it will be to tolerate and accommodate discordant views on areas of public policy.

Public Management

Understanding how public policies are arrived at and then implemented is a critical issue in TSO advocacy (Najam, this volume). Formal procedures for setting policy agendas, developing policy options and content and then putting policy into practice, may be well established and work as intended in some countries. But for many others the policy process is a jungle or maze (Grindle and Thomas, 1991; Wuyts et al, 1992). Deciding which role to play at which part of the process becomes an art as much as a science. Moreover, it is often a highly personalized process where relationships count as much as the rationale and the evidence. A difficulty for TSOs, therefore, is that the competencies to access policy actors may not be learnable or transferable from one organization to another. It also means that if TSOs do not take care, they may be vulnerable to a policy maker who moves up, on or out of a long drawn-out process. Both issues can have a negative impact on effectiveness.

The second element in public management is the ethos, stance, competence and honesty of the bureaucracy, coupled to its stance towards other policy actors and to public oversight more generally. Aziz Khan (1997), a member of the Indian Administrative Service not renowned for its sensitivity towards citizens, was seconded to a local NGDO. After examining a number of cases of TSO involvement in public policy processes, from an insider's perspective he details what public servants are sensitive to in terms of advocacy by TSOs. He treats NGDO policy advocacy as 'selling in the market place of ideas'. His assessment is that obtaining a positive response from civil servants requires untainted TSO leadership, credibility as an advocate, a credible agenda, credible packaging, many backers, appropriate sales strategies and tactics, high quality of work done and professionalism in approach.[14]

Finally, TSO effectiveness in advocacy will depend on the degree to which the bureaucracy and administration of policies is meant to be inclusive and participatory in the sense of citizens having some control over decisions. Where this is not the case, TSOs will find it much harder to find openings and claim a right to be heard. Put another way, if the principle of people's participation does not live within the civil service, advocacy is disadvantaged irrespective of what the political leadership may say.

This point leads to the fourth factor in TSO effectiveness, the institutional interests of the different parties involved.

Institutional Interests

Najam, in this volume, draws attention to an important distinction between TSO roles and TSO goals, which are too often confused. He stresses that a TSO's goal in advocacy is to co-opt government into its agenda and that this also applies in reverse, such that governments would like to co-opt TSOs into supporting government policies. From his viewpoint, confrontation is one strategy to achieve co-optation as a goal. The issue for advocacy effectiveness becomes one of selecting the right strategies and tactics to move, in Najam's phrasing 'co-opt', government towards the TSO's position. Confrontation, complementarity and collaboration can all feature in the co-optive repertoire used by both parties.

What drives this process are the institutional interests – rather than the supposed comparative advantages – of both parties. In other words, the name of the game is to engage – and choosing not to engage can be a significant form of engagement[15] – in ways which protect or further organizational viability and legitimacy in the eyes of legitimate stakeholders. The key to negotiation is to move beyond a stated policy position to the institutional interests lying behind it and then judging the extent to which they can be used either as points of leverage or even shifted. For example, donor agencies have an institutional interest in disbursing funds. It is politically embarrassing not to be able to allocate grants and then go to parliament and ask for budget maintenance or increases. TSO agendas which offer respite from this problem are of a different order from those suggesting that a development service be modified in a way which will save money. A necessary advocacy competence for TSOs is therefore to gain deep insight into organizational behaviour and its interpretation.

COMPLICATING CONCLUSIONS

The foregoing analysis gives little more than an overview of where the combined experience of voluntary and non-governmental development organizations might lead in terms of understanding, and perhaps improving, their effectiveness in advocacy. Obviously, the model is an approximation of a complex reality, one which is being influenced by a number of global shifts. In addition to an area of future research noted above, the analysis brings forward three issues that may deserve research attention.

First, aided and abetted by communications technology, the erosion of national sovereignty is increasing. One response is to create higher level structures, such as regional trading and defence associations, which may or may not have a super-governance authority, a weak example of which is the European Parliament. Simultaneously, adoption of the principle of subsidiarity is devolving some authority downwards to governance structures which enjoy their own mandates from the population. The Scottish Parliament will be a new example of this. For TSOs in Britain, policy advocacy may have to deal with public decision making diffused over three or more levels of governance.

The situation with regard to influencing policy in the South is made more complex because of the roles played by international financial institutions. Governance in these bodies is undemocratic. Weighted voting biases power towards borrowers at the cost of lenders. The necessary formal, politically empowering democratic coupling between types and levels of governance producing public policies is available to Europeans, but not to many citizens of the South. Though unevenly spread and of widely differing significance between countries, diffusion of governance is for TSOs in the South a disempowering factor in their advocacy effectiveness. The complex strategies and tactics applied to deal with this fact would benefit from systematic study.

Secondly, with diffuse governance, the issue of political responsibility for policy positions adopted by public-serving TSOs comes to the fore (Jordan and van Tuijl, 1997). In other words, how can TSOs be held accountable for their national advocacy agendas when these are pursued beyond national borders in engagement with influential institutions like the MDBs? What checks and balances are needed to ensure that they do not undermine domestic politics and policy processes, effectively disenfranchizing the publics concerned? The pertinence of this question is sharpened by contending policy positions adopted between TSOs. Again, systematic enquiry is called for.

Finally, what should and can be done to enable TSOs to operate from a position of reasonable autonomy in the game of policy co-optation? For, while Najam's point is valid, the fact remains that an ability to be a meaningful policy advocate requires that TSOs maintain sufficient civic rootedness to be credible. Present resource trends raise doubts about this ability. A critical appraisal may conclude that intermediary voluntary and non-governmental development organizations are less well able to pursue advocacy goals and roles than their member-serving counterparts. Such an appraisal needs to be made.

ENDNOTES

1 No agreed conventions exist for differentiating between nonprofit organizations involved in domestic or overseas issues, nor between them in terms of their country of origin, or the developed or developing world. In this chapter, voluntary organizations will be regarded as nonprofits working domestically in the Organisation for Economic Cooperation and Development (OECD) countries – the North. The term NGDO is used for both nonprofits originating in Northern countries working overseas or on overseas issues and for nonprofits in developing countries – the South – which operate domestically and internationally when it comes to policy. In both cases, the term third sector organizations (TSOs) will be used to denote VOs and NGDOs collectively.

2 The Week's Charity was established in the 15th century to purchase faggots with which to burn witches (Whitaker, 1974: 11).

3 The policing function of charities in the UK is carried out by the Charity Commission, in the US by the Internal Revenue Service.

4 The British have charity laws not to be found in France or Spain. Consequently, many ex-British colonies exhibit not just legal constraints on NGDO policy advocacy, but a culture of government which mediates against it and which must therefore be overcome. Ex-colonies of other powers do not face the same barriers.

5 To assist countries without nonprofit laws, the World Bank has financed the production of a guide produced by the International Centre for Non Profit Law (World Bank, 1997b). The charge of imposing a US style and interpretation of what VOs and NGDOs are was not long in coming.

6 Some movements, and subsequent NGDO leaders, found inspiration from Catholic Liberation theology, others from Marxist-Leninism, others from principles of social democracy. Traces of these roots are still to be found in the factionalism between NGDOs and the differences in their policy stance towards successive elected regimes. The Philippines is a good example (Alegre, 1996).

7 A significant number of Latin American NGDOs were formed by intellectual refugees from universities, and functioned as think tanks for the left. Examples are IBASE in Brazil and CEPES in Peru. Their agenda has always been policy reform.

8 A more balanced view appears to be emerging about the indispensable roles of governance which must be done well (World Bank, 1997a).

9 Borrowing governments are less happy about this trend, and increasingly raise concerns about the legitimacy and accountability of the NGOs now appearing at the policy table (Mohammed, 1997).

10 For other summaries see Lee, 1994; Madrinan, 1995; Thomas, 1995; Van Rooy, 1997.

11 This proposition is probably bad news for TSOs in the UK's ex-colonies which have inherited adversarial systems.

12 Examples are the political foundations in Germany and co-financing *Stichtings* in The Netherlands.

13 The authors used freedom of speech as a proxy for democracy.

14 An extended treatment can be found in Fowler, 1997: 124–127.

15 Deciding to be an outsider in an advocacy process can be as of profound a significance as a statement made about the process. The degree of significance is proportional to the standing and credibility of the non-engaging TSO in the specific policy area.

BIBLIOGRAPHY

Alegre, A (ed) (1996) *Trends and Traditions, Challenges and Choices: A Strategic Study of Philippine NGOs*, Atoneo Center for Social Policy and Public Affairs, Manila

anon (1997) 'Non-governmental organizations and policy advocacy in Tanzania: critical advocacy skills', *World Development*, review manuscript

Fowler, A (1992) 'Distant obligations: speculations on NGO funding and the global market', *Review of African Political Economy*, No 55, pp9–29

Fowler, A (1997) *Striking A Balance: A Guide to Enhancing the Effectiveness of Non-Governmental Organisations in International Development*, Earthscan, London

Grindle, M and Thomas, J (1991) *Public Choices and Policy Change: The Political Economy of Reform in Developing Countries*, Johns Hopkins University, Baltimore

Jordan, L and van Tuijl, P (1997) 'Political responsibility in NGO advocacy: exploring shapes of global democracy', Bank Information Center/NOVIB, Washington, DC/The Hague

Khan, A (1997) *Shaping Policy: Do NGOs Matter?* Society for Participatory Research in Asia, New Delhi

Lee, R (1994) 'From projects to advocacy', *Development and Democracy*, No 7, pp34–43

Madrinan, C (1995) 'Influencing policy – the NGO lobby on multilateral development banks', *Institutional Development*, Vol 2, No 1, pp69–74

McCarthy, K (1989) 'The voluntary sector overseas: notes from the field', *Working Papers*, Center for the Study of Philanthropy, City University of New York, draft

Mohammed, A (1997) 'Notes on MDB conditionality on governance', in *International Monetary and Financial Issues for the 1990s*, pp139–145, Research Papers for the Group of 24, Vol III, United Nations, New York and Geneva

Najam, A (1996) 'Understanding the third sector: revisiting the prince, the merchant and the citizen', *Nonprofit Management and Leadership*, Vol 7, No 2, pp203–219

Nelson, P (forthcoming) 'Conflict, legitimacy and effectiveness: who speaks for whom in transnational NGO networks lobbying the World Bank', *Nonprofit and Voluntary Sector Quarterly*

Nerfin, M (1986) 'Neither prince nor merchant: citizen – an introduction to the third system', *IFDA Dossier*, No 56, pp3–29

ODI (1996) 'The impact of NGO development projects', Briefing Paper No 2, Overseas Development Institute, London, May

Pfeffer, J and Salancik, G (1978) *The External Control of Organizations: A Resource Dependence Perspective*, Harper and Row, New York

Randon, A and 6, P (1994) 'Constraining campaigning: the legal treatment of non-profit policy advocacy in 24 countries', *Voluntas*, Vol 5, No 1, pp27–58

Salamon, L M and Anheier, H (1994) *The Emerging Sector: An Overview*, Institute for Policy Studies, Johns Hopkins University, Baltimore

Smillie, I (1995) *The Alms Bazaar: Altruism under Fire – Non-profit Organizations and International Development*, IT Publications, London

Smith, B (1990) *More Than Altruism: The Politics of Private Foreign Aid*, Princeton University Press, New Jersey

Thomas, A (1994) 'Does democracy matter? A comparison of NGOs' influence on environmental policies in Zimbabwe and Botswana', GECOU (Global Environmental Change – Open University) Workshop, 16th May, Milton Keynes

Thomas, B (1995) 'Exploring the basics of advocacy I–III', *Exchanges*, Nos 9–11, ACTIONAID, Bangalore

Van Rooy, A (1997) 'The growing influence of NGOs in world conferences: Canadian and British lobbying at the 1974 World Food Conference and the 1992 Earth Summit', *World Development*, Vol 25, No 1

Whitaker, B (1974) *The Foundations: An Anatomy of Philanthropy and Society*, Eyre Methuen, London

World Bank (1997a) *The State in a Changing World*, World Development Report, Oxford University Press, Oxford

World Bank (1997b) *Handbook on Good Practices for Laws Relating to Non-Governmental Organisations*, (Discussion Draft), Environment Department, The World Bank, Washington, DC

Wuyts, M, Mackintosh, M and Hewitt, T (eds) (1992) *Development Policy and Public Action*, Open University/Oxford University Press, Milton Keynes/Oxford

13

Legitimacy and Values in NGOs and Voluntary Organizations: Some Sceptical Thoughts

Michael Edwards

ASPECTS OF LEGITIMACY

Legitimacy is generally understood as having the right to be and do something in society – a sense that an organization is lawful, proper, admissable and justified in doing what it does and saying what it says, and that it continues to enjoy the support of an identifiable constituency. In the NGO literature at least, questions about legitimacy are rarely discussed explicitly – a consequence perhaps of widespread assumptions about 'closeness to the poor' and 'attachment to values' that persisted up until the more questioning climate of the mid-1990s. Legitimacy in membership bodies is claimed, first and foremost, through democratic processes (like elections or less formal sanctions) by which these constituencies hold the organization formally accountable for what it does (Pratten and Ali Baldo, 1995).

But most intermediary voluntary organizations and development NGOs are not membership organizations in this sense, though they may have supporters and volunteers who have at least some of the rights and responsibilities of members. Their legitimacy is claimed and maintained through demonstrated conformity with laws and regulations, accepted practice standards, public expectations, the terms of the contracts they sign and the values they espouse. The expectation (in much NGO rhetoric and writing) is that it is conformity with values in this list that provides the bottom line in claiming legitimacy in this way. The assumption that NGOs are values-based organizations is often used to demonstrate their comparative advantage in some areas of development work, in contrast to governments and businesses (Edwards and Hulme, 1995; Fowler, 1997). By injecting values such as equity and non-discrimination, the rights of current and future generations, and their own visions of justice and emancipation into markets, politics and social action, NGOs and voluntary organizations can help to transform the systems and structures that exclude or marginalize certain groups at certain times. NGOs are widely-perceived as keepers of the moral flame – born in and loyal to unpopular causes and the interests of those with less economic power and political voice (Van Rooy, 1997).

But is this true? The explicit treatment of values as a significant factor in management and decision making is increasingly common among voluntary organizations (Paton, this volume), but less so among development NGOs (Fowler, 1997; Zadek, 1996). NGOs usually have a more implicit understanding of the place of values in their work, expressed through the different roles they adopt and the causes they defend in society – a good example of the general differences between the two sets of organizations and their literatures highlighted by Lewis (this volume). In my experience NGOs may speak about the primacy of values in their mission statements but less often do they operationalize values in day to day practice, organizational structure and processes. They are far more likely to discuss legitimacy in terms of one or more of the following:

- legal compliance (being seen to remain within the framework of charity or nonprofit legislation and accountability, and regulatory frameworks);
- effective oversight by governing bodies (usually their boards of trustees);
- extent and continuity of public support (retaining the public's faith that the organization does what it says it does, and is what it says it is);
- voluntary (ie non-coerced or pressurized) requests for assistance from other bodies ('we are legitimate because people ask us for help' as one UK NGO staffer put it to me recently);
- technical expertise, usefulness as a source of information, and credibility (where NGOs are designated as legitimate participants in policy debates or project implementation by other legitimate authorities, such as a government ministry or the World Bank);
- demonstrable representativeness (of the views of supporters, partners and others) when claiming to lobby or advocate a particular position; and
- transparent performance monitoring and clear accountability procedures.

Some sense of values is implicit in most of these criteria, but it is the last one – legitimacy through accountability – that is most explicitly value-laden. NGOs do not have to be member-controlled to be legitimate, but they do have to be accountable for what they achieve if their claims to legitimacy are to be sustained (Edwards and Hulme, 1995). A focus on performance and accountability immediately begs a number of questions: Performance on what? Accountability to whom? Measured by which criteria (Pearce, 1997)? Being held accountable for delivery according to the targets set in a service contract   is   clearly   different   from   being   held accountable in relation to broader processes of democratization and social change. The accountability of market-based institutions (through supply and demand) is not the same as that of social actors (through popular support and sanction). Roles and identities have different implications for the ways in which legitimacy is claimed and the place of values in claiming it. So questions of legitimacy involve judgements and choices, struggles and negotiations about what NGOs do and who has what rights to influence organizational decisions. And values – especially the ones which govern how power and authority are exercised inside organizations, between them, and across society at large – are central to resolving these questions.

ROLES, RELATIONSHIPS, VALUES AND LEGITIMACY

Among NGOs, the focus of activity is increasingly turning to large scale service delivery under a broader donor-led privatization agenda, albeit with social goals (such as gender equity) and institutional development added in where the internal and external context allows (a trend especially well-illustrated in the case of Bangladesh: Hashemi, 1995 and this volume). A similar trend took hold among voluntary organizations in industrialized countries in the 1980s amid the rhetoric of public–private partnership and the widespread privatization of the welfare state. In both cases, there is less official support available for social mobilization or large scale protest and struggle by grassroots movements. More support has been forthcoming for NGO activities related to democratization, since this is currently flavour of the month among donor agencies, but this is usually defined quite narrowly in terms of Western liberal norms (Blair, 1997), and delivered just like any other service (with targets like the number of citizens trained by the end of the financial year, or specified increases in the proportion of women registered to vote). In these service-related activities, performance is measured according to managerial or market values of efficiency and effectiveness – levels of satisfaction among clients and purchasers with the quality of the services provided, unit costs and trends in cost recovery, technical standards and comprehensiveness of coverage (Paton, this volume). It is interesting that voluntary organizations in industrialized countries seem to have been able to maintain a sense of social values and downward accountability even under the influence of the contract culture that has engulfed them, partly through the development of the service-user movement in countries like the UK and the US (Taylor, this volume; CFVS, 1996). Among development NGOs any genuine sense of accountability (or even consultation) to/with users or beneficiaries is rare (Edwards and Hulme, 1995).

Because of their continued financial dependence on institutional donors, NGOs tend to accept these performance measures while simultaneously trying to have a deeper-level impact on power relations and social exclusion. Whether they do make a difference at this level is a controversial question well-illustrated by claims and counter-claims about the success of the Bangladesh Rural Advancement Committee (BRAC) and other NGOs in combining large scale service delivery (credit, health and education) with institutional development and social mobilization in Bangladesh (Hashemi, 1995 and this volume; Montgomery, 1996; Rao and Kelleher, 1995). In cases like Bangladesh a focus on service delivery is understandable given widespread state and market failure, the size of gaps in the provision of even the most basic of services, anti-NGO sentiments among religious groups, journalists and others, deeply-entrenched social and political elites and a government which is extremely wary of any other form of NGO activity. Nevertheless, it is important to remember that NGOs always have some room to manoeuvre and that their legitimacy is always contested by different actors – states, donors, other elements of civil society and NGO staff themselves. In the same way Paton (this volume) highlights the trade-offs and perhaps irresolvable conflicts that emerge between the values attached to different roles and relationships in UK voluntary organizations.

The point is the same in both cases: all NGOs and voluntary organizations must be explicit about which values are central to their claims to legitimacy, which values are more important than others if there are trade-offs to be made between them (as there often are in real world management and decision making), and how these trade-offs are arrived at. For example, hierarchy and standardization are probably essential to reduce unit costs in service delivery above a certain scale, but participation, flexibility and time and space for iteration are essential to promote social and institutional change; a rights-based approach to health and education implies a very different relationship between user and provider than access according to purchasing power in private provision (whether NGO programmes or commercial operations); accountability to funders and regulators signifies a different priority in the ordering of values than cases where accountability to clients or beneficiaries is considered paramount. While in theory such multiple accountabilities can be managed effectively, this is rarely true in practice (Edwards and Hulme, 1995). None of these are either/or choices, but nonetheless they do imply that choices will be made. NGOs are often unclear about these choices and how to handle them, partly because they are such hybrid organizations (containing elements of both market-based institutions and social actors), partly because most lack the autonomy to make real choices in the first place (dependent as they are on short term funding and official permission to operate), and partly because few have thought enough about where they want to go in the future, and what choices are required to get there.

For NGOs and voluntary organizations that are content to be service providers on contract to states and donors, mixed accountability and a hazy connection between values and legitimacy are problematic but manageable – facts of life, so to speak. But for those who want to focus on other roles such as social mobilization, democratization and advocacy (with service delivery restricted to a temporary or innovation role), such a muddled state of affairs is more dangerous. In these roles, the indirect avenues for claiming legitimacy through performance examined in brief above may not be appropriate or acceptable: legitimacy here *does* depend on more formal accountability mechanisms to those whose interests NGOs claim to speak for, represent, defend, protect or advance. And that requires an explicit focus on non-market values such as social rootedness, democratic management and communication, and the primacy awarded to building the organizational capacity of disenfranchized groups to speak and act for themselves, and the space and opportunities to use it. Unless these values are operationalized in the agency's systems and structures, the tensions and conflicts between stated values and actual performance tend to increase, and it becomes more and more difficult to hold the organization together, especially where there are strong disagreements about mission and strategy among different groups of staff. That is what is happening to many NGOs today.

Legitimacy and accountability in this sense do not have to be perfectly representative of, or responsive solely to, grassroots concerns – there would be less debate and fewer new ideas if that criterion were rigidly enforced. 'No-one requires DAWN (an international women's network) to be elected by every woman in the world before it is regarded as a voice for women' (Van Rooy, 1997: 110). In any case, the structure of governance in most NGOs precludes this (with authority vested in non-elected trustees appointed only from the country of registration: Tandon, 1995). But NGOs and voluntary organizations do have to adhere to what Fowler (1997) calls 'authentic partnership' if they are to play a legitimate role as social actors – to be intimately connected to a constituency in some way, formally responsive to their concerns, and accountable for the quality of the partnerships they develop with others. Although there are examples of genuinely reciprocal and mutually open and accountable relationships between NGOs in different countries (Gaventa, this volume; Brown, this volume), in the real world of foreign aid they are rare. Many NGOs are only weakly connected in this sense, and problems do arise when the link between stated values and the reality of partnership is broken.

Some of the clearest examples of this problem come from the world of advocacy, where more powerful Northern NGOs have sometimes claimed a false legitimacy in speaking on behalf of constituencies in the South they do not represent, and have taken up policy positions which have not been rooted in proper consultation with Southern partners (Najam, this volume). In the case of the IDA (International Development Association – the soft loan arm of the World Bank) funding in the mid-1990s, environmental NGOs in the US claimed to be representing a Southern consensus in lobbying against replenishment because of the social and environmental costs of even this form of foreign aid, when Southern NGOs were arguing the opposite case, albeit simultaneously requesting more checks and balances on how IDA funds were to be spent (Nelson, 1996). In addition, pressure by NGO alliances on the World Bank to adopt tougher social and environmental conditionality has increased the influence of the international financial institutions over Southern governments, thus eroding the local democratic processes on which sustainable change depends (Nelson,

1996). In Indonesia, major differences arose between Northern and Southern partners in campaigns related to World Bank-funded dams and industrial development projects, which were never democratically resolved (Cleary, 1995). Without careful planning and the deliberate intent to promote internal accountability, the same patterns can re-occur in policy alliances which link Southern NGOs with grassroots organizations in the same country (Covey, 1995). In cases like these, NGO values – particularly the traditional bottom line of empowering poor people to speak and act for themselves – are submerged under institutional agendas and more powerful voices among intermediaries, especially those with more resources and access to decision makers in the North.

This issue – the balance between direct action by NGOs and devoting NGO resources to supporting action by others – is one of the major fault-lines which will define the evolution of the NGO sector over the next ten years. It provides an illustration of the wider tensions that are emerging between developmental imperatives (the things that NGOs should be doing to fulfil their social mission), and institutional imperatives (the things they tend to do because of bureaucratic inertia or funding pressures: Edwards, 1996). To some extent this is an artificial distinction, because agencies tend to move back and forth across a continuum between these sets of imperatives all the time, mixing elements from one column with those from the other in response to both internal dynamics and pressures from a changing external environment. But the choices these imperatives embody are real enough. Hashemi (this volume) uses the example of Gono Shahajjo Sangstha (GSS) to show how NGO strategies in Bangladesh have turned away from building organizations of poor people to building up the NGO itself, but similar evidence could be cited from the North, where increasing numbers of NGOs are investing in fundraising in countries like India and Brazil to their own benefit, instead of supporting local NGOs to develop financial roots in their own societies.

This is a natural consequence of the trend among NGOs everywhere to internalize market values and dilute the links to a social base. In both cases contextual factors could be cited to explain these decisions – the political climate in Bangladesh which makes conscientization and grassroots organization dangerous, and the increasingly competitive fundraising environment in many industrialized countries which leads NGOs to look for new markets and techniques. But context by itself does not justify organizational choices – even where room to manoeuvre is restricted some still exists, and wherever it does, questions about legitimacy will remain. For Northern NGOs working internationally there is the additional problem that legitimacy has to be substantiated in many different countries, which means convincing authorities in each one that the NGO conforms with all the criteria listed at the outset of this chapter. As more questions are raised about the role, added value, accountability and effectiveness of Northern NGOs by governments, researchers and journalists, and NGOs and grassroots organizations in both North and South, this becomes more and more difficult (Edwards, 1996).

Table 13.1 *Developmental and Institutional Imperatives in NGOs*

Developmental Imperatives	Institutional Imperatives
Bottom line: empowering marginalized groups for independent action	Bottom line: size, income, market share, profile
Downplay the role of the intermediary; encourage marginalized groups to speak with their own voice	Accentuate the role of the intermediary; speak on behalf of marginalized groups
Democratic governance; less hierarchy; more reciprocity; focus on stakeholders	More hierarchy; less reciprocity; focus on donors and beneficiaries
Multiple accountability; honesty; transparency; sharing of information	Accountability upwards; secrecy; exaggerate successes and disguise failures
Maintain independence and flexibility; take risks	Increasing dependence on government funds; standardization; bureaucracy
Address the causes of marginalization; defend values of service and cooperation	Deal with symptoms; internalize orthodoxies even when antithetical to mission (eg competition)
Long term goals drive decision making; programme criteria led	Short term interests drive decision making; marketing criteria led
Rooted in broader movements for change; alliances with other groups; look outwards	Isolated from broader movements for change; incorporate others into your structures
Maximize resources to the sharp end; cooperate to reduce overheads and transaction costs	Duplicate delivery mechanisms (eg separate field offices) and materials; resources increasingly consumed by headquarters
Maintain focus and continuity, critical mass and distinctive competence	Opportunism – go where the funds are; increasing spread of activities and countries

Source: CFVS, 1996

LEGITIMACY AND VALUES: QUESTIONS FOR PRACTICE

Although the answers will be different, the basic questions facing NGOs and voluntary organizations about legitimacy and values are similar in all contexts. First, why do values matter? If contextual factors and interpretations of values vary widely across cultures and organizations, and if other institutions (like businesses and government bureaucracies) also claim to be values-based (as increasingly they do), there is no reason why there should be a single, universal framework of values based management. But the *choice* to be values-based has to be a conscious one, consciously carried through. Legitimacy through conformity with values is too important simply to be assumed. If values are really not the bottom line, better to say so in public.

Secondly, if NGOs do claim to be values-based, what values are we talking about, and which values matter most? Are some values common to all roles and relationships, while others are more specific? If so, when do organizations have to choose between them and how can different values be accommodated or married together? This question is especially important wherever role conflict exists and organizations are financially dependent on powerful institutions (or effectively colonized by states: Hashemi, this volume), since this greatly reduces their room to manoeuvre.

Thirdly, how can NGOs operationalize the values they do select throughout their management systems and decision making procedures? Are they prepared to make these values the bottom line in deciding what they do; how are they held accountable, and whose voices count? A lack of clarity about this question means that NGOs may indeed be legitimate, but are unsure in themselves because they lack the means to demonstrate if and how they are. There *are* methods to do this (such as social audits, the use of participatory monitoring and evaluation systems, and NGO codes of conduct), but they are still in their infancy. Most codes, for example, are purely voluntary, have only weak enforcement mechanisms, and lack the independent verification by users or beneficiaries that is an essential part of accountability procedures for all types of organization. The first article in the LICROSS/VOLAGS (League of Red Cross and Red Crescent Societies and voluntary agencies) code of conduct for humanitarian emergencies states that 'the humanitarian imperative comes first', but what does that imperative actually mean (Christopolous, 1997)? Who decides? Who arbitrates if there is disagreement? Unless NGOs answer these questions for themselves they are likely to find that other authorities take action to enforce greater transparency and accountability – in the form of independent ombudsmen, famine relief commissioners (de Waal, 1997), or other complaints procedures. The trouble with being values-based is that someone, somewhere is liable to check up on whether you are putting your values into practice. It is not a decision to be taken lightly, as Save the Children USA and other child sponsorship agencies discovered when exposed for just this sort of malfeasance in a series of books and newspaper articles during 1997 (Maren, 1997).

Most NGOs are weak in addressing all three of these sets of questions, so they tend to retreat into simplistic ways of defining legitimacy (as described at the beginning of this chapter), and/or they become increasingly confused about who they really are and what they stand for, hoping that institutional survival won't be overly threatened by continued fudge and compromise. This is unlikely to be good enough in the more critical world of foreign aid and third sector contracting in the 21st century. If NGOs and voluntary organizations do call themselves values-based organizations, let's see some concrete proof that they practice what they preach; if they are not, let's be honest about that too; and if the answer is 'maybe' (as it is in all hybrid institutions), then agencies should be able to show clearly and transparently how trade-offs and conflicts between different values have been managed and resolved.

In my view it is precisely this issue – the role of values in claiming legitimacy – that lies at the heart of the dilemma that faces NGOs and voluntary organizations today, and which provides the most promising route out of the confusion, co-option and hijackings that confront the sector in most countries. Although the evidence is far from conclusive (and no organization can afford to stand still), there *are* signs that NGOs are losing touch with the values of social solidarity which originally motivated them as they move further and further into the market and its orthodoxies. This is often an unconscious process, and nearly always a gradual one, but the result is the same – an erosion of the roots that legitimize NGOs as independent actors in their own societies, and consequently an increasing question mark over their legitimacy as actors in an emerging global civil society (Hulme and Edwards, 1997). The re-interpretation of mission statements, constant restructurings and continuous rethinking that mark the NGO sector out at present in many countries reflect this basic anxiety about the future, and what it means to be non-governmental in such a rapidly changing world. The solution to this condition may be a new set of roles and relationships (as I and others have argued elsewhere – Edwards and Hulme, 1995; Fowler, 1997; Smillie, 1994; Sogge, 1996), or simply greater honesty about the realities and limitations of current practice. Honesty is surely the absolute bottom line in any discussion of values, and any practice of partnership. Being, becoming and remaining a truly values-based organization presents all NGOs and voluntary agencies with an extremely complex and demanding agenda. But there is a payoff – any organization that pursues this agenda will be clearer about its role in the 21st century, and better able to fulfil it effectively.

BIBLIOGRAPHY

Blair, H (1997) 'Donors, democratisation and civil society: relating theory to practice', in Hulme, D and Edwards, M (eds) *Too Close for Comfort: NGOs, States and Donors*, Macmillan, London and St Martins Press, New York

CFVS (1996) *Meeting the Challenge of Change: Voluntary Action into the 21st Century*, Commission on the Future of the Voluntary Sector, London

Christopolous, I (1997) *Local Service Institutions and the Humanitarian Imperative*, paper presented to the Manchester University Conference on Public Sector Management in the 21st Century

Cleary, S (1995) 'In whose interest? NGO advocacy campaigns and the poorest', *International Relations*, Vol 12, No 5, pp9–36

Covey, J (1995) 'Accountability and effectiveness in NGO policy alliances', in Edwards, M and Hulme, D (eds), *Beyond the Magic Bullet: NGO Performance and Accountability in the Post-Cold War World*, Earthscan, London and Kumarian Press, West Hartford

de Waal, A (1997) *Famine Crimes*, James Currey, London

Edwards, M (1996) 'International development NGOs: legitimacy, accountability, regulation and roles', in *Meeting the Challenge of Change: Voluntary Action into the 21st Century*, Commission on the Future of the Voluntary Sector, London

Edwards, M and Hulme, D (eds) (1995) *Beyond the Magic Bullet: NGO Performance and Accountability in the Post-Cold War World*, Earthscan, London and Kumarian Press, West Hartford

Fowler, A (1997) *Striking A Balance: A Guide to Enhancing the Effectiveness of NGOs in International Development*, Earthscan, London

Hashemi, S (1995) 'NGO accountability in Bangladesh: beneficiaries, donors and the state', in Edwards, M and Hulme, D (eds), op cit

Hulme, D and Edwards, M (eds) (1997) *Too Close for Comfort: NGOs, States and Donors*, Macmillan, London and St Martins Press, New York

Maren, M (1997) *The Road to Hell*, The Free Press, New York

Montgomery, R (1996) 'Disciplining or protecting the poor?' *Journal of International Development*, Vol 8, No 2, pp289–305

Nelson, P (1996) 'Internationalising economic and environmental policy: transnational NGO networks and the World Bank's expanding influence', *Millennium*, Vol 25, No 3

Pearce, J (1997) 'Between co-option and irrelevance? Latin American NGOs in the 1990s', in Hulme, D and Edwards, M (eds), op cit

Pratten, D and Ali Baldo, S (1995) 'Return to the roots: processes of legitimacy in Sudanese migrant associations', in Edwards, M and Hulme, D (eds), op cit

Rao, A and Kelleher, D (1995) 'Engendering organisations: the BRAC case', *IDS Bulletin*, Vol 26, No 3, pp69–78

Smillie, I (1994) *The Alms Bazaar: Altruism Under Fire*, IT Publications, London

Sogge, D (1996) *Compassion and Calculation: the Politics of Private Foreign Aid*, Pluto Press, London

Tandon, R (1995) 'Board games: governance and accountability in NGOs', in Edwards, M and Hulme, D (eds), op cit

Van Rooy, A (1997) 'The growing influence of NGOs in world conferences', *World Development*, Vol 25, No 1, pp93–114

Zadek, S (1996) *Value-Based Organisation*, New Economics Foundation, London

Postscript: Reshaping the Third Sector

David Lewis

This book has begun to explore the reshaping of the third sector at the level of research and action. While the third sector concept allows us to explore non-governmental and voluntary action organized beyond the state and the market, the papers in this volume reveal the complexity of global third sector issues. Common challenges exist between North and South, but there are also problems of generalizing both within and between these contexts. Third sector organizations everywhere are concerned with a vast range of different activities from social welfare service delivery to advocacy and social change, from grassroots self-help among the poor to middle class charitable work, and from small scale informal associations to large professionalized bureaucracies. Some third sector organizations are closer to states, some closer to markets and many have a hybrid character. Some third sector organizations choose to emphasize their public identity while others see themselves as essentially private.

It is however clear that parts of the global third sector are undergoing far-reaching change. It is no longer possible for researchers to sustain a dualist vision of voluntary organizations or nonprofit organizations in the North providing welfare services to better-off populations and NGOs in the South fighting poverty, as the parallel universes of the nonprofit and the non-governmental literatures have implied by their separateness. Poverty and growing inequality are global phenomena which increasingly cut across both Northern and Southern contexts. A recent Christian Aid (Lockwood and Madden, 1997: 1) report on globalization points out that people everywhere have been affected by change, but in different ways:

> *Some have done well out the rapid changes, but others have been left behind: whether they are workers in Europe whose industries are*

disappearing, or the peoples of whole countries (many in Africa) which have dropped out of the race for economic growth.

There are people that the state has failed in countries as different as Bangladesh and the UK, helping to create the rationale for third sector welfare organizations and organizations working towards policy change. There are people that the market has failed, creating other types of third sector organization such as alternative credit providers and mutual societies. In Bangladesh one response was the establishment of the Grameen Bank, while in Britain the growth of local exchange trading systems (LETS) has increasingly been documented as a form of mutual financial support (eg Croall, 1998).

Processes of globalization have impacted both on our conceptual understanding of voluntary action around the world and on the shape of third sector activities at the level of action. As researchers, the need to make conceptual links and exchange ideas between the universes will be a priority as the study of third sectors grows to become a more established field of academic study. As activists and practitioners, globalization may require that we work locally and establish links between communities of both North and South, as well as networking to build upon the newer foci for global action such as the recent series of UN summit conferences and alliances such as CIVICUS.

The contributions to this volume have shown that learning and exchange between third sector organizations is not a straightforward process of linking around common interests. While Gaventa (this volume) shows how there can perhaps be win–win partnerships between organizations and communities in North and South, there are also massive inequalities of power and complex dimensions of difference. While Brown (this volume) shows the potential of learning from difference, his case studies also highlight the dangers and conflicts which may follow. There is value to be gained in learning from difference just as much as from similarity, but inequalities in power and resources can cause conflict and can pose problems for synthesis. There are both opportunities and constraints with hazards to learning and exchange.

In the first chapter of this book the argument was made that there may be advantages in seeking ways to bridge the gap which exists between the two parallel universes of third sector research literatures. This first step in the pooling of insights from both literatures that this book represents shows that there are important areas from which organizations in North and South might learn from each other. For example, Baig's (this volume) discussion of governance issues for NGOs in Pakistan emphasizes the uncertain context in which NGOs operate. It also draws powerful parallels between the types of organizational problems experienced by some NGOs in the Indian subcontinent and those raised in Harris's (this volume) overview of research on the governing bodies of third sector organizations in the UK and the US.

Despite the massive differences in the scale of problems between most Northern and Southern contexts there are some common themes for third sector research: improving governance; strengthening organizational legitimacy; understanding whether organizations can be made more effective in their work; analysing the relationships between policy context and organization; and uncovering more of the small scale, informal areas of the third sector. Both sets of literatures show the ways in which most third sector organizations seek, for example, to claim legitimacy through performance and yet little evidence is yet available to sustain this approach. Research also suggests that many third sector organizations in both North and South continue to find themselves confused about their values and the extent to which these might differ from those found in other types of organizations. Approaches to the evaluation of third sector organizations appear to be quite weak in both North and South and despite the raised expectations about the performance of these organizations there is no consensus about exactly what is meant by evaluation or the techniques through which it might best be carried out.

There are still gaps and areas of weakness in both literatures. For example, in the NGO literature the focus has been largely on those organizations working in developing countries which are to some extent linked or associated with the international aid industry or which are formal and bureaucratic in structure. Far less attention has been given to other kinds of third sector organizations found in many countries such as self-help associations, burial societies and religious community organizations, as Salamon and Anheier (this volume) illustrate. There is a related gap in the nonprofit literature in which some researchers have observed a similar bias towards larger formal organizations at the expense of grassroots associations (Horton Smith, 1997). The NGO literature needs more work in the area of organization and management, while the nonprofit literature neglects campaigning and social change organizations and issues. A key challenge for both literatures is that the global diversity of organizational models and cultures needs to be better understood.

This book has focused on the separateness of the two literatures and the growing interconnectedness of global third sector organizations and problems. It remains to be seen whether claims for diminution of the explanatory power of concepts such as North and South may turn out to be a little premature. However, the sophistication of many parts of the third sector in the South is now apparent and exchanged ideas now flow both ways.

In bringing together these researchers, this book has attempted to initiate debate and discussion on these themes. The future agenda is a wide one. There is also a range of related practical, political and academic dilemmas which are becoming more important in international third sector research and which have only been partly discussed here. These include:

- the domination of Southern research agendas by Northern researchers;

- tensions between theory and practice and researchers and practitioners; and
- debates concerning different perspectives on what constitutes development.

Some of these issues have been touched upon in the material which has been presented in this volume, but each is likely to continue or gain in importance over the coming years. Third sector researchers will perhaps need to escape the artificial limitations on perspective which may sometimes constrain them, while keeping in mind the massive diversity of third sector organizations and contexts which exist.

BIBLIOGRAPHY

Croall, J (1998) *LETS Act Locally: The Growth of Local Exchange Trading Systems*, Calouste Gulbenkian Foundation, London
Horton Smith, D (1997) 'Grassroots associations are important: some theory and a review of the impact literature', *Nonprofit and Voluntary Sector Quarterly*, Vol 26, No 3, pp269–306
Lockwood, M and Madden, P (1997) *Closer Together, Further Apart: A Discussion Paper on Globalisation*, Christian Aid, London

Index

Page numbers in **bold** refer to boxes, figures and tables